Mark Haye

The British
Communist Left

A contribution
to the history
of the
revolutionary
movement
1914 - 1945

Preface by the ICC

We live in a moribund social order which does all it can to make its potential gravedigger forget that it has a history; and to imprison the working class in the immediate present is equivalent to making it lose sight of itself altogether, because the working class is a historic class or it is nothing. This makes it all the more important that revolutionary minorities combat the prevailing ideology by reclaiming the real history of their class, not only from the prevailing immediatism, but also from the numerous falsified and pseudo-revolutionary interpretations of the past offered by currents such as Stalinism, Trotskyism or anarchism. This is all the more true when it comes specifically to the tradition of the communist left, which has for decades suffered either from being written out of the story of the workers' struggle altogether, or presented in the most caricatured manner by those whom official society recognises as the guardians of 'revolutionary history'.

The International Communist Current has devoted numerous articles in its press to the history of the communist left, as well as three books - on the Italian, Dutch/German and Russian lefts. We thus welcome this new contribution on the British left communists, written by a long-standing sympathiser, and actively encourage our readers to study it and respond to it. While not assuming responsibility for every last formulation in the book, we are in fundamental agreement with its approach, overall content and conclusions, and will be assisting the author in distributing it in Britain and internationally. We also recommend readers to refer to the 15-part series of articles 'The struggle for the class party in Britain' which appeared in the ICC's paper in Britain, World Revolution, between numbers 198 and 237. This series, which we will re-publish on our website, examined the development of the revolutionary political tendencies in Britain during the 19th century and up to the first world war; the present volume takes up the thread in the years around the war and the revolutionary wave which it provoked.

ISBN 1-897980-11-6

Publications of the ICC	*(write without mentioning the name)*
Accion Proletaria	Apartado Correos 258, Valencia, SPAIN.
Communist Internationalist	POB 25, NIT, Faridabad, 121001 Haryana, INDIA.
Internacionalismo	Apartado Postal 20674, San Martin, Caracas 1020A, VENEZUELA.
Internationalism	Post Office Box 288, New York, NY 10018-0288, USA.
Internationalisme	BP 1134 Bruxelles, 1000 Bruxelles, BELGIUM.
Internationell Revolution	Box 21 106, 100 31 Stockholm, SWEDEN.
Revolucion Mundial	Apdo. Post. 15-024, CP 02600, Distrito Federal, MEXICO.
Revolution Internationale	RI, Mail Boxes 153, 108 Rue Damremont, 75018, Paris, FRANCE.
Rivoluzione Internazionale	CP 469, 80100 Napoli, ITALY.
Weltrevolution	Postfach 410308, 50863 Koln, GERMANY.
Weltrevolution	Postfach 2216, CH-8026, Zurich, SWITZERLAND.
Wereld Revolutie	P.O.Box 339, 2800 AH Gouda, NETHERLANDS.
World Revolution	BM Box 869, London, WC1N 3XX, GREAT BRITAIN.

ICC Website	http://www.internationalism.org
e-mail addresses:	
From Great Britain use	uk@internationalism.org
From India use	India@internationalism.org
From rest of the world use	international@internationalism.org

Contents

Introduction

Over eighty years ago the left communists in Britain were a target of Lenin's polemic *Left Wing Communism, An Infantile Disorder*, which singled out for criticism two of its best-known representatives – Sylvia Pankhurst and William Gallacher – for their opposition to supporting the Labour Party or participating in elections.

Since then, there have been numerous studies of the revolutionary movement in Britain, written from a variety of political perspectives, but very few indeed have dealt adequately with the history of left communism, let alone with the relevance of its positions for today. Even among serious historians of the period there is a tendency to treat left communism as an 'extremist' offshoot from the mainstream, and Stalinist and Trotskyist historians have either ignored it completely or misused Lenin's polemic to dismiss it inaccurately as 'sectarian' or 'ultra left'.

In fact, the left communists were among the tiny minority of revolutionaries in Britain who upheld the principle of internationalism in August 1914, denouncing the Second International for its betrayal and actively opposing the imperialist war. They were the most enthusiastic supporters of the October revolution in Russia, defending the Bolsheviks against the bourgeoisie's lies about a 'coup d'etat', and calling for revolution at home as the only real way for British workers to show their solidarity. Far from being 'ultra left', the left communists were the original left wing of the Communist International (CI). They were among the CI's earliest and most active supporters in this country, contributing to its work and helping to forge practical links between communist groups in western Europe (including the German, Dutch and Italian lefts). In the tortuous negotiations to form a communist party in Britain, the left communists fought for unity on the basis of a clear break with the Second International and all the methods and tactics of reformism. When the CI's leadership switched its support away from the left and adopted opportunist tactics in order to foster unity with the larger centrist parties, the British left communists took up this fight inside the International itself, arguing forcefully at its second congress against any compromise with opportunism alongside the other lefts. On their return they entered the newly-formed Communist Party of Great Britain (CPGB) to fight for their positions.

However, the revolutionary wave was already on the ebb. The group around Sylvia Pankhurst attempted to form a left opposition inside the CPGB but was quickly expelled. At the same time the German, Dutch and Bulgarian lefts were forced out of the International. Several years before the emergence of Trotsky's Left Opposition, and in a more profound way, the left communists began to analyse the reasons for the degeneration of the Communist International and the Russian revolution. Pankhurst's paper, the *Workers' Dreadnought*, became the most important English language journal of the international communist left, exposing the CPGB's betrayals of Bolshevism's revolutionary principles, and publishing Herman Gorter's reply to Lenin's arguments in *Left Wing Communism* and other key texts of the Dutch, German and Russian lefts, before it finally ceased in 1924.

While the *Dreadnought* group was the clearest expression of left communism in Britain, there were still militants inside the CPGB who continued to resist the move to the right and opposed any compromise with the Labour Party, before the early 'Bolshevisation' of the party finally stifled this opposition in 1922. With the deepening defeat of the working class, the left was too weak and isolated to prevent the final triumph of opportunism in the International and its official party in Britain. The CPGB subsequently became a most loyal servant of the Stalinist regime.

Some of the communist left's positions were kept alive during the depths of the counter-revolution by those who called themselves 'anti-parliamentary' or 'council' communists. Active mainly on Clydeside, influenced by anarchism but also by the surviving Dutch and German lefts, these revolutionaries stubbornly continued to denounce the Labour Party and trade unions and to highlight the counter-revolutionary nature of the Stalinist regime in Russia. Despite giving support to the bourgeois republican government in Spain, the British council communists upheld an internationalist position in the second world war (unlike the Trotskyists who were led by the reactionary logic of anti-fascism and 'defence of the USSR' to take sides in the massacre), finally dissolving when it became clear there would be no revolutionary wave at the end of the war.

In a country where working class politics is all too often identified with the trade unions and the Labour Party, and where the very idea of revolution can still be portrayed as alien to the British experience, the history of left communism is proof that there is a deep tradition within the British proletariat of principled opposition to parliamentarism and reformism, and an understanding of the need for a workers' revolution against the bourgeois democratic state.

This revolutionary tradition almost disappeared in the counter-revolution which descended on the working class following its great assault on capitalism, buried as 'un-British' or perverted by Stalinism to fit the dictates of the Russian state's foreign policy. Left communism was reduced to a few brief references to 'anarcho-syndicalists', 'sectarians' or 'purists' in the footnotes of official Stalinist histories.[1] Sylvia Pankhurst was remembered chiefly as a suffragette or as the anti-fascist she later became, while William Gallacher became a Stalinist MP and publicly recanted his past as a 'left sectarian'.[2] On the other hand, more independent-minded histories of the Communist Party of Great Britain, which were largely written from a social democratic, reformist perspective, tended to see 'official communism' as imposing itself on a 'naturally evolving' (that is, reformist) British movement, and viewed dissidents like Pankhurst more as 'victims' of Lenin's manipulations, whose mistake was to agree to enter a party 'artificially' created by the Bolsheviks and controlled from Moscow.[3]

The reappearance of the historic crisis of capitalism in the late 1960s provoked massive social movements and workers' struggles, finally signalling the return of the proletariat to the stage of history. In Britain this led to the rediscovery by a new generation of militants of the ideas of the 'old' workers' movement and the history of anti-parliamentary opposition. Revolutionary minorities began to re-emerge, mainly from splits in leftism and libertarianism, which identified with the positions of the left communists and re-appropriated their history.[4] The resurgence of class struggle, however, also led to the growth of leftist ideas and organisations, and to a large extent the Stalinist historiography of the CPGB was eclipsed by a Trotskyist version which shared many of the same characteristics, repeating Lenin's criticisms of the 'infantile left' and defending as 'Leninist' orthodoxy the CI's opportunist positions on parliamentarism, trade unionism and united fronts with the social democratic butchers.[5] This period did see some more sympathetic studies (for example Raymond Challinor's history of the Socialist Labour Party[6]), but by the 1980s there were far fewer works of original research appearing, and none challenging what might be termed the leftist version of history.

The notable exception was Mark Shipway's study of what he called 'anti-parliamentary communism'.[7] This was a detailed history of both Pankhurst's *Workers' Dreadnought* group and the 'anarchist communist' current around Guy Aldred. Shipway rightly criticised leftist interpretations of history which treated left communism, in his colourful phrase, as "an 'infantile' tributary flowing into the Leninist mainstream, later to emerge as an effluent which disappears into the void."[8] He described the evolution of these groups' political positions and their struggle against the counter-revolution, concluding that only they upheld a genuine vision of communism. But he could not hide the fact that he was dealing here with two disparate political currents; one whose main influence was post-war left communism, the other nineteenth century Bakuninite anarchism.[9] To paper over the differences he created an artificial political theory of 'anti-parliamentary communism', with its own basic principles and definition of communism to distinguish it from 'orthodox communism'; that is, Bolshevism. This was an a-historical approach, which ignored the fact that at the height of the revolutionary wave the left communists defended precisely the same vision of communism as the Bolsheviks. It also excluded those revolutionaries who defended positions against the Labour Party and trade unions but did not totally oppose electoral activity. In reality even among anti-parliamentary communists there was a whole range of different tactics on this question. More seriously, Shipway did not confront the reactionary nature of some of the views expressed by the anti-parliamentary communists about the supposed bourgeois nature of Bolshevism and the Russian revolution, or Aldred's nihilistic conclusions in the mid-1930s about the nature of Marxism itself, which threw into question the whole experience of the workers' movement. In this sense, his approach gave support to what could be termed a 'councilist' or 'anarcho-Marxist' version of history, and while his was a serious study, other products of this milieu were much cruder in displaying their anti-Bolshevik prejudices, claiming, for example, that the Comintern 'tricked' the left communists into becoming its 'accomplices' – a claim which essentially mirrors the social democratic version of history...[10]

Shipway's study is now over 15 years old. Many groups and publications of the anarcho-Marxist milieu (like *Wildcat* which reprinted material by Pankhurst and the anti-parliamentary communists) are defunct. The political climate for research into revolutionary history changed dramatically with the collapse of the so-called 'communist' bloc in 1989-91. This explosive event, which in fact marked a dramatic deepening of capitalism's own crisis, was (and is) presented as the demise of Marxism. Not surprisingly there has been a tendency to reject the whole experience of the Russian revolution as leading inevitably to the gulag, and Marxism itself as inherently totalitarian. After several waves of increasingly threatening struggles, the international working class has been deeply disoriented by the bourgeoisie's propaganda campaigns about the 'end of communism', and has suffered the most profound retreat in its combativity and consciousness since the end of the counter-revolution in the 1960s.

The final death of the CPGB in 1991 prompted a proliferation of books and articles ranging from fawning obituaries by neo-Stalinist descendants, who are naturally unapologetic about the party's anti-working class activities,[11] to more critical-sounding treatments by various representatives of Trotskyism. As part of its own effort to fill the gap in the market for a 'mass party' left by the CPGB, the 'Trotskyist-derived' Socialist Workers' Party, for example, published a history portraying itself as the genuine defender of 'Leninist' orthodoxy against the CP.[12] In spite of its denunciation of Stalinism, the Trotskyist movement today defends a state capitalist programme founded on all the opportunist mistakes of the early CI, which renders it incapable of honestly re-appraising the past for its lessons. Even a serious, supposedly non-sectarian journal like *Revolutionary History* tries to avoid any serious coverage of currents to the left of Trotskyism and, when challenged to a more informed debate about left communism in Britain, considers it sufficient to repeat Lenin's denunciation of the 'infantile' left'.[13] Other obituaries of the CPGB, reflecting the attachment of its former supporters to social democracy, conclude that the party should either never have existed at all, or simply acted as a pressure group inside the much larger and influential Labour Party.[14]

Generally there has been a decline of interest in the political history of the workers' movement and a trend instead towards cultural, biographical and literary approaches, which focus on local events, the lives of individual activists, or the 'social and cultural history' of the CPGB, whose betrayals – along with their vital political lessons for the working class – are thus made to disappear into the rich tapestry of British labour movement history.[15] A more specific product of this trend has been the growth of a 'revisionist' school which throws into question the control exercised by the Stalinist apparatus over the national communist parties and argues that the CPGB had a greater degree of local autonomy than hitherto accepted by 'cold war' historians. This not only flies in the face of the historical evidence but also serves to whitewash the crimes of Stalinism, promoting instead a supposedly more acceptable, home-grown version of its politics which is no less anti-working class.[16]

But there have also been some more positive developments, despite the very difficult conditions. Amidst signs that the working class is recovering its militancy, the deepening of the capitalist crisis and the brutal realities of the 'war on terror' are bringing a new generation towards genuine revolutionary politics. The established groups of the communist left have been able to maintain and even extend their influence (perhaps most dramatically in Russia, birthplace of the world revolution), and to find a new readership for material about the history of left communism as part of their intervention in this developing revolutionary milieu.[17]

This history of the British communist left is written in the same spirit. Although undertaken as an individual project, it has been produced with the active support and collaboration the International Communist Current, while the other communist left groups have been invited to comment and to contribute.[18] It should be clear therefore that it does not pretend to be 'neutral'; rather it is intended as a sympathetic but honest study, whose focus is not on personalities, local events or aspects of social and cultural history, but firmly on the political positions defended by the communist left, tracing the evolution of these positions within the left trend of the workers' movement from 1914 through to 1945. Against the leftist version of history it argues that the communist left was in political continuity with Russian Bolshevism and German Spartacism, and played a vanguard role in the struggle against the degeneration of the Russian revolution long before the emergence of Trotsky's opposition. Against both the reformist and anarcho-Marxist versions of history it argues that the communist left was absolutely correct to fight for its positions inside the CPGB and the Communist International, as a fraction of the same international communist movement. Suspicious of secondary sources and existing histories, it draws wherever possible on original sources, including previously unavailable party archive material. In order to promote a more informed debate it also includes a selection of original texts which illustrate the positions of the left at key stages of its development.

In the face of all the lies about the 'end of communism', the story of the communist left's struggle is still very relevant for revolutionaries, and for this reason the approach is also critical, identifying the main mistakes made by the British communist left and drawing their lessons for today. Its strengths and weaknesses are considered in the context of other fractions of the international left communist movement. The British left did not command the mass support enjoyed by the KAPD in Germany or Bordiga's Abstentionist Fraction in Italy. Nor did it produce theoretical works to compare with those of of Luxemburg, Pannekoek or Gorter. The communist left was strongest where the revolutionary wave reached its highest peaks: in Germany, Italy and Russia itself. Here it was able to gain a real influence in the working class and make the greatest contribution to understanding the realities of the new epoch of capitalist decadence. In Britain the left was forced to struggle against a powerful and experienced bourgeoisie, and a vast tide of reformist ideas and practices in the working class. On the other hand, it was well placed to offer crucial insights into the realities of the new period; after all Britain was the first industrialised capitalist nation and therefore the first to display many of the symptoms of capitalism's decay. Above all, the struggle of the British communist left was a very practical one for the construction of a clear and principled organisation of revolutionaries. In this it displayed all the characteristic stubbornness of this fraction of the world proletariat, refusing to entirely give up despite the might of the enemies ranged against it.

The struggle fought by the British communist left for a class party remains to be fought anew today, albeit in different historical conditions, in order to lead the final assault of the proletariat to destroy capitalism once and for all. In the struggle before us, the history of left communism in Britain provides not only a rich source of lessons but also an inspiration.

Notes

1 For example, see James Klugmann, *History of the Communist Party of Great Britain,* vol.1, Lawrence & Wishart, 1968, p.57.

2 See *Revolt on the Clyde,* Lawrence and Wishart, 1936, p.251.

3 For example, see Henry Pelling, *The British Communist Party. A Historical Profile,* Adam & Charles Black, 1958; Walter Kendall, *The Revolutionary Movement in Britain 1900-21,* Weidenfeld & Nicholson, 1969, and L.J. MacFarlane, *The British Communist Party. Its origin and development until 1929,* MacGibbon & Kee, 1966.

4 For example, *World Revolution* in London and *Revolutionary Perspectives* in Scotland, both formed from splits in the libertarian group *Solidarity.* In Liverpool, *Workers' Voice* was formed by a group of militants breaking with the shop stewards' movement, who re-published many texts from the *Workers' Dreadnought* by Pankhurst and other left communists.

5 For example, see M. Woodhouse and B. Pearce, for whom the main enemies of the early CPGB were

not opportunism and centrism but sectarianism and syndicalism (*Essays on the History of Communism in Britain*, New Park, 1975). In a brief footnote they cursorily dismiss Pankhurst's organisation as a perfect expression of "a-political revolutionary syndicalism" (n.p.62).

6 *The Origins of British Bolshevism*, Croom Helm, 1977. Challinor's agenda however was to justify rank and file unionism; his history is highly selective and misleading, and fails to challenge the political basis of Lenin's 'mistakes' in the CI's opportunist policies.

7 *Anti-Parliamentary Communism: the Movement for Workers' Councils in Britain, 1917-1945*, Macmillan, 1988.

8 *Ibid.*, p.xii.

9 *Ibid.*, p.xi.

10 Bob Jones, *Left-Wing Communism in Britain 1917-21...An Infantile Disorder?*, Pirate Press, 1991.

11 For example, see Andrew Murray, *The Communist Party of Great Britain. A Historical Analysis to 1941*, Communist Liaison, 1995. For Murray, the high point of the CPGB was during 'third period' Stalinism. The left communists are referred to in passing as 'doctrinaire sectarians'.

12 J. Eaden & D. Renton, *The Communist Party of Great Britain since 1920*, Palgrave Macmillan, 2002.

13 See John McIlroy's reply in *Revolutionary History*, vol.8, no.2, 2002, pp.282-287.

14 For example, see Willie Thompson, *The Good Old Cause* [sic!]: *British Communism 1920-1991*, Pluto Press, 1992.

15 For example, see the misleadingly titled *Opening the Books,* whioch is more revealingly sub-titled *Essays on the Social and Cultural History of the British Communist Party* (G. Andrews, N. Fishman & K. Morgan (Eds.), Pluto Press, 1995). Only one of these essays deals even tangentially with the period of the post-war revolutionary wave.

16 For example, see the work of Andrew Thorpe, Matthew Worley, Phil Watson *et al.*

17 The International Communist Current (ICC) has published in English *The Italian Communist Left 1926-1945 (*1992), and *The Dutch and German Communist Left (*2001). See also publications of the International Bureau for the Revolutionary Party, and the International Communist Party (*Communist Program*).

18 It is a mark of the sectarianism which unfortunately dogs the communist left milieu that neither the IBRP nor the ICP made any formal response to this invitation.

Chapter 1

War

The final outbreak of war in 1914 revealed the extent of the opportunist rot within the mass organisations built up by the working class in the period of capitalism's ascendancy. Despite all its formal declarations against war, the Second International died on August 4th, when the Socialist Parties of the main belligerent powers all voted for war credits. In Germany and France the trade unions proclaimed a *union sacrée*, banning all strikes and declaring themselves for the mobilisation of the nation's forces for war. The leaders of the main parties of the International became avid supporters of the war and recruiting sergeants for the slaughter. Through its call for national defence in the war of imperialism, social democracy betrayed the historic interests of the working class.

In Britain, after decades of class collaboration, the loyalty of the trade unions and the Labour Party was never seriously in doubt. Immediately on Britain's declaration of war the Labour Party made it clear it would not obstruct the war effort and on 7th August its leaders in parliament voted for special war grants. Both the Labour Party and the Trades Union Congress proclaimed an 'industrial truce' for the duration and agreed to end all labour disputes. By mid-August 1914 they had fully lined up behind the British bourgeoisie's war effort and agreed to help in its recruiting drive, later entering the coalition government. In return for their support, the leaders of the 'Labour Movement' demanded a greater say in the running of the war, and union officials, already well implanted in the state apparatus, took on the role of ensuring production in the factories, disciplining the working class in the name of the war effort, and later helping to administer conscription through their role in the tribunals hearing the cases of conscientious objectors. In this way, the Labour Party and the trade unions passed definitively over to the camp of the bourgeoisie.

The left's intransigent defence of internationalism

The first duty of revolutionaries in the face of this historic betrayal was to defend the international interests of the proletariat, as expressed in the original watchword of the workers' movement: "Workers of the world unite!"

Not all the individual parties of the Second International capitulated on the outbreak of war, and even in the larger social democratic parties that had supported the war, there were internationalist tendencies that opposed the slaughter. Among the belligerent powers, the Russian social democrats – both Bolshevik and

Menshevik – united temporarily to abstain from the vote on war credits and disclaim all responsibility for the war, while in Serbia the two Socialist deputies voted against war credits and denounced the war as imperialist. The Socialist Party of Italy also took a position against the war, along with the Bulgarian Social Democratic Workers' Party (the 'Tesniaks' or 'Narrow' Social Democrats). A few tiny minorities called for a revolutionary struggle against their own government, including in Germany the *Internationale* and *Lichstrahlen* groups and the Bremen Left; in Russia the Bolsheviks and the *Nashe Slovo* group around Trotsky and Martov, and elements of Latvian and Polish Social Democracy; in France some syndicalists and sections of the Socialist Party, and in Holland the *Tribune* group around Pannekoek and Gorter.

In almost all cases, these defenders of internationalism emerged from within the social democratic parties themselves, where they had been amongst the most determined fighters against the growth of opportunism in the International, and for a revolutionary position against war. Revolutionaries like Lenin and the Bolsheviks in Russia, and Karl Liebknecht and Rosa Luxemburg in Germany, were actually putting into practice the position formally adopted by the Second International at its Stuttgart Congress in 1907, which pledged the social democratic parties, in the event of war breaking out, to "strive with all their power to make use of the violent economic and political crisis brought about by the war to rouse the people, and thereby hasten the abolition of capitalist class rule."[1] This only proved that, when it came to the test, it was the left that intransigently defended the International's genuine socialist positions.

In the British Labour Party, initially at least there was some resistance to the war; while the trade union leaders who dominated the party were among the most enthusiastic supporters of the war, many of its leadership positions were held by the ostensibly socialist Independent Labour Party, whose leader, Ramsay MacDonald, was chairman of the Labour Party in parliament. Five of the seven ILP-sponsored Labour MPs at first disassociated themselves from Labour's support for the war, and MacDonald resigned as party chairman, but once the war had started the majority came out in support of the government's recruiting campaign, MacDonald arguing that "whatever our views may be of the origins of the war, we must go through with it."[2]

The earliest and most consistent defender of a revolutionary position against the war in Britain was the group around John Maclean and the Glasgow District Council of the British Socialist Party. The BSP, led by Hyndman a notorious pro-imperialist, had declared its wholehearted support for Britain's entry into the war and called for an allied victory. The party's war manifesto backed "the right of nations to defend their national existence by force of arms" and called for the defeat of "Prussian militarism", while Hyndman personally praised the "splendid resistance" of "plucky little Belgium", claiming that "...everybody must eagerly desire the defeat of Germany..."[3] The BSP's pro-war attitude was defined even more explicitly in a later statement which advised party members to accept (with a few provisos) invitations to take part in the government's recruiting campaigns: "Recognising that the national freedom and independence of this country are threatened by Prussian militarism, the Party naturally desires to see the prosecution of the war to a speedy and successful issue..."[4] Both these chauvinist statements were signed by the entire executive committee, which included representatives of the left and centre of the party (Albert Inkpin and EC Fairchild). But even as the BSP was proclaiming its support for King and Country, Maclean and his supporters were carrying out anti-war propaganda at factory gates on

Clydeside, where mass meetings of workers passed resolutions calling for an end to the war and sent fraternal greetings to workers of all nations.[5] In September 1914, Maclean argued that: "Our first business is to hate the British capitalist system that, with 'business as usual', means the continued robbery of the workers... It is our business as socialists to develop 'class patriotism', refusing to murder one another for a sordid world capitalism."[6] In the first issue of his own paper the *Vanguard*, started as a riposte to Hyndman's pro-war *Justice*, Maclean set out his belief that the only alternative to war now was revolution: "This monstrous war shows that the day of social pottering or reform is past... We do not think national wars are of benefit to the workers so we shall oppose all national wars as we oppose this one. The only war that is worth fighting is the class war..."[7] He explained the conflict as a product of imperialist rivalries; unless this war ended in revolution, further world imperialist wars were inevitable.

Maclean's internationalist tendency, however, co-existed in a party still controlled by a rabidly chauvinist leadership. A determined struggle for the organisation was necessary to exclude those who had betrayed internationalism and win the party over to a revolutionary position against the war.

In the decade before the war, the left wing of the BSP had waged a bitter struggle against the growing nationalism of the party leadership. In particular, the left fought to disassociate the party from Hyndman's public advocacy of a big navy and to obtain its adherence to the official position of the Second International against war. The left was strongest in East London, and in Scotland where Maclean and the Glasgow branches carried out anti-militarist propaganda. In both areas, émigré Marxists from Russian and East European social democracy played a leading role. The left was successful in gaining representation on the party's executive, and in late 1912 narrowly won endorsement for its own clear rejection of militarism and imperialism.[8] But, in the face of a counter-attack by the right, the opposition revealed a tendency to hesitate; two of its representatives failed to attend the next executive meeting in February 1913, giving the leadership a majority of one in voting to suspend the resolution and allow the party to decide on the question of maintaining a British navy. At the 1913 party conference, the centre in the party did all it could to prevent a split on such a 'non-essential point', proposing that members should be "free to hold any opinion they like on subjects apart from socialism"! As one delegate bluntly put it: "first and foremost they must have socialist unity." In the end, the left's anti-militarist resolution was never voted on and Hyndman, while still airing his "strong conviction" that a very powerful navy was "indispensable" to Britain, agreed to keep quiet for the sake of the party. In a display of phoney unity, a resolution was then adopted pledging the BSP to oppose the growth of militarism as an integral part of the Second International. For the left this proved a Pyrrhic victory. The right, in danger of losing its grip on the party, had been rescued by centrist conciliation.[9]

The working class paid heavily for this failure; at the outbreak of the first imperialist world war, one of the very few Marxist organisations in Britain, so painfully built up during the preceding period of capitalist prosperity, remained in the hands of a right-wing chauvinist clique which proceeded to offer its enthusiastic support to the slaughter, dragging the whole notion of proletarian internationalism down into the mud with it.

The leadership's first tentative efforts to mobilise the party behind the bourgeoisie's war effort did, however, provoke a swift reaction from internationalists in the party, who found growing support among the membership. The right was forced to avoid a national conference in 1915 to prevent this opposition from uniting; at the six regional conferences held instead, the mass of the party rejected both social chauvinist *and* revolutionary positions, narrowly adopting an 'india rubber' resolution which in fact justified the British war effort.[10] Again the leadership survived by allowing the 'expression of opinion', but there was a running battle over the party's press, which continued to present the views of the chauvinists, and in 1916 Hyndman and his supporters set up a 'Socialist National Defence Committee' which effectively operated as an arm of the government in the party; the organisational struggle turned violent and anti-war militants found themselves being set up for state repression by their own leadership.

A split was clearly inevitable, but the opposition, despite gaining a majority on the executive, still hesitated to take the initiative. Within this opposition there appeared a more clearly defined centrist current, mainly around Fairchild in East London, which resolutely avoided any call for action against the war and restricted itself to calls for peace, demanding that all action calculated to endanger national defence should be avoided.[11] The *Vanguard* group at this point called on the party to choose its camp: either the revolutionary left, or Hyndman and the old International. However, with Maclean's imprisonment and the closure of the *Vanguard* in 1916, political leadership of the opposition passed by default to the London grouping, which began publication of its own journal *The Call* in February 1916, urging peace and still calling on the Second International to 'act'. At the 1916 party conference, the Hyndmanites were finally isolated and walked out, but even now they were not excluded and the debates at the conference clearly revealed the centrist confusions of the majority. While supporting calls for an early end to the war, the party restricted itself to a demand for the immediate re-establishment of the Second International "as the necessary preliminary to a united campaign in favour of peace."[12] Essentially the new BSP leadership deeply feared a British military defeat and did all it could to avoid any action that might jeopardise an allied victory.

The chauvinism and opportunism of the BSP's predecessor, the Social Democratic Federation, had already prompted splits, and alienated many socialists in the already fragmented British movement. The Socialist Labour Party, formed in 1903 as a result of the 'Impossibilist revolt' in the SDF, stated in its press on the outbreak of war: "Our attitude is neither pro-German nor pro-British, but anti-capitalist and all that it stands for in every country of the world. The capitalist class of all nations are our real enemies, and it is against them that we direct all our attack." It also denounced the leaders of the International who had failed to give a direction to workers and had: "...delivered them into the hands of the capitalists to be butchered in droves until the conflict ceases for want of victims." The failure of the international socialist movement was "the direct outcome of its leaders and thinkers having forsaken the revolutionary traditions of socialism." But when it came to anti-war action the SLP could only advise socialists at this moment "to endeavour to lend some stability to working class organisations; to get them to take a calm view of the entire situation, and see how the very existence of their organisations is menaced..."[13] In fact, despite its initial anti-war pronouncements, the SLP took no official position on the war, and divergences soon emerged within the party, between those like Muir, the *Socialist's* editor, who argued that a German victory must be opposed and that British workers should therefore join the army and defend their country; and those who argued that workers had no country to defend, that the only justified war was the class war, and therefore the workers should refuse to take up arms even in the event of invasion. After a public debate in the pages of the *Socialist*, the defencists were finally won over, and at a special conference in April 1915 the party finally took a position against the war. This, however, stopped short of active opposition: the resolutions adopted merely demanded "a stoppage of the war and a peace arranged along the lines laid down by Karl Liebknecht."[14] The SLP's 1916 party conference merely demanded, "that the government shall immediately take steps to terminate hostilities."[15] In practice, many SLP militants were in the forefront of anti-war activity, especially on Clydeside alongside John Maclean and his supporters.

The other 'Impossibilist' organisation, the Socialist Party of Great Britain formed in 1904, merely declared in August 1914 that: "...no interests are at stake justifying the shedding of a single drop of working class blood... Having no quarrel with the working class of any country, we extend to our fellow workers of all lands the expression of our goodwill and socialist fraternity..."[16]

Other socialists who took a more or less internationalist line included the group around Sylvia Pankhurst in the East End of London. This was mainly composed of working class women who had broken from the official women's suffrage movement over the latter's support for the war. Although initially its position against the war was largely on pacifist grounds, the group was very active in organising anti-war demonstrations in London, and became more militant as the slaughter went on, its paper, the *Women's Dreadnought*, quoting the anti-war writings of Liebknecht and the Bolsheviks.

On the anarchist wing of the workers' movement, there were also elements who took a stand, including the 'anarchist-communists' around Guy Aldred, who had undertaken anti-militarist propaganda before the war and now denounced the workers' betrayal in ringing terms: "The socialists of Europe have betrayed the workers of the world... The syndicalists of France have united with the social democrats of Germany to deluge Europe with proletarian blood."[17] Aldred's position, however, was tinged with anarchist individualism, blaming the European workers themselves for the war as "jingo sheep, devoted to their devourers – the capitalist shepherds."[18] Among other groups in the anarchist milieu, the *Freedom* group broke from Kropotkin's pro-war stance after an initial struggle and came out against. Most of the pre-war syndicalist organisations simply collapsed on the outbreak of war.

Zimmerwald: the revolutionary left regroups its forces

After the initial shock of the war and the betrayal of social democracy, the revolutionary left began to regroup its forces. The question posed was whether the old International could be rebuilt or if a new, revolutionary International was now necessary. The Bolsheviks answered as early as November 1914 that "The Second International is dead, overcome by opportunism." Their position was clear: "Down with opportunism, and long live the Third International."[19] With the old International's leaders now fully backing their respective imperialisms and refusing to take any action to bring the social democrats of the belligerent nations together, its central organ, the International Socialist Bureau, was completely impotent, and it was eventually on the initiative of the Italian Socialist Party that a first unofficial international socialist conference was held at Zimmerwald in September 1915. This brought together some of the most important currents of the revolutionary left, including the Bolsheviks, along with representatives of the pacifist centre. The left's own draft resolutions and anti-war manifesto, which called for the revolutionary overthrow of capitalism, were rejected by the majority, which restricted itself to a call for peace. But the conference was an important step in the regroupment of revolutionaries against the war and enabled the left to establish itself as an organised fraction which later, following a second conference at Kienthal in April 1916, became the nucleus of the Third International.[20]

In Britain, the British Socialist Party had placed all its hopes in the ISB to secure peace, but the British section of the Bureau included the Labour Party, which fully supported the war and systematically blocked any attempt at common action. Both the BSP and the Independent Labour Party agreed to send delegates to Zimmerwald but were denied passports. The BSP executive welcomed the outcome of the conference but still primarily saw it as a way of prompting the International to 'act', and remained opposed to any move to form a new international organisation in opposition to the ISB.[21] The London opposition was hesitant in its support for Zimmerwald, giving 'friendly aid' to the international commission established to progress its work while repeating its own demand that the ISB 'act'.[22] In contrast, John Maclean enthusiastically reported the conference in the *Vanguard,* interpreting its manifesto as a call for "the class war for social democracy" and denouncing the ISB's efforts to keep the sides apart: "...this conference clearly indicates that the International itself will go on. The traitors to the International will have to be treated later on."[23] His collaborator Peter Petroff, who had close contacts with the movement abroad, was best able to analyse the political character of Zimmerwald, giving it his support and repeating his earlier call for the building of a new International, but pointing out that its manifesto did not call for revolutionary action against the war.[23]

The Socialist Labour Party had been kept informed of the anti-war movement abroad through its own émigré contacts. In November 1914 the *Socialist* had published a summary of an article by Anton Pannekoek on the collapse of the Second International, which located the reason in the failure of its parliamentary tactics; identified the emergence of a new period of the labour movement requiring new policies of attack and mass action as advocated by the left wing of the German Socialist Party; and envisaged a new International based on these tactics. The *Socialist* defended the Zimmerwald conference as laying the foundation of a new International and denounced the pro-war socialists, with whom all common action was now impossible:

> We are at the parting of the ways. Every day the cleavage between the socialists remaining true to the International and the pro-war socialists is becoming more and more marked. The socialists welcome any sign that points to the regeneration of the International; the pro-war socialists oppose any coming together of the proletarian parties of the belligerent nations...[25]

Sylvia Pankhurst also gave support to Zimmerwald in her paper the *Women's Dreadnought,* like many in the workers' movement seeing in it a practical hope for peace. This grouping was still in the process of evolving towards a revolutionary position against the war; an evolution marked by the newspaper's change of name to the *Workers' Dreadnought* in 1917.

From their initial isolation, by late 1915 at least some of the scattered revolutionary forces in Britain had taken their first steps towards international regroupment based on a clear political break with the social chauvinists, but also by distinguishing their position from that of the pacifist centre.

The need for a struggle against the social chauvinists – and the 'centre'

In 1916, in the midst of the inter-imperialist conflict, Lenin defined the three main political tendencies in the workers' movement which had emerged during the war:

1. The social chauvinists, i.e. socialists in word and chauvinists in deed, who had gone over to the bourgeoisie through their support for national defence;

2. The internationalists, represented by the Bolsheviks and the left at Zimmerwald, who called for a revolutionary struggle against the war;

3. The 'centre', consisting of those who vacillated between the social chauvinists and the real internationalists.

The 'centre' were internationalist in word and chauvinist in deed, 'cowardly opportunists': "The crux of the matter is that the 'centre' is not convinced of the necessity for a revolution against one's own government; it does not preach revolution; it does not carry on a wholehearted revolutionary struggle; and in order to evade such a struggle it resorts to the tritest ultra-'Marxist'-sounding excuses..."[26] While the centre had not passed over to the bourgeois camp like the social chauvinists, it had not broken from the methods and practices of the workers' movement in the period when reforms were possible, and had yet to recognise the realities of the new epoch opened up by the war; the epoch of wars and revolutions.

In Britain, the Labour Party and the trade union leaders, together with the Fabians and the Hyndmanite leadership of the BSP, easily fell into the social chauvinist category.

Of the centre or 'swamp', the Independent Labour Party was a classic example; its leadership was far too deeply embedded in the leadership of the Labour Party to take a clear stand against the war, while the membership largely opposed the war on pacifist grounds, avoiding any action against the Allied war effort. The ILP's war manifesto eloquently expressed solidarity with the workers of Germany and Austria "across the roar of the guns", but stopped short of calling for an anti-war struggle and affirmed that: "Our nationality and independence, which are dear to us, we are ready to defend..."[27]

Into the swamp also fell the majority of the opposition in the BSP, although here we can distinguish a definite right wing, represented by the social pacifist tendency around Fairchild which had taken over the leadership after the departure of the Hyndmanites; and a more vaguely defined left wing which was open to the influence of the revolutionary left. But centrism also constituted an ever-present danger to the revolutionary movement, expressed in a tendency to hesitate, or to attempt to conciliate between opposing interests when confronted with the necessity for an intransigent defence of revolutionary positions.

Nor did the early break of the 'Impossibilists' from the SDF's opportunism inevitably lead them to avoid centrist confusion and defend a clear position on the war. The Socialist Labour Party was initially disoriented and only belatedly adopted an official position against the war which fell short of advocating practical anti-war action, while the Socialist Party of Great Britain simply washed its hands of the whole affair and played no part in anti-war activity, thus representing, in Lenin's terms, a social pacifist rather than a revolutionary tendency.

It was the internationalists of the *Vanguard* group, with their call for all action against the government whatever the consequences for military defeat, who best represented the revolutionary interests of the proletariat. It is no accident that this tendency in Britain arose in a party that in the pre-war years had seen a determined struggle by its own internationalist left wing for the official policies of the Second International. As we have seen, the internationalists had emerged from within the organisations of social democracy themselves, where they had been the most intransigent defenders of the International's positions against militarism and war.

While the organisations of social democracy remained in the hands of the social chauvinists it was necessary for the left to wage a struggle to remove them if possible from their positions and expel them from the proletarian movement; but, where they proved too deeply entrenched, at the very least to win over as many militants as possible to a revolutionary position. Given the vital historic role of its organisations in the struggle to destroy capitalism, the proletariat could not afford to concede a single position to the class enemy. This was the struggle fought so intransigently by revolutionaries like Rosa Luxemburg, who argued strongly against abandoning the German Socialist Party and defended the need to remain within it as long as possible, in order to try to reconquer the party from below.

In Britain, this basic principle of the Marxist movement was not well understood. Whereas in Germany opposition to the war came out of the mass social democratic party built up by the proletariat in the preceding period of capitalist expansion, in Britain the socialist movement had been dominated from its very beginning by small sects, isolated from the masses and prone to sectarianism and splits. It is a reflection on the indigenous revolutionary movement that it was the émigré Marxists in the BSP – many schooled in the hard conditions and organisational struggles of Russian social democracy – who had most clearly assimilated this lesson, and it was because of this that, unlike the 'Impossibilists' and other oppositionists before them, they were so careful to avoid giving the Hyndmanites a pretext to throw them out of the organisation. Despite their failure to unseat the Hyndmanites before the war, this strategy of patient, determined struggle eventually paid off, and then, once the chauvinists had been isolated, the émigré Marxists were among the most vigorous in calling for their expulsion.[28] Many others who formally defended an internationalist position simply turned their backs on the fate of social democracy; the 'anarchist-communist' Guy Aldred, for example, who had left the Social Democratic Federation in 1906, later commented, with typical egoism, that: "It took me a year to sense that social democracy was capitalism and careerism... It took me a few years longer to realise how completely anti-socialist it was. The SDF was an anti-Marxist and careerist organisation from the start."[29] Aldred's verbal radicalism – by 1909 he was calling for the formation of a new International to replace the Second, which had "supplanted the Marxist communism of the First" – masked an all too typical disdain for the workers' struggles and the organisations so painstakingly built up in the preceding period.

This inability to grasp the importance of staying inside proletarian organisations to fight for revolutionary positions, reflecting the historical influence of anarchism on such questions in the British revolutionary movement, was to be a recurring obstacle in the struggle to form a new class party in Britain.

War and revolution are vital tests for revolutionaries. By supporting national defence in the imperialist war, the right wing of the workers' movement, including in Britain the Labour Party and the trade union leadership, passed over to the camp of the bourgeoisie. The centre and the left proved by their continued defence of the basic internationalist interests of the working class that they remained within the proletarian camp, but only the left defended the need for a revolutionary struggle against the war. By breaking with the social chauvinists and identifying with the Zimmerwald movement, the left had taken the first necessary steps towards the regroupment of revolutionaries at an international level. But a political struggle against the centre and against the influence of centrism within the ranks of the workers' movement was still an essential condition for the creation of a new party and a new International. An equally important condition for this was the presence of revolutionaries within the working class, to intervene in the workers' struggles and give them a revolutionary direction. It was the workers' own efforts to defend themselves against the attacks on their conditions that was to lay the ground for a revolutionary struggle against the war and strengthen the left in its struggle against chauvinism and social pacifism.

Notes

1 See J. Riddell (Ed.), *Lenin's Struggle for a Revolutionary International, vol. 1, Documents: 1907-1916 The preparatory years,* Monad, 1984, pp.1-47. This crucial section was put forward by Rosa Luxemburg on behalf of the left in the International.

2 Quoted in James Hinton, *Labour and Socialism,* Wheatsheaf, 1983, p.100.

3 *Justice,* 13 August 1914.

4 'Statement of the Executive Committee', *Justice,* 17 September 1914.

5 Letter from 'JM', *Justice,* 17 August 1914.

6 *Justice,* 17 September 1914.

7 *Vanguard,* October 1915.

8 See 'Resolution at a meeting of the Executive Committee on 14 December 1912', *BSP Report of the Second Annual Conference, 1913,* p.37.

9 *BSP Report of the Second Annual Conference, 1913,* pp.16-18.

10 See *Justice,* 4 March 1915.

11 See Fairchild's proposed resolution in *Justice,* 28 October 1915.

12 *BSP Report of the Fifth Annual Conference, 1916,* pp.11-13. A Hyndmanite minority remained within the conference: significantly, a resolution from the militant Kentish Town Branch committing the party to fighting "the only war - the class war" was passed by the lowest number of votes (55), with 13 delegates voting against.

13 *Socialist,* September 1914.

14 Conference report, *Socialist,* June 1915. Raymond Challinor, in his sympathetic study of the SLP (*The Origins of British Bolshevism,* Croom Helm, 1977), is misleading about the party's response to the war, claiming that it "never wavered from its stand of proletarian internationalism" (p.124). He does not mention the emergence of a defencist tendency which included the editor of its paper, and even quotes selectively from Muir's own arguments to support his claim that the party adopted a revolutionary defeatist position against the war (see p.126). The defencist nature of Muir's position, which was heavily justified by the use of Marx's arguments for supporting wars in the 19th Century, is clear from a reading of the complete text (see *Socialist,* November 1914, January 1915).

15 *Socialist,* May 1916.

16 *Socialist Standard,* September 1914.

17 *Spur,* September 1914.

18 *Socialism and War,* Bakunin Press, London, 1915, p.10.

19 Lenin, 'The position and tasks of the Socialist International', November 1914, in Riddell, *op. cit.,* p.164.

20 For further details including documents of the Zimmerwald Conference, see Riddell, *op. cit.,* pp.276-325.

21 *BSP Report of the Fifth Annual Conference, 1916.* See also 'Statement of the EC' in *Justice,* 16 December 1915.

22 *The Call,* 24 February 1916.

23 *Vanguard,* October 1915.

24 *Vanguard*, December 1915. See text no. 1.

25 *Socialist*, February 1916. The author was Alexander Sirnis, a little known émigré socialist who appears to have had close links with the Bolsheviks and the Spartacists. Sirnis was a member of the BSP but contributed numerous translations of texts by Lenin and others to the *Socialist*. He left the BSP in September 1917 because of its 'political opportunism'. He died in November 1918 (See Challinor, *op. cit.*, p.167)

26 Lenin, 'The tasks of the proletariat in our revolution', in *Lenin on Britain,* Progress, third revised edition, 1973, p.283.

27 Manifesto of the National Council of ILP, *Labour Leader,* 13 August 1914.

28 See Walter Kendall, *The Revolutionary Movement in Britain 1900-21*, Weidenfeld & Nicholson, 1969, n., p.351.

29 Guy Aldred, *No Traitors Gait!,* Strickland Press, 1955, p.112.

Chapter 2

Revolution

The collapse of the Second International and social democracy's definitive betrayal, while disarming the working class and temporarily putting a brake on its struggles, did not constitute a decisive blow, and the genuine euphoria with which thousands of workers greeted the war (in Britain, for example, nearly a quarter of a million miners volunteered for military service in the first nine months) began to evaporate as ever greater sacrifices were demanded in the name of the war effort. In order to prosecute the war the bourgeoisie was forced to push through a whole series of repressive measures with the support of the trade unions, amounting in effect to the militarisation of labour. In such conditions the class 'truce' imposed by the Labour Party and trade unions could not hold, and when it did break the workers were forced to struggle against their own union leaders and confront the capitalist state directly.

The working class lays the basis for the new party

As early as February 1915, engineering workers on the Clyde struck for higher wages against the union executive and formed their own unofficial strike committee. Rent strikes also began. In July, 200,000 South Wales miners struck in defiance of the Munitions Act and forced concessions from the government, while in November 1915 transport workers in Dublin paralysed the docks. Unofficial shop stewards' committees grew up all over country. The introduction of conscription in 1916 provoked further strikes by Clydeside engineering workers, which were only cut short by the wholesale arrest and imprisonment of the strike leaders (including John Maclean). The centre of resistance now moved to England with a strike by engineering workers in Sheffield in November 1916, and in the following March further repressive government measures led to renewed unrest which spread throughout England, eventually involving over 200,000 workers; the largest strike movement of the war.

These struggles were part of a rising international movement. Protests against the war began in Germany in 1915, when 15,000 demonstrators in Berlin marched against the war. There were also numerous strikes in Austria, against the orders of the unions. On 1st May 1916 10,000 workers in Berlin demonstrated against the war: Karl Leibknecht shouted "Down with the war! The main enemy is at home!" and was promptly arrested, sparking huge protests which led to a political mass strike against his imprisonment. There were also struggles against hunger and price rises. The Russian workers launched economic strikes against hunger, misery and increased exploitation. At the front, there were growing desertions and mutinies, especially in the Russian, German and French armies.

In the midst of the slaughter, these struggles opened up revolutionary possibilities. Despite their initial isolation, those few revolutionaries who had remained faithful to the cause of the proletariat in 1914 now found opportunities to win a hearing in the workers' struggles, and to put forward a revolutionary perspective against the war. The group around John Maclean was very active in the unofficial strike movements on Clydeside. Against the prevalent disdain of British socialists for the class's immediate struggles, Maclean saw every determined struggle of the workers as a preparation for socialism, and the *Vanguard* goup put its efforts into connecting all the different struggles on immediate issues – wages, rent rises, the 'dilution' of skilled labour – into a class-wide offensive to end the war, calling on the Clyde workers to adopt the tactic of the political strike along the lines of the pre-war European mass strikes:

> We rest assured that our comrades in the various works will incessantly urge this aspect on their shopmates, and so prepare the ground for the next great counter-move of our class in the raging class warfare – raging more than even during the Great Unrest period of three or four years ago ... the only way to fight the class war is by accepting every challenge of the master class and throwing down more challenges ourselves. Every determined fight binds the workers together more and more, and so prepares for the final conflict. Every battle lifts the curtain more and more, and clears the heads of our class to their robbed and enslaved conditions, and so prepares them for the acceptance of our full gospel of socialism, and the full development of the class struggle to the end of establishing socialism.[1]

The *Vanguard* group also intervened in Clyde Workers' Committee, the body set up by the militant shop stewards to co-ordinate their struggle against the Munitions Act, urging it to organise swift, determined mass action against the threat of conscription. But after criticising the Committee's leadership for refusing to deal with the issue of the war, the group was expelled from its meetings. Maclean was led to question the Committee's ability to respond to the needs of the class struggle, calling on the workers if necessary to "take the initiative into their own hands."[2] The unofficial shop stewards' committees thrown up during the war were primarily an expression of the struggle of skilled engineering workers against the erosion of hard-won pre-war gains, largely restricting their activity to a militant shopfloor defence of conditions which avoided the question of the war and the need to develop a revolutionary perspective for the class struggle.[3] Only the revolutionary left around Maclean consistently intervened in the workers' struggles to call for a class struggle against the war.

The Socialist Labour Party had a strong presence on Clydeside, where some of its militants played a leading role in the Clyde Workers' Committee. The SLP failed, however, to raise the question of the war or to give the struggles a revolutionary perspective, pandering instead to the syndicalist ideas of the majority and restricting its intervention to a call for nationalisation and workers' self-management of the munitions industry. The SLP leadership saw the shop stewards' committees as a step towards the building of new, industrial unions in opposition to the old craft unions. During the 1917 engineering workers' strikes the *Socialist* did however call for an extension of the struggle to other sectors, and through its active involvement in these struggles a section of the SLP began to move away from a dogmatic attachment to building new permanent forms of organisation and relate more closely to developments within the workers' struggles.[4] Meanwhile, from its initial focus on the fight for women's suffrage, the small group in the East End of London around Sylvia Pankhurst also moved closer to the workers' struggles to defend their conditions, actively denouncing the imperialist war at mass demonstrations and leading protests to the government against repression and the hunger and misery imposed on the working class.

In this way, through their active intervention in the growing struggles against the war, revolutionaries gained a small but significant hearing for internationalist positions within the working class, as part of an international movement against the war. The outbreak of revolution in Russia in February 1917, only three years after capitalism had plunged the world into the massacre, was a spectacular confirmation of the revolutionary perspective of this movement. In November 1918 the German navy mutinied and workers' and soldiers' councils emerged overnight in almost every German city, threatening a situation of dual power and forcing the bourgeoisie to hurriedly declare an armistice in order to be able to deal with the proletarian threat. As the SLP observed: "For the first time in history a great world war had been ended by the action of the workers."[5] The imperialist war was turning into a civil war.

To revolutionaries in Britain, these events appeared as the first steps in the world revolution. John Maclean, newly released from prison after huge workers' demonstrations in his support, wrote: "This is the class war on an international basis, a class war that must and will be fought out to the logical conclusion - the extinction of capitalism everywhere. The question for us in Britain is how we must act in playing our part in this world conflict."[6] The SLP was also in no doubt that a revolutionary situation was opening up: "Russia and Germany, with their soviets, have lifted socialism beyond the mere conjectures of theoretical speculation. The social revolution is on now. It is for us in this country to bring it to its consummation."[7] In the *Dreadnought*, Pankhurst pointed out that the armistice was the "fruits of the Russian revolution, which has evoked a workers' revolution also in Germany." The real war for freedom was only beginning.[8]

The actual situation in Britain at the end of the war appeared to confirm these revolutionary conclusions. In January 1918 the Clyde munitions workers had threatened a political strike against conscription, calling for action to end the war. After the armistice the British bourgeoisie faced widespread discontent, with strikes at home and abroad, unrest in the armed forces and even in the police. Clydeside became the focus of a growing movement for shorter working hours, led by engineering workers, miners and dockers, supported reluctantly by the trade unions. In January 1919, 70,000 workers in Glasgow responded to a general strike call issued by a joint committee of local trade unions and the unofficial Clyde Workers' Committee. The strike spread rapidly to other sectors across Scotland, with mass pickets of five to ten thousand workers bringing out factories along the Clyde. Racing to get ahead of the movement the Scottish TUC called for a general strike throughout Scotland. There were expressions of solidarity from workers in Barrow and other English centres, while at the same time in Belfast a struggle by 60,000 engineering and shipbuilding workers for a 44 hour week led to a general strike, with the city practically under the control of the strike committee.

The British bourgeoisie, fearing a massive extension of these economic struggles, now used the same tactic as its German counterpart during the Berlin insurrection the previous month, using repression to try to provoke the workers into a premature action. A peaceful demonstration of 30,000 workers in Glasgow's George Square was viciously attacked by police, leaving 53 injured. The strike leaders were arrested. Overnight, trainloads of troops were brought in and the city was effectively put under military occupation with armed guards, machine guns, tanks and barbed wire.

The British workers, including their revolutionary minorities, were totally unprepared for a direct confrontation with the state. The original strike call had been made without any prior effort to co-ordinate solidarity action in the rest of the country, and in the absence of a revolutionary leadership the strike movement quickly declined. With the notable exception of John Maclean, British revolutionaries lacked any strategy or tactics for the struggle, typically restricting themselves to general statements of support.[9] Maclean's strategy, based on his analysis of the international situation and the level of class consciousness among the mass of the workers in Britain, was to engage British capitalism so that it would be unable to pursue its policy of crushing the Russian workers, and to develop a revolution in Britain by unifying the working class, both employed and unemployed, around the demand for a drastic reduction of working hours: "Here we have the economic issue that can unify the workers in the war against capitalism."[10] At the level of tactics, he threw his efforts into strengthening the workers' unofficial organisations and building links with other sectors, in particular with the Lanarkshire miners and workers in the north of England. He tried unsuccessfully to persuade the organisers to postpone the Clyde strike, in order to ensure the best conditions for the effective extension of the struggle. He also argued against the planned peaceful demonstration in Glasgow and warned the workers to take measures to protect themselves.[11] In his balance sheet of the defeat of these struggles, Maclean was forced to conclude that the failure of the Clyde and Belfast strikes was "due more to the lack of working class ripeness than to batons, tanks, and machine guns...", and he highlighted in particular the failure of the struggles to extend.[12]

With hindsight, we can see that this was the high point of the post-war revolutionary wave in Britain. The bourgeoisie's decisive action had nipped in the bud any direct revolutionary threat, while growing unemployment among former munitions workers rapidly destroyed the bargaining power of the shop stewards and allowed the trade unions to regain control of the unofficial movement. By March 1919, in an almost throwaway line, the SLP was reporting that, "The general industrial situation [on the Clyde] is quiescent, with unemployment on the increase."[13] Potentially dangerous strikes by the miners and other industrial sectors were headed off by government concessions, while hastened demobilisation helped to defuse unrest in the armed forces.

Internationally, the early part of 1919 also saw a series of significant setbacks for the proletariat, especially in Germany where, despite the warnings of the Communist Party (KPD), premature attempts at insurrections in Berlin and Bremen led to the massacre of thousands, including the KPD leaders Karl Leibknecht and Rosa Luxemburg, at the hands of troops directed by the social democratic regime. In Bavaria, another short-lived attempt to set up a soviet republic was similarly drowned in blood. By successfully preventing the development of a unified mass movement in Germany, the bourgeoisie was able to break the backbone of the European proletariat's revolutionary struggles, then to pick off and crush the dispersed and often premature uprisings that followed. Despite these defeats, however, the working class still possessed enormous reserves of combativity and continued to show great willingness to go onto the attack; in March a soviet republic was proclaimed in Hungary, which encouraged workers' uprisings in Poland and Austria. In Britain, the most powerful battalions of the class – the miners, railway workers, transport workers and engineers – still threatened to unleash huge struggles against the government.

There was plenty of evidence therefore that the perspective was still towards world revolution. A significant factor in the defeats in Germany and Hungary, but also in Britain, was the absence of strong communist parties with the necessary influence to be able to warn the workers against the provocations of the bourgeoisie and to prevent precipitate actions, as the Bolsheviks had successfully been able to do during the July Days in Petrograd in 1917. The hard work of constructing such organisations at an international level was now an urgent necessity if the working class was to avoid further defeats and return to the offensive against capitalism

The split between the reformist and revolutionary wings of the workers' movement

The February revolution in Russia was greeted with widespread and genuine enthusiasm by the British working class. The left saw in these events the first step towards a proletarian revolution, exposing the hypocrisy of the British bourgeoisie's 'support' for the February revolution and identifying with the Bolsheviks, emphasising that it was the workers' and soldiers' councils which had overthrown the Tsarist regime:

> In so far as the Russian revolution has cleared away the paraphernalia of medieval feudalism it was a glorious step in social evolution, and as such, all socialists welcome it; but across the triumph of Russian capitalism there looms the spectre of international socialism. British capitalism welcomed the success of its class in Russia: but it is gravely disturbed as to how far the workers will carry the revolution of which they compose the left wing and the driving force.[14]

For the left, the first task of the working class in the belligerent countries was to take revolutionary action to prevent the crushing of the Russian workers: "if Russian socialism is crushed by the capitalist forces it will be harder still...to throw off the yoke when it becomes more unbearable than ever... Sympathy with Russia is nothing if we cannot strike a blow at our own chains."[15] But the leadership of the British Socialist Party still avoided drawing such a conclusion: in a resolution put forward by Fairchild for the Executive Committee, the Party's 1917 conference limited itself to abstract propaganda against 'despotism and militarism', and for the restoration of the Second International.[16] Together with the Independent Labour Party, the BSP attempted to bring together the revolutionary and reformist wings of the workers' movement in support of the Russian revolution. The Leeds Convention of June 1917 saw the extraordinary spectacle of well known social pacifist leaders of the British Labour Movement like Ramsay MacDonald hailing the Russian revolution, asserting their enthusiasm for the dictatorship of the proletariat and calling for workers' and soldiers' councils on the Russian model! A resolution calling for the formation of 'councils of workmen and soldiers' made it clear that their intended role, far from being organs of proletarian power, was "to work strenuously for a peace made by the peoples of the various countries" and to "generally support the work of the trade unions."[17] The mover of this resolution, the Labour MP Anderson, went out of his way to reassure the delegates, who were mostly from local Labour Parties and trade unions, that this was not at all intended to be a threat to the state.[18]

Behind all this posturing lay a more sinister purpose: for the leaders of the Labour Party and the trade unions this was a rehearsal for the role they would be called on to play if the British workers decided to take their own revolutionary action in support of their Russian comrades; the same bloody role their German counterparts were to perform so enthusiastically when they crushed the Berlin insurrection in January 1919. In the calls for spurious soviets to be set up under the control of the trade unions we can see the shape of the counter-revolutionary strategy the left wing of the bourgeoisie was preparing to deal with this threat; by absorbing an upsurge of working class militancy into a more flexible local union apparatus under the cover of revolutionary rhetoric. The Labour leaders' specific role for the capitalist state was to alert the rest of the bourgeoisie to the need for such a strategy.[19]

The overthrow of the Russian provisional government and the seizure of power by the soviets in October 1917 signalled the irreversible split between the reformist and revolutionary wings of the workers' movement. The left instinctively recognised the significance of these events; the SLP, for example, under the banner "Hail! Revolutionary, Socialist Russia", proclaimed that, "The workers in Russia have now taken control of affairs in their country."[20] The impact on the WSF was even more dramatic, prompting the group almost overnight to shed many of its pacifist and parliamentary illusions and become a resolute supporter of soviet power. In their defence of the Russian revolution against the attacks of the bourgeoisie, both groups adopted almost identical positions:

– *full support for the seizure of political power by the working class, and recognition of the role of the soviets.* The WSF, for example, was clear that "The council of workers' and soldiers' deputies...was the power that made the revolution..."[21]; in fact, "...the soviets created the revolution. They sprang into being at its outbreak, they carried through the deposition of the czar in March, and every subsequent advance has been initiated by the soviets."[22]

– *solidarity with the Bolsheviks against all the lies in the capitalist press about a 'coup d'etat':*

Their opponents strive to make it appear that Lenin and his party are a handful of people which has imposed its domination upon the unwilling Russian people; but it is the workers' and soldiers' council which has now deposed Kerensky and the provisional government, and itself becoming the government has chosen Lenin to be its prime minister...[23]

– *full support for the action of the Bolsheviks in dispersing the constituent assembly.* The WSF highlighted:

The failure the elections for the constituent assembly, even though decided by adult suffrage ballot, to return members prepared to support the policy of the soviets... As a representative body, an organisation such as the All-Russian workers', soldiers', sailors' and peasants' council is more closely in touch with and more directly represents its constituents than the constituent assembly, or any existing parliament.[24]

Through their active solidarity with the October revolution against the bourgeoisie's barrage of lies, both the SLP and the WSF passed the test of a revolutionary organisation with some honour. Others, however, failed miserably. Faced with the choice of supporting either workers' soviets or bourgeois constituent assembly, the SPGB, for example, showed its dogmatic attachment to the institutions of bourgeois democracy by backing the latter as expressing, at least in part, "the will of the Russian people". Instead of creating their own mass organisations, according to the SPGB the Russian workers should have supported the constituent assembly because "the franchise presents to the workers the way to their emancipation. Until the workers learn to use this instrument properly they are not fit or ready for socialism."[25] In this way, the SPGB added its own small voice to the bourgeoisie's propaganda campaigns in defence of democracy and against the very idea of revolution.

The best elements in the anarchist movement showed more class solidarity: the Glasgow Anarchist Group around Guy Aldred, for example, defended the Russian revolution and the necessity for the dictatorship of the proletariat against those anarchists who from the very beginning asserted that the Bolsheviks were no better than any other government. Aldred argued that: "those anarchists who oppose the dictatorship as a transitional measure are getting dangerously close to supporting the cause of the reactionaries... If abstract anarchism is opposed to the social revolution...it must be repudiated by every soldier of the red flag."[26]

The British Socialist Party greeted the seizure of power by the Russian proletariat as the first step in the international social revolution. But while for the SLP and WSF the logical next step was to call for sympathetic action by British workers to defend the Russian bastion and end the war, the BSP's leadership still hesitated. From 1917 onwards BSP was a prime example of a centrist party moving leftwards under the pressure of events. With the departure of its right-wing chauvinist leadership in 1916, the party had found itself led not by Maclean and the revolutionary left but by the social pacifist tendency around Fairchild and Alexander, which resisted the efforts of the revolutionary forces to found a new International and made all anti-war action conditional on the 'reconstitution' of the Second International. It made no attempt to conduct agitation in the armed forces or to intervene in the workers' struggles to give them a revolutionary anti-war perspective. Nor was any effort made to carry out clandestine work or to make contact with the left abroad. But with the course of history flowing rapidly towards class confrontations, and with more and more strikes breaking out on the home front, conditions were favourable to the left in the party, which was strengthened, as in the pre-war period, by an influx of new militants coming directly from the struggles in the factories, where BSP members like William Gallacher had become active, without the party's direction, in the unofficial shop stewards' movement. The left, again without official sanction, also made closer links with the revolutionary movement abroad, particularly in Russia. Émigré members like Petroff, Rothstein and Chicherin contributed to Trotsky's journal *Nashe Slovo*, which was widely distributed in this country and in turn acted as an influence on the left in the BSP.

At the BSP's 1918 conference the membership expressed its support for the Russian revolution in very general terms.[27] The interventions of left-wing delegates revealed the underlying pressures building up in the party: J.F. Hodgson, for example, observed that the October revolution had meant "driving a wedge between the reformist section of the socialist movement and the revolutionary section", and "A good many people in this country who had posed as revolutionaries had proved to be reformists..."[28] The conference had shown "that we were going more and more towards the left, while certain other people were going towards the right."[29] Typically it was Maclean who, giving vent to deep frustrations at the party's lack of action in the face of British military intervention, most clearly argued the need for a revolutionary position:

> There is a spirit of revolution developing inside the workshop, and we should be watching our enemy at home so as to seize the opportunity at any movement to down capitalism... What is wanted is not pious resolutions in support of our Russian comrades, but to use every action of the British government for the advancement of our own cause. We should get our comrades to...talk and think revolution... We are in the rapids of revolution...we should go forward from this moment determined to focus all activity and energy into one unified movement...to arouse class consciousness and revolutionary feeling among the workers.[30]

Only one month after making this speech, Maclean was arrested and sentenced to five years imprisonment for sedition; a calculated act of repression by the British bourgeoisie which robbed the revolutionary movement in Britain of its most able and determined leader at a moment when the threat of revolution at home seemed most imminent.

For the time being, the reformists in the BSP's leadership remained in place, albeit under mounting pressure from the party's left wing. It was the founding of the Third International in March 1919 that finally brought the struggle inside the BSP to a head. The party was still formally committed to the reconstruction of the Second International 'on Marxian lines', but fundamentally the leadership rejected the relevance of the Russian revolution to Britain and repudiated any idea that the British workers were about to abandon constitutionalism; the reconstruction of the International on the basis of a revolutionary programme was therefore invalid.[31] The left called on the party to choose its camp: either with the Bolsheviks in the revolutionary Third International; or with the anti-revolutionary patriotic, opportunist, and pacifist socialists in the Second.[32] The split finally came at the annual party conference in April 1919. Under pressure from the left, the executive put forward a resolution (dubbed 'sovietist') committing the party to support a world revolution that would overthrow capitalism and establish soviet power. Fairchild attempted to delete all reference to soviets but was overwhelmingly defeated and Maclean accused him openly of going over to the enemy. The right was now completely isolated, but on the question of support for the Third International there were still signs of vacillation, and in the end the leadership avoided taking a position by proposing a ballot of the membership. Sylvia Pankhurst congratulated the BSP on having declared for soviets in Britain, but:

> ...the BSP has not quite made up its mind yet to throw in its lot with the socialist revolution. It could not decide whether to sever its connection with the sham International of Henderson, Huysmans, Vandervelde, Thomas and their kind...or with the Red International, the Third International... Not being quite sure to which International it will belong, the BSP conference has referred the question to its branches. On that decision hangs the future of the BSP.[33]

The ensuing ballot showed an overwhelming majority of branches in favour of affiliating to the Third International and Fairchild and Alexander finally withdrew from the party in October 1919. This did not, however, by any means signify the defeat of centrism within the BSP.

The Socialist Labour Party also identified itself with the Third International, expressing its support for its founding congress "in the desire to unite the forces of the world revolution."[34] But the SLP did not vote to join until March 1921. Despite its boast that it was at the head of the revolutionary movement for socialism in Britain, the SLP did not sufficiently grasp the importance of regroupment at an international level. The strength of the Workers' Socialist Federation, on the other hand, was precisely its practical grasp of internationalism; the WSF enthusiastically embraced the call for a new International, severing its links with the Second at its annual conference in June 1919 and instructing its executive committee to link up with the Third.[35]

In 1914 those few revolutionaries who remained faithful to internationalism had appeared to be in a hopeless minority, isolated from the working class. Within three years, the correctness of their stand was spectacularly confirmed by the successful seizure of political power by the workers in Russia, and the revolutionary wave of struggles that erupted to end the war. It was the resurgence of class struggle which created the objective conditions for the regroupment of revolutionaries and for a new world party of the proletariat to replace the reactionary Second International. The initiative of the Bolsheviks in convening a new International was an absolutely vital step in this process. Far from being premature, it was if anything late in relation to the immediate tasks facing the working class: to avoid all the traps laid by the bourgeoisie and to return to the offensive against capitalism, armed with strong communist parties capable of playing a decisive role in the mass struggles to come.

Notes

1 *Vanguard,* December 1915.
2 *Ibid.*
3 See Gallacher in the *Worker,* 29 January 1916, cited in Kendall, *op. cit.,* p.116.
4 See *Socialist,* June 1917, July 1917.
5 *Ibid.,* November 1918.
6 *The Call,* 23 January 1919.
7 *Socialist,* November 1918.
8 *Workers' Dreadnought,* 16 November 1918.
9 For example, see Sylvia Pankhurst's editorial in the *Workers' Dreadnought,* 8 February 1919: "Socialists must support all strikes..."
10 *The Call,* 23 January 1919.
11 See Kendall, *op. cit.,* p.139.
12 *Worker,* 12 April 1919, reprinted in Nan Milton (Ed.), *John Maclean. In the Rapids of Revolution. Essays, Articles and Letters 1902-23,* Allison & Busby, 1978, p.155.
13 *Socialist,* 13 March 1919.
14 Supplement to the *Socialist,* April 1917. For the SLP see also *Socialist,* June 1917. For the WSF, see *Woman's Dreadnought,* 24 March and 30 June 1917.
15 *Socialist,* August 1917.
16 *BSP Report of the Sixth Annual Conference, 1917,* pp.10-11.
17 *What Happened at Leeds,* Pelican Press, 1917, reprinted in *British Labour and the Russian Revolution,* Spokesman, n.d., p.29.
18 *Ibid.,* pp.30-31.

19 For example see Anderson's speech in the House of Commons, *ibid.*, pp.11-13.
20 *Socialist*, December 1917.
21 *Workers' Dreadnought* , 17 November 1917.
22 *Ibid.*, 26 January 1918.
23 *Ibid.*, 17 November 1917.
24 *Ibid.*
25 *Socialist Standard*, May 1919.
26 *Spur*, September 1919, quoted in John Quail, *The Slow Burning Fuse*, Granada, 1978, p.299.
27 See *BSP Report of the Seventh Annual Conference, 1918*, p.15.
28 *Ibid.*
29 *Ibid.*, p.16. Hodgson was elected to the executive committee at the conference.
30 *BSP Report of the Seventh Annual Conference, 1918*, pp.16-17 (wording slightly amended to read in first person).
31 E.C. Fairchild in *The Call*, 24 October 1918.
32 See text no. 2.
33 *Workers' Dreadnought*, 26 April 1919.
34 Conference report in the *Socialist*, 24 April 1919.
35 *Workers' Dreadnought*, 14 June 1919.

Chapter 3

Programme

Comrades! Our task today is to discuss and adopt a programme. In undertaking this task, we are not activated solely by the consideration that yesterday we founded a new party and that a new party must formulate a programme. Great historical movements have been the determining causes of today's deliberations. The time has arrived when the entire socialist programme of the proletariat has to be established on a new foundation. (Rosa Luxemburg at the founding congress of the German Communist Party, 1918)[1]

The formation of the Communist Party of Great Britain is usually described in terms of the protracted negotiations between the main participating socialist groups to form a single organisation. But as Rosa Luxemburg well understood, the creation of a class party is more than just a merger of existing organisations; it is also a vital moment in the clarification of the historic programme of the proletarian movement; of its ultimate goals, and the methods and tactics needed to achieve them. What was the programmatic basis upon which the new class party in Britain was to be founded? More specifically, what was the level of clarity achieved by the different revolutionary tendencies in Britain on the change of historic period, and its implications for the methods and tactics to be used by the proletariat to destroy capitalism?

The decay of capitalism

The Third International was founded on the recognition that capitalism had entered into a new phase of its existence, as its platform proclaimed: "A new epoch is born! The epoch of the dissolution of capitalism, of its inner disintegration. The epoch of the communist revolution of the proletariat!"[2] The immediate task of the proletariat was to destroy the old bourgeois state power and replace it with its own dictatorship based on the soviets or workers' councils.

This understanding that capitalism had definitively left behind its phase of progressive expansion did not appear out of the blue but was the product of the pre-war political struggle waged by the left – in particular the Bolsheviks, the Dutch Tribunists and the left wing of the German Socialist Party – against the revisionist theories of Bernstein and others on the right wing of the Second International, who began to argue that capitalism was capable of overcoming its own inner contradictions, and that the struggle for gradual reforms alone could result in a peaceful transition to socialism. Against these arguments, Rosa Luxemburg demonstrated in her 1899 pamphlet *Reform or Revolution* that the rise of militarism and state control were symptoms of the sharpening contradictions of capitalism that, far from denying the validity of Marxism, were actually confirming the conditions for the proletarian revolution.[3] For the left, the outbreak of world war was the definitive proof that capitalism was no longer a progressive social system, making the communist revolution both a necessity and a practical possibility.

The left in Britain not only participated in this political struggle as part of European social democracy, but also made its own contribution to the Marxist understanding of the changing conditions for the class struggle in the most advanced capitalist countries. As early as the 1880s William Morris, for example, identified the rise of imperialism as a response to capitalism's increasingly desperate need for new markets:

...the one thing for which our thrice accursed civilisation craves, as the stifling man for fresh air, is new markets; fresh countries must be conquered by it which are not manufacturing and are producers of raw material, so that 'civilised' manufactures can be forced on them. All wars now waged, under whatever pretences, are really wars for the great prizes in the world market."[4]

The left in Britain fought vigorously against local variants of revisionism like Fabianism, and against the growth of 'state socialist' ideas, making an explicit link between the tendencies towards state capitalism at home and imperialism abroad: "Imperialism...is in its essence nothing but the application outside the British Isles of that socio-political principle which, when applied at home, leads to 'state socialism'. That principle is the organisation and the consolidation by the power of the state of...the interests of the capitalist classes."[5] State socialism simply meant that the state bureaucacy would become the sole exploiter of the working class. This represented "capitalism at its worst point of development."[6]

The Socialist Labour Party in particular developed quite a sophisticated analysis of state capitalism, arguing that even the Liberal government's welfare measures – despite offering some minimal improvements in the conditions of the working class – were fundamentally "a preliminary measure towards the bureaucratic enslavement of the people."[7] For the SLP, the final outbreak of the world war and the insatiable demands of the war economy greatly intensified this tendency, confirming the reactionary consequences of any support for more state control:

Nationalisation or 'state socialism' so far from being a method of working class progress to socialism, has become the very life blood and method of the most militant and aggressive imperialism... State control means the highest form of capitalism, and will create the industrial warfare of whole empires and groups of empires... Thus, along the road of nationalisation or state ownership, instead of meeting socialism, freedom and peace, we find competition intensified, wage slavery, militarism, and, in the distance, the bloodstained fields of future battlefields.[8]

Three years of bloodstained battlefields enabled the clearest elements of the SLP to conclude that capitalism, like the social systems that preceded it, had now definitely entered into its epoch of decadence.[9] Although this conclusion was influenced by a mechanistic vision of the system's 'inevitable' dissolution, it was based on the solid Marxist position that the war was essentially the product of capitalism's historic crisis of overproduction. Echoing Rosa Luxemburg, William Paul, for example, argued that in order to avert this crisis, the capitalist class had been forced to divert the productive forces into waste production, particularly of armaments, and finally to go to war in order to re-divide a saturated world market.[0]

There was also an understanding among revolutionaries that the war could not solve this crisis, and that unless the working class was able to destroy capitalism once and for all, the perspective would be one of further imperialist bloodbaths. On the revolutionary left wing of the BSP, John Maclean was probably the clearest in drawing the lessons of the economic struggle between capitalist states in the new period to ominously predict a second, even more destructive round of butchery, which threw into question the whole basis of any future struggle for reforms:

> The increased output of commodities...will necessitate larger markets abroad, and hence a larger empire. The same will apply to other capitalist countries. This must develop a more intense economic war than led up to the present war, and so precipitate the world into a bloodier business than we are steeped in just now. The temporary advantage the workers may get in shorter hours and higher wages with higher purchasing power will then be swept away in the destruction of millions of good lives and fabulous masses of wealth.[11]

These were vital insights by the most advanced minorities of the British workers' movement into the roots of the world war and its profound significance for the struggle for socialism.

New methods and tactics

The brutal realities of this new epoch threw into question all the methods and tactics of the previous period. A gradual and largely peaceful struggle for reforms based on the use of parliament and the trade unions was no longer valid; instead, as the platform of the Third International proclaimed, "The revolutionary epoch demands that the proletariat use those methods of struggle which concentrate its entire energy, namely the methods of mass action leading logically to direct clashes with the bourgeois state machine in open struggle."[12] The earliest statements of the International were entirely focused on developing a revolutionary struggle for soviet power; all other tactics were subordinated to this task. The theses drafted by Lenin for the founding congress, for example, declared that the practical tasks of the communist parties in countries where soviet power was not yet established were:

> 1. To explain to the broad masses of the working class the historical meaning of the political and practical necessity of a new proletarian democracy which must replace bourgeois democracy and parliamentarism.
> 2. To extend and build up workers' councils in all branches of industry, in the army and navy, and also amongst agricultural workers and small peasants.
> 3. To win an assured, conscious communist majority in the councils.[13]

29

Questions such as the precise attitude to be adopted towards bourgeois parliaments, and tactics to be employed in the trade unions, still remained to be clarified. On these and other issues the Bolsheviks recognised the need to adopt an open attitude. Furthermore, by founding the International partly on the German Spartacists' programme, and by inviting into its ranks the anarchists and syndicalists, the Bolsheviks were explicitly accepting those who defended anti-parliamentary and anti-trade union positions.[14] Among those who supported the principles of soviet power and the dictatorship of the proletariat, these were still matters for debate and clarification.

Parliament or soviets?

The experience of the Russian revolution, and in particular the Bolsheviks' dissolution of the constituent assembly, appeared as definitive proof to many revolutionaries that parliamentary action must now be discarded in favour of the struggle for soviets. The bourgeoisie made full use of elections and democratic mystifications, particularly in western and central Europe, to deflect the threat of revolution and prevent the spread of workers' councils. Not surprisingly, there were strong tendencies in the earliest communist parties to oppose any participation in parliaments: at the founding congress of the German Communist Party (KPD) in December 1918, for example, the majority voted against the leadership to boycott the national assembly. The Austrian and Polish Communist Parties also boycotted elections in early 1919. In Italy, the intransigent Marxist left of the Socialist Party (PSI) around Amadeo Bordiga and the journal *Il Soviet*, established the Communist Abstentionist Fraction in 1918. While clearly distancing itself from the anarchists, the Fraction insisted that the communist party could only be formed on the basis of renouncing electoral and parliamentary action.[15]

Despite their disagreements on the question of whether to participate in elections, revolutionaries like Rosa Luxemburg were agreed that bourgeois parliaments were so many "bastions of the counter-revolution" that would have to be destroyed.[16] The question therefore was how best to bring about this destruction and advance the struggle for soviet power.

In Britain, the wartime struggles had encouraged the growth of anti-parliamentary attitudes in the working class, particularly among younger generations of workers. The unofficial shop stewards' movement which had grown up was strongly (though not exclusively) anti-parliamentary, albeit largely from a syndicalist viewpoint which tended to see any electoral activity as a diversion from the primary struggle for workshop control.[17] The anarchists tended to be anti-parliamentary in principle, although in practice the tactics they adopted varied; the 'anarchist-communist' Guy Aldred, for example, was not opposed to the standing of candidates in elections as long as they pledged not to take their seats (the so-called 'Sinn Fein tactic').[18]

Among groups sympathetic to the Third International, only the small Workers' Socialist Federation adopted an abstentionist position similar to the German, Polish and Austrian communist parties. This group saw workers' councils as the machinery of the future soviet republic in Britain and emphasised their role as directly representative bodies of the working class. During the 1918 general election the WSF called for the overthrow of parliament. It confirmed this position at its June 1919 conference, refusing to take part in elections in favour of working for the formation of workers' committees and soviets.[19] However, throughout the negotiations to form a communist party the WSF emphasised that, while it was opposed to parliamentary action, it saw this as a question of tactics rather than of principle.[20] This distinguished it from the anarchists who were opposed to any participation in parliament in principle, and aligned it with Marxists in the International who considered abstention from electoral activity absolutely necessary in the struggle for soviet power in order to make a clean break with opportunism.

The Socialist Labour Party supported the use of parliamentary action as part of the De Leonist strategy to capture control of the capitalist state through the ballot box while building up industrial unions to take control of the factories. On the only occasion when the SLP stood parliamentary candidates in the 1918 general election, it was still formally on the basis of this strategy. However, just before the war as a result of its debate on state capitalism, the SLP had rejected the use of bourgeois parliaments for anything but agitation purposes.[21] There were also persistent anti-parliamentary tendencies within the party, and during 1919 several London branches broke away to form the Communist League which rejected parliamentary action.[22] After an open debate in its press, the SLP leadership came out in favour of the continued use of parliament for agitation purposes, although it called for abstention from the ballot box on certain occasions.[23]

At the time of the 1918 general election the British Socialist Party was still formally committed to a parliamentary road to socialism as part of the Labour Party. In practice, the BSP's position was a half-way house between reformism and revolution; its election manifesto made abstract calls for a social revolution and referred to the soviets as "the most democratic form of government", but it called on workers to vote for socialist and Labour candidates in order to "speed the socialist republic."[24] Only John Maclean stood openly as a socialist, the remaining fifteen BSP candidates running under the Labour Party banner.[25]

Parliamentary democracy versus soviet power was the central issue in the struggle between the party's reformist and revolutionary wings in 1918-1919. For the left, Theodore Rothstein pointed to the growing tendency of the capitalist state to by-pass parliament and govern through what was in effect an 'executive committee' of the ruling class:

It is this essential feature of parliament which makes it a mere talking shop, bereft of all capacity and will for action, and which must necessarily sterilise all reforming or revolutionary effort on the part of its Labour or socialist members... The growing distrust of the workers of this (as of every other) country in parliamentary government as a capitalist arrangement is therefore well founded, and it ought to be our business to deepen and to spread this distrust in such a way as to turn it into an opposition. To that end, however, we must also bring forward positive arguments by explaining the advantages of the soviet system.

But for Rothstein this did not imply an abandonment of parliamentary activity; on the contrary: "So long as the masses are still interested in parliament and attach importance to its proceedings, we should be fools, if not criminals, if we abstained from making use of its opportunities."[26] Some anti-parliamentary tendencies did emerge within the BSP, particularly among those (like Gallacher) who had become active in the shop stewards' movement and shared its syndicalist-influenced rejection of parliamentary activity. But on the whole the left wing of the BSP did not reject the continued use of parliamentary action. The reformist wing was finally defeated on the question of parliamentary versus soviet power, but this did not result in the adoption of an official position on the use of parliament for agitation only. Instead, following an open debate, the party simply dropped its former policy and the whole idea that parliament could be used as an instrument of revolution ceased to appear in its press. This centrist avoidance of a clear position hid the fact that a sizeable minority of the party remained attached to the old methods and tactics of parliamentarism and electoral activity, particularly at a local level.

Trade unions or soviets?

The Third International at first adopted an open attitude to the question of the trade unions, recognising that in Germany and Britain, for example, the workers had created new, alternative forms of organisation to wage their struggles. Bukharin, in his introductory remarks to the platform adopted at the founding congress, acknowledged that, while in Russia the trade unions were seen as having a positive role in the socialist reconstruction of society, in Germany they were acting against the proletariat and were already being replaced:

> The trade unions there no longer play any kind of positive role. We cannot work out any kind of concrete line on this, and therefore we say only that, in general terms, to manage the enterprises, institutions must be created that the proletariat can rely on, that are closely bound to production and embedded in the production process. If in Britain, for example, there are shop stewards committees or some kind of other organisations that stand close to the productive process, then they, like our trade unions or the German factory and plant committees, will serve as a basis of administration in socialist society.[27]

In Germany, the question of the correct tactics to be adopted towards the unions was an immediate one facing the newly-formed communist party; during the war the struggle between workers and unions had developed into open confrontations, leading to the formation of workers' councils. Despite the social democrats' efforts to try to refurbish their image, most communists remained outside the official unions (or were expelled anyway), and raised the slogan "Get out of the unions!" The debate at the KPD's founding congress therefore focused on building alternatives; speaking for the leadership, Luxemburg completely agreed that the goal of the struggle was the "liquidation" of the unions, which had become "organisations of the bourgeois state and of capitalist class rule."[28] However, she firmly opposed the idea of building new unitary organisations in the factories; instead it was necessary to develop the workers' councils as the real vehicles for unifying the political and economic struggles of the working class, and she argued strongly against any premature split from the unions that left the power of their existing leadership intact.

In Britain, the revolutionary wave did not lead to direct confrontations with the official unions or to the formation of workers' councils. The British trade unions, despite their enthusiastic support for the war effort, could still count a membership of nearly eight million in 1919. But the workers' struggles did show definite tendencies to go beyond and against the union apparatus through the creation of unofficial shop stewards' and workers' committees, and for revolutionaries the debate was essentially the same as in Germany: how to encourage anti-union tendencies and develop revolutionary alternatives as a step towards the emergence of workers' councils.

It was the left that most clearly recognised that the struggle for soviet power implied a struggle against the trade unions. For Sylvia Pankhurst, the experience of the German revolution showed that "The trade unions as we know them today in this country, will oppose, not foster, the growth of soviets."[29] But until there was a viable alternative in their place, the unions could not simply be ignored; the task of revolutionaries was to propagandise within them for the formation of workers' committees as the forerunners of the soviets, and to support any rank and file movement that emerged to oppose to the union bureaucracy.[30]

The anarchists took a more radical-sounding stance, denouncing the unions as part of the capitalist state and calling for revolutionary socialism as an alternative. As early as 1911 Guy Aldred had observed the tendency for the trade unions to become "an essential department or expression of the bourgeois state." But this view hid a strong tendency to dismiss any struggle by the working class for economic demands: for Aldred, the involvement of workers in any struggles for higher wages was a "worthless palliative effort" and doomed to failure; the only alternative was revolution.[31]

For the De Leonists, the question was not whether the official unions needed to be opposed, but what alternative was to be put in their place: industrial unions or soviets? Since its formation, the SLP had defended the position that the existing craft-based unions had become a bulwark of capitalism: the task of the working class was to organise itself into new, industry-wide unions which, once strong enough, would form their own political party to "demand the surrender of the capitalist class" and institute a"general lock-out" of the capitalists; after this the industrial unions would furnish the administrative machinery for "directing industry in the socialist commonwealth."[32] In practice, the SLP was able to avoid the reactionary consequences of this vision of a peaceful overthrow of capitalism, and as a result of its intervention in the pre-war mass strikes shed some of its sectarianism, prompting the departure of some of the most dogmatic De Leonists. But the SLP still formally adhered to the De Leonist programme; it saw the Russian revolution as a vindication of industrial unionism because of the introduction of workers' control in the factories, and even at the height of the revolutionary wave in November 1918 it still proposed that the workers should first form industrial unions as a means of then establishing soviet power.[33] Not surprisingly, this contradictory position heightened the tensions between those who remained wedded to the letter of De Leonism, and those who, through their active involvement in the wartime unofficial movement, essentially saw the shop stewards' and workers' committees as embryo soviets. The SLP's leadership avoided a split on this question by changing the party's constitution to urge the formation of workshop committees, while at the same time declaring the principle of industrial unionism "inviolate."[34] Industrial unionism continued to be a popular tactic in the British revolutionary movement in its wider sense of promoting the move from craft-based to industry-wide class organisation.[35]

One of the key factors in the British Socialist Party's move towards revolutionary positions had been the active involvement of its militants in the wartime class struggle. At its 1918 conference the party welcomed the shop stewards' movement as "a change in working class organisation rendered essential by altered conditions of capitalist production", and decided to advocate industrial unionism "as a class conscious weapon for the workers to fight the capitalist class."[36] The whole question of trade unionism was an issue in the debate between the party's revolutionary and reformist wings. Against the reformists' arguments, Theodore Rothstein argued that the trade unions were conservative organisations whose very role was predicated on capitalism's continued existence; revolutionaries should therefore encourage the growth of unofficial shop stewards' and workers' committees as the forerunners of soviets. The BSP left wing embraced the need to develop unofficial, soviet-style bodies within the existing unions, but it avoided drawing the logical conclusion that this would inevitably lead to an open confrontation with the union apparatus; Rothstein, for example, argued contradictorily that this tactic should be pursued without attacking or even antagonising the existing unions because they would still have a role to play in the "socialist reconstruction of society."[37] The BSP's propaganda at the height of the revolutionary wave spread illusions in the possibility of the workers defending themselves through 'their' unions, focusing on criticisms of individual union leaders like J.H. Thomas and calling for the reorganisation of the TUC. Despite the party's overwhelming acceptance of soviet power at its 1919 conference, it made little or no mention of the need for workers' councils; and where it did it implied that these could arise out of and embrace the local union apparatus.[38] On the eve of the Communist Party's formation, the BSP merely reiterated its support for industrial unionism and called on the trade unions to unite their forces to overthrow the wage system.[41]

The revolutionary left in the BSP failed to separate itself from this orientation. Some of those active in the shop stewards' movement, influenced by syndicalism, simply distanced themselves from the party.[39] John MacLean's whole post war revolutionary strategy was based on developing unofficial movements to pressure the union leadership into calling a general strike; he looked first to the miners' union and then to the Triple Alliance to lead this offensive against capitalism. Even after the successful counter-attack of the capitalist state, in which the trade unions played a vital role, MacLean continued to argue for a 'special committee' of the TUC to be appointed to lead a general strike, and spread illusions in radical-sounding union leaders like Robert Smillie of the miners. At no time did MacLean address the role of the soviets, remarkably failing even to mention them in his writings on the lessons of the October revolution.[40]

It was those like the grouping around Pankhurst and the clearest sections of the SLP who best understood the role of the trade unions as the last bulwark of capitalism, and the need to strengthen any tendency to go beyond and against them in order to prepare the ground for the formation of workers' councils. Unlike the anarchists, the Marxist left at no point rejected the need to work inside the trade unions; indeed at this time it still expressed illusions in the possibility of transforming their structure from within through rank and file control.[42] This reflected the heterogeneity of understanding in the whole working class on this question at the height of the revolutionary wave, especially in Britain where the workers had pioneered trade unions as mass defensive organisations of the class in capitalism's ascendance.

The Labour Party: a party of the bourgeoisie?

The Third International was founded on the basis that, by supporting the imperialist war, the social democratic parties had definiively passed over to the camp of the bourgeoisie.[43] By actively participating in the crushing of the workers' uprisings, especially in Germany, the social democrats demonstrated that they had now assumed the role of out-and-out butchers of the proletariat. The Bolsheviks' closest sympathisers in Britain were quick to warn that, given the opportunity, Labour Party leaders like Ramsay McDonald would massacre the workers just as mercilessly as Noske and Scheidemann.

The fact that the British Labour Party was formed by, and largely composed of, the trade unions, was from the beginning a source of some confusion in the socialist movement, and whether to work inside it was a matter of real debate for British Marxists before the first world war, with valid arguments put forward for and against.[44] Supporters of affiliation pointed to the Labour Party's supposed 'peculiarities'; that it was a federation of trades unions, co-operative societies and socialist societies, and hence not even a political party in the usual sense of the term, whose loose structure uniquely allowed freedom of criticism to socialists... The fundamental problem was the Labour Party's late formation right at the end of capitalism's progressive era when the conditions for a struggle for real reforms were fast disappearing, and as a result it was dominated by deeply opportunist political forces shaped by decades of class collaboration.

When the Labour Party applied to join the Socialist International in 1908 this confusion about whether it was a political party or a trade union-type body was exploited by the opportunist tendency within the International's leadership; Kautsky, for example, while conceding the LP did not expressly accept the class struggle, argued that "'in practice' the Labour Party conducts this struggle, and adopts its standpoint, inasmuch as the party is organised independently of the bourgeois parties."[45] Lenin, speaking for the revolutionary left, rejected this argument; while he accepted the logic that the Labour Party must be admitted if it was "the parliamentary representation of the trade unions", he argued that in practice the Labour Party was not independent of the bourgeois Liberal Party and did not pursue a fully independent class policy. However, he believed that the Labour Party represented "the first step on the part of the really proletarian organisations of Britain towards a conscious class policy and towards and socialist workers' party."[46] In the end, in an expression of centrism, the International adopted both positions. Arguments about the 'peculiarities' of the Labour Party were to re-emerge in the debate about the affiliation of communists in 1920.

The SDF's leadership had at first supported affiliation as part of its own opportunist turn towards the trade union bureaucracy and the ILP, but very quickly agreed to disaffiliate faced with the failure of this opportunism and with growing internal opposition. This came partly from the 'Impossibilists' in the organisation who from the start were strongly opposed to any collaboration with 'non-socialist' bodies, but also from the broader left wing of the SDF. Even Theodore Rothstein, who fought for the SDF to become a real social democratic party of the working class and bitterly attacked the Impossibilists as "traitors to socialism", conceded that re-affiliation would be a surrender of political principle. Increasingly the left found it necessary to denounce the Labour Party's betrayals of workers struggling to defend themselves, and its attitude became inseparable from the broader struggle of the left against opportunism in the Second International. When the British Socialist Party applied to affiliate to the Labour Party in 1913, it was as a direct result of pressure from the International's leadership; within a year the International was dead, its main leaders had gone over to the class enemy, and the Labour Party had become a faithful recruiting sergeant for the British bourgeoisie's war effort. Despite this definitive betrayal, the BSP's leadership continued to argue that the Labour Party was the political expression of the British working class.[47] The BSP's deep reluctance to break from the Labour Party was to constitute the single biggest obstacle to the regorupment of revolutionaries in Britain.

Significantly, from the start there were moves by the left in the BSP to sever links with the Labour Party. At the 1918 conference, for example, several delegates expressed their failure to understand how the BSP could remain affiliated to a party whose leaders acted as "recruiting sergeants and labour lieutenants of the capitalist class."[48] Maclean argued that the working class should have nothing to do with the Labour Party, which was "bound up at present with capitalism and fighting socialism." The task for revolutionaries was to develop "a force and organisation that would sweep the Labour Party on one side and develop the workers' class consciousness."[49] The leadership of the BSP, at this time still in the hands of the social pacifists, was strongly opposed to any move to disaffiliate, arguing that "Whether we liked it or not, the Labour Party, including ourselves, was the political movement of the working class."[50] In the end, the potentially dangerous call for a vote by the membership was avoided through a procedural fudge, but calls from within the BSP to dis-affiliate continued right up until the merger of the party into the CPGB in July 1920.

The Workers' Socialist Federation developed an intransigent opposition to communists having any dealings with the Labour Party, based on its own very practical experience of trying to change it from within. Pankhurst attended the 1918 Labour conference as a BSP delegate where, in a stormy speech, constantly interrupted and shouted down, she denounced the party's complicity in the government's attacks on Russia abroad and the working class at home. The WSF at this time was still hopeful that the Labour Party could be developed in a anti-capitalist direction, and supported the party's decision to finally end the electoral truce, for example, as "a step, but only a very small step, towards Labour's independence."[51] The group's activity inside the Labour Party represented a phase in its political evolution from reformist activity to revolutionary positions. It finally broke from the Labour Party in June 1919 when it declared for the Third International.[52] Significantly it had envisaged such a break even when it decided to affiliate early in 1918.[53]

A minimum programme or a revolutionary programme?

In the period of capitalism's ascendance it had been absolutely necessary for the workers' movement to struggle for reforms such as the limitation of the working day, the right to organise and the right to vote, as preconditions for the further development of the class struggle. The struggle of the left wing in the SDF before the first world war was in part a struggle to turn the organisation into a real party of the class, with a programme of democratic reforms along the lines of continental social democracy.[54] Even the 'Impossibilists', who were strongly against any involvement in reformist activity, did not reject reforms *per se*: the SLP, for example, raised demands in local elections for the eight hour day and a minimum wage, and adopted the position that, if elected to parliament or local government, it would vote for certain "palliative measures."[55] But the development of capitalism itself was eroding the conditions for any meaningful, lasting reforms, and the SLP found it necessary to try to distinguish genuine 'palliatives' from what were in reality state capitalist measures. This distinction became increasingly difficult to make, and on the eve of the first world war, following a debate ostensibly about its electoral policy, the party rejected any further support for capitalist legislation, on the grounds that the development of state bureaucracy was now being consciously encouraged by the ruling class as a means of preventing revolution.[56] The SLP still formally defended the obsolete and confused programme of De Leon, but in practice the most advanced elements in the party were able to develop further important insights into the features of the class struggle in capitalist decadence, including, as the following passage written at the height of the Clyde strike shows: the tendency towards workers' spontaneous self-organisation in struggles for immediate demands; the potential for these struggles to be transformed into political confrontations with the capitalist state, and the role of communists in giving expression to the ultimate goals of the workers' own demands:

We are passing through a revolutionary period. Since 1914 we have passed through several... but the present one is more intense and extensive than any of its predecessors... The distinguishing feature of a revolutionary period is the fact that the workers revolt spontaneously and that the driving force of the rebellion comes from below. Another symptom...is the break down of the traditional organisations of labour, such as the conservative trade unions, and the rapid rise of new, flexible, and unofficial workshop committees, which are manned by the rank and file... To us, a revolutionary period is pregnant with immense potentialities...it means we must translate the instinctive revolt of the masses into the conscious will to carry through the social revolution... it must be our clear duty to give concrete expression to the manifold demands of the workers and to organise them to enforce that expression... There is only one definite manner by means of which long hours, low wages, unemployment and lack of houses, and the other million grievances can be seriously tackled and that is by the workers taking over the means of production and controlling these themselves. To do this requires organisation. But the striking masses have spontaneously created such an organisation. That organisation is the unofficial workers' committees, which are springing up everywhere. These committees, representing every department in every mill, mine, railway or plant, contain the elements of an organisation which can transform capitalism into a soviet republic. (...)

The peculiar nature of a revolutionary period is that while the fight at present is one for shorter hours, etc., it may become a political struggle at any moment should the government take up some drastic and brutal attitude towards the strikers. We must be on the alert to use every turn of the revolt for our revolutionary mission.

The revolutionary period reveals the character of the class war. But the mere blind, instinctive struggle of the workers against their masters cannot overthrow capitalism and establish communism. Into that struggle every revolutionary socialist must throw himself or herself and give the masses a battle cry. And our battle cry must be: All power to the workers' committees![57]

It was more through its practical attachment to the struggle for soviet power that the WSF was able to grasp the essential points of a revolutionary programme for the new period. In the struggle for a class party it clearly contrasted the old

37

struggle for reforms and parliamentary and trade union action with the overthrow of capitalism by the workers' revolution and the dictatorship of the working class based on the soviets. Against nationalisation it posed the socialisation and workers' control of all production, distribution and exchange as steps towards communism. The weapon of the proletariat in this struggle was "the political strike and revolutionary industrial action organised by the communists."[58]

The leading elements of the left wing in the BSP also recognised that the old minimum programme, inherited from the previous period of 'social peace' could no longer apply, at least "in full."[59] But unlike the clearest elements in the WSF and SLP, the left in the BSP found it very difficult to decisively break from the parliamentary and local electoral activity of the previous period.

On the key questions of principles and tactics which animated the struggle for the class party in Britain – the attitude of communists to the Labour Party, the use of parliamentarism and trade union action – it was the left trend in the revolutionary movement which most firmly grasped the meaning of the new period for the proletariat's struggle. By actively working for revolution at home it most clearly expressed its practical support for the programmes of Bolshevism and Spartacism. The WSF's enthusiastic support for soviet power, for example, coupled with its intensely practical internationalism, enabled it to overcome its reformist illusions and to grasp the essentials of the communist programme very quickly. The left was also able to draw on the lessons of the struggle of the pre-war internationalist left in the Second International and of the Zimmerwald Left; this was a particular strength of the revolutionary left around John Maclean in the BSP. The left also demonstrated the most intransigent attachment to the Marxist method, which explains how at least some of the 'Impossibilists' in the SLP were able to overcome their party's dogmatism and sectarianism and deepen the Marxist understanding of state capitalism and its implications for the programme of the working class.

The weaknesses of the workers' movement in Britain have often been noted. But the British left still made an important contribution to understanding the change in conditions for the class struggle in the most advanced capitalist countries. It was able to do this firstly because it was well placed in Britain, the first industrialised capitalist nation, to observe the symptoms of capitalism's decay; and secondly, because it was an integral part of an international movement, linked by a web of political, organisational and personal connections to the Russian Bolsheviks, the German Spartacists, the Dutch Tribunists and the Italian Abstentionists... The British left participated alongside the Russian, German, Dutch and Italian lefts in the same political struggles: as part of the internationalist left in the Second International against revisionism and opportunism; then as part of the Zimmerwald Left against social chauvinism and centrism. In this context, it becomes clear that the abstentionist position defended by the WSF, for example, was not the 'extreme' view of a tiny fringe group, but the position taken up by a strong left wing tendency in early Third International, based on the lessons of the Bolsheviks' experience in 1917. Conversely, we can see that the support of groups like the BSP for work in the Labour Party and parliament was not some 'natural' response to British conditions, but an expression of the difficulty for the revolutionary movement to break with the obsolete ideas and practices of capitalism's ascendance. The struggle for a class party in Britain was in part a struggle led by the left to clarify the implications of the change in period for the class struggle, and to ensure that the programme of the new party was based on the needs of the new period of capitalism's decay.

Notes

1 Rosa Luxemburg, 'Speech to the founding convention of the German Communist Party', in Mary-Alice Waters (Ed.), *Rosa Luxemburg Speaks*, Pathfinder, 1970, p.405.

2 Jane Degras (Ed.), *The Communist International 1919-1943. Documents, vol. 1*, Frank Cass, 1971, p.18.

3 'Reform or Revolution' is included in Waters, *op. cit.*, pp.36-90. Luxemburg further analysed the economic roots of capitalism's historic crisis in *The Accumulation of Capital* (1913).

4 *Commonweal*, 19 February 1887.

5 Theodore Rothstein, *Social Democrat*, 15 December 1901, p.360.

6 *Socialist*, June 1912.

7 *Ibid.*, October 1913.

8 *Ibid.*, October 1916.

9 William Paul, *The State: Its Origin and Function*, SLP Press, 1917.

10 See, for example, *Socialist*, May 1917.

11 John Maclean, *The War after the War*, Scottish Labour College pamphlet, 1917, reprinted in Nan Milton (Ed.), *John Maclean. In the Rapids of Revolution. Essays, Articles and Letters 1902-23*, Allison & Busby, 1978, p.135.

12 'Platform of the Communist International', 1919, Degras, *op. cit.*, p.23.

13 'Theses on bourgeois democracy and proletarian dictatorship', 1919, *Ibid.*, p.16.

14 Written by Rosa Luxemburg in December 1918, *What the Spartacus League Wants* set out immediate measures to defend the German revolution including the abolition of all bourgeois parliaments and their replacement with workers' and soldiers' councils. Making no reference at all to the official unions, it called instead for the election of councils in every factory and the appointment of a central body to lead the mass strike movement (John Riddell (Ed.), *The German Revolution and the Debate on Soviet Power*, Pathfinder, 1986, pp.118-126).

15 See International Communist Current, *The Italian Communist Left, 1926-45*, 1992, p.18.

16 Rosa Luxemburg in the 'Discussion on the National Assembly', Riddell, *op. cit.*, p.177.

17 See, for example, W.F. Watson of the London Workers' Committee in *Workers' Dreadnought*, 14 December 1918.

18 See Mark Shipway, *Anti-Parliamentary Communism: the Movement for Workers' Councils in Britain, 1917-1945*, Macmillan, 1988, pp.9-10.

19 *Workers' Dreadnought*, 14 June 1919.

20 *Ibid.*, 10 April 1920.

21 See *Socialist*, April 1914. The party also rejected any further agitation for adult suffrage.

22 'Proposed constitution of the Communist League', n.d. [1919]. The League, which was an amalgamation of SLP branches and the Communist Propaganda Groups animated by the anarchist-communist Guy Aldred, was short-lived, publishing only three issues of its paper, the *Communist*.

23 For example in local elections at Paisley in 1920 (*Socialist*, 5 February 1920).

24 *The Call*, 21 November 1918.

25 The imprisoned John Maclean ran with the backing of the local Labour Party but not the national executive (see Kendall, *op. cit.*, p. 309.)

26 *The Call*, 5 June 1919.

27 Bukharin, 'Report on the Platform', in J. Riddell (Ed.), *Founding the Communist International, Proceedings and documents of the First Congress, March 1919*, Pathfinder, 1987, pp.128-129.

28 In J. Riddell (Ed.), *The German revolution and the debate on soviet power, Documents: 1918-1919, Preparing the Founding Congress*, Pathfinder, 1986, p.190.

29 *Workers' Dreadnought*, 24 July 1920.

30 See, for example, *Workers' Dreadnought*, 6 September 1919, 10 April 1920.

31 Guy Aldred, *Trade Unionism and the Class War*, London, Bakunin Press, 1919.

32 *The SLP: Its Aims and Methods*, 1908.

33 *Socialist*, November 1918.

34 *Ibid.*, April 1919.

35 For the WSF, see *Workers' Dreadnought*, 10 April 1920.

36 *BSP Report of the Seventh Annual Conference, 1918*, p.26.

37 *The Call*, 12 June 1919.

38 *Ibid.*, 9 October 1919.

39 See, for example, the letter from Gallacher in the *Workers' Dreadnought*, 21 February 1920. Gallacher was the author, with J.R. Campbell, of the influential pamphlet *Direct Action: An Outline of Workshop and Social Organisation* (1919), which defended the revolutionary tasks of the soviets

(reprinted by Pluto Press, London, 1972).

40 See, for example, *The Call*, 6 November 1919, in Milton, *op. cit.*, pp.211-214.

41 *BSP, Report of Ninth Annual Conference, 1920*, p.24.

42 See *Workers' Dreadnought*, 24 July 1920. The *Dreadnought* group was particularly influenced by its contacts in the South Wales coalfields, where a strong rank and file movement appeared to be able to dictate policy to the Miners' Federation.

43 See the 'Manifesto of the Communist International to the proletariat of the entire world', written by Trotsky (Degras, *op. cit.*, p.46).

44 See Martin Crick, *The History of the Social Democratic Federation*, Ryburn, 1994, pp.165-166.

45 Quoted in Lenin, *Lenin on Britain*, Progress, third revised edition, 1973, p.96.

46 Lenin, *op. cit.*, p.97.

47 The BSP applied for affiliation to the national Labour Party in June 1914 following a referendum of its membership. The Labour Party's executive referred the application to its next annual conference, but due to the war this was postponed, finally being accepted at its 1916 conference. BSP delegates attended the Labour Party conference in 1917 for the first time in sixteen years.

48 See the speech of B. Allen of the North West Ham branch (*BSP Report of the Seventh Annual Conference, 1918*, p.26).

49 *Ibid.*, p.30. Continued support for affiliation came from some of the Northern branches, where the BSP had been more successful in gaining influence in local Labour Parties, and from the Russian émigré Joe Fineberg, who still clung to the vision of a long term struggle within the Labour Party to transform it into a socialist party, pointing to the example of the Bolsheviks who remained inside the soviets to fight against Kerensky (p.29).

50 *Ibid.*, p.27.

51 *Workers' Dreadnought*, 6 July 1918.

52 The WSF instructed its branches to withdraw from the Labour Party, although in August 1919 it was reported that the Poplar Branch had joined a Labour Party procession, leading to its expulsion from Poplar Trades Council and Labour Party (WSF Committee meeting minutes, 7 August 1919, Pankhurst Papers).

53 See WSF Committee minutes, 22 February 1918, and minutes of general meeting, 15 April 1918 (Pankhurst Papers).

54 See, for example, Theodore Rothstein, *Social Democrat*, June 1900.

55 See the report of the SLP conference, *Socialist*, August 1912. This position, known as the 'Budgen-Murphy letter' (originally a response to a reader's query), was accepted by only a small majority, and led to the departure of five Lancashire branches who denounced it as 'reformist'.

56 *Socialist*, October 1913.

57 *Ibid.*, 30 January 1919.

58 *Workers' Dreadnought*, 21 February 1920.

59 'John Bryan', *The Call*, November 1919.

Chapter 4

Party

"Opportunism is our main enemy." (Lenin at the Second Congress of the Communist International)[1]

In the struggle for a class party, the main enemy as Lenin recognised was the opportunism of the right: that is, the tendency for elements of the workers' movement under the pressure of capitalist ideology to make concessions to the political positions of the bourgeoisie. While the right wing of the Second International had definitively gone over to the capitalist camp, the struggle against opportunism had by no means ended with the formation of the Third International. The struggle to create a communist party in Britain was above all a political struggle led by the left against both the opportunist right, which essentially wanted a party that would act as an appendage to social democracy; and the centre, which instead of choosing sides with either social democracy and communism, attempted to conciliate between the two.

This political struggle between the left, centre and right trends in the workers' movement cut across organisational boundaries,and within the existing organisations to a varying extent we can identify right, centre and left tendencies, which evolved under the impact of the revolutionary wave and played a dynamic role in the unity negotiations to form a communist party.

The right-wing leadership of the **Independent Labour Party** was implacably hostile to Bolshevism and the Third International, and withdrew from the unity negotiations at an early stage. In the centre of the party there was growing disillusionment with the Second International and a strong tendency on the left that was sympathetic to the Third. In early 1920 the Scottish and Welsh sections of the ILP voted to sever connections with the Second and affiliate to the Third. The party's 1920 conference voted almost 4 to 1 to withdraw from the Second International, but the right, by combining with the centre, managed to prevent a vote to join the Third. This prompted the formation of an organised left fraction to try to win the party over. The 'ILP Left Wing' (with its own paper, *International)*, pursued an internal struggle for affiliation to the Third International, but failed to win significant support. Politically it was unable to break definitively from parliamentarism and remained equivocal about support for soviet power; Pankhurst's conclusion was that "Until the Left Wing of the ILP has made up its mind to plump for the soviets and work for the complete abolition of parliament, it will not be ready to join the Third International."[2] The Left Wing finally merged into the CPGB after the ILP's 1921 conference, adding around 500 members to the new party.

The final departure of the social pacifist leadership of the **British Socialist Party** in late 1919 left a sizeable social democratic minority still intact within the party, with a political base among those holding positions as officials in local government and the trade unions. After decades of involvement in reformist activities the right had become attached to the institutions of the capitalist state, and essentially saw itself as the left wing of the Labour Party. At the 1920 BSP conference, BSP member Joe Vaughan, mayor of Bethnal Green and president of the local trades and labour council, greeted delegates by applauding "The spade work of the SDF and afterwards of the BSP [which] had resulted in the recent victories of the Labour Party at the borough council elections."[3] At the same conference, a motion committing party candidates for parliamentary and local elections to "stand as socialists based on the class war" was defeated by 48 to 26 votes,[4] while an amendment toning down the party's commitment to the dictatorship of the proletariat and soviet power was supported by a quarter of the delegates present, clearly indicating the strength of this social democratic minority in the party.[5]

The BSP's endorsement of soviet power, the dictatorship of the proletariat and affiliation to the Third International was a definite result of the move leftwards by the party's rank and file. But the leadership which replaced the social pacifist tendency represented the centre rather than the revolutionary left. During the unity negotiations this leadership revealed strong tendencies to try to conciliate towards reformism; faced with a clear political choice between the Second and Third Internationals, the centre of the BSP was deeply reluctant to break decisively from the Labour Party and from parliamentary and trade union activity, essentially because it feared a loss of influence within the institutions of social democracy. This centrist tendency, which included figures from previous struggles of the left against the Hyndmanites and social pacifists like Albert Inkpin and J.F. Hodgson, in turn came under growing pressure from a section of the party's rank and file which opposed affiliation to the Labour Party and parliamentary action.

The original invitation to the founding of the Third International had been addressed not to the BSP as a whole but to "The left elements of the British Socialist Party (in particular the group represented by Maclean)."[6] There is no doubt that the Bolsheviks saw Maclean's tendency as the nucleus of a communist party in Britain. The failure of Maclean and his supporters to a constitute themselves as a fraction to win over the party was a serious setback for the revolutionary left. The party leadership which replaced the social pacifists represented not the revolutionary left but a more amorphous grouping of centre and left tendencies, which showed strong tendencies to conciliate towards reformist positions on key questions. The British bourgeoisie did its best to destroy Maclean, and his brutal imprisonment, involving hunger strikes, forced feeding and solitary confinement, undoubtedly took its toll on his physical and mental health, but his political weaknesses were more fundamental; Maclean underestimated the importance of waging a struggle for the organisation, himself admitting that "during the war he and others had worked on BSP lines, but had not stressed the matter of the party."[7] The left in the BSP had also been weakened by the imprisonment or departure for Russia of many of the émigré Marxists who had formed the backbone of the opposition to opportunism and centrism in the party since the turn of the century. In the absence of a strong revolutionary left block in the BSP, the struggle against opportunism and centrism was taken up by smaller left groupings, in particular the non-sectarian wing of the Socialist Labour Party, and the Workers' Socialist Federation.

The **Socialist Labour Party** claimed that the Russian revolution had merely confirmed the correctness of its own methods and tactics. In fact it opened up growing tensions in the party between those who were open to new developments in the class struggle, and those who remained attached to the letter of the De Leonist programme. These tensions focused on the question of regroupment: between the supporters of unity, led by an influential group which included Tom Bell (the party's secretary), Arthur MacManus (editor of the *Socialist)*, William Paul and J.T. Murphy; and the more sectarian De Leonist elements who still retained a strong grip on the party.

The tensions in the SLP did not therefore correspond to a straightforward left-right split, both wings of the party being at least formally committed to the same obsolete political programme, although there was certainly a 'centre' in the party influenced by the arguments of both sides. The crucial issue for the SLP was sectarianism, and the willingness of the party to open itself up to the need for regroupment to form a class party. The argument of the pro-unity faction that the struggle in the party was between 'practical revolutionary realists' and 'abstract doctrinaires' was therefore essentially correct. But by signalling their willingness to compromise for the sake of unity, the 'realists' undermined their own ability to stand firm against opportunism.

The **Workers' Socialist Federation**, the smallest of the main participating organisations in the unity negotiations, had emerged out of the women's suffrage movement and in 1919, according to Pankhurst, still consisted largely of women. But its commitment to soviet power increasingly attracted supporters from the workers' struggles, and the WSF made close links with the London Workers' Committee, and the militant movements among the London dockers and the South Wales miners. It was also very active in the national "Hands Off Russia" movement.

As its name suggests, the WSF remained a relatively loose organisation, animated by Sylvia Pankhurst (who remained the *Dreadnought*'s owner as well as its editor) and a small group of comrades from the women's suffrage struggles, who were often the clearest on political questions and on the need for a strong communist party. Pankhurst's powerful personality and her practical grasp of internationalism allowed the group to exercise an influence in the unity negotiations out of proportion to its size, but the WSF's opposition to parliamentary action attracted a heterogeneous mix of syndicalists, anarchists and others who were anti-parliamentarists in principle, and this, together with a lack of rigour in its internal organisation, was to become a source of tension within the group.

By extending an invitation to the **shop stewards, syndicalists and anarchists** and others moving in the direction of the revolutionary left, the Bolsheviks were explicitly accepting into the International those genuine supporters of soviet power who were opposed to parliamentary action, arguing that it was "necessary to form a bloc with those elements in the revolutionary workers' movement who, although they did not formerly belong to socialist parties, now stand by and large for the proletarian dictatorship in the form of soviet power."[8]

Were the shop stewards and workers' committees to be treated as political organisations, or as the equivalent of the soviets, that is, mass organisations open to all workers? The Bolsheviks had adopted an open attitude on this question. The left tended to argue that the communist party as a political organisation should include only class conscious revolutionaries (the position defended by the WSF.)[9] In fact, due to post-war unemployment the shop stewards' movement represented only a militant minority of workers, albeit politically heterogeneous. Some of the shop stewards' leaders played a major role in the unity negotiations as members of their respective organisations, especially the SLP. Others, more syndicalist-minded, did not see the importance of a political party or rejected the need for it outright. Nationally, the shop stewards' and workers' committee movement only decided to affiliate to the Third International in January 1920, and did not take an active part in the struggle for a communist party until after the CI's second congress that summer.

The best elements in the syndicalist movement responded positively to the need for a political party, in particular the South Wales Socialist Society (SWSS), which was a federation of local groups active in the coalfields. Anti-parliamentary in principle and strongly opposed to affiliation to the Labour Party, the SWSS closely aligned itself with the WSF in the early unity negotiations, but its loose organisation and deeply localist outlook eventually led to its dissolution, and the main body of the SWSS became an SLP branch in March 1920.[10] Some elements in the anarchist movement also expressed their support for communist unity: for example the Glasgow Anarchist Group around Guy Aldred, which regrouped with some London SLP branches in March 1919 to form the Communist League. In May 1920 Aldred's group changed its name to the Glasgow Communist Group "to emphasise the need for communist unity."[11] In practice Aldred's support for unity was platonic; his vision went no further than a loose federation of anti-parliamentary groups and stopped well short of a centralised class party. The Communist League itself was short-lived, and many members left to support the struggle for a communist party, Aldred later blaming its 'destruction' on "Lenin-adoring elements" (i.e. the WSF).

The left on the offensive

From the beginning it was the opportunism of the right and not the sectarianism of the left that presented the main obstacle to communist unity in Britain. In fact, the left could if anything be accused of not being firm enough against the right, and it was certainly the left tendencies in each of the major groups that provided the main impulse towards regroupment.

In April 1918 there was a first tentative step towards unity when, faced with an extension of conscription, the BSP opened discussions with the WSF on merging the two organisations. Fairchild rejected the WSF's proposal that the organisation should decide between bourgeois democracy and proletarian dictatorship, and when the BSP proposed Fairchild as co-editor of the proposed joint paper, the WSF concluded that it could not agree to the merger. But it retained amicable relations with the BSP and Pankhurst even joined the BSP's delegation to the 1918 Labour Party conference, speaking for its resolution that Labour MPs should leave the government.[12]

At the BSP's 1918 conference, left-wing delegates like William McLaine, a leader of the national shop stewards' movement, argued that the BSP was closer to the SLP than the ILP; the two organisations were already collaborating in Clydeside and other areas, and as there were no differences of principle between them they should discuss amalgamation.[13]

In the SLP itself, elements of the leadership began to call on the party to shed its doctrinairism and work for unity with other revolutionary tendencies. In January 1919, after hearing a report of discussions with the BSP and ILP, a special conference voted to suspend the party's constitution and endorsed a manifesto proposed by Bell, MacManus, Murphy and Paul as a basis for unity. An official Unity Committee was mandated which met with the other parties in March 1919. The manifesto itself was a hybrid of orthodox De Leonism and revolutionary positions, and was intended as much to paper over the cracks in the SLP as to form the basis for unity.[14]

The withdrawal of the ILP from the unity negotiations and the departure of the BSP's reformist leadership marked a very necessary split with the right, but the BSP still remained firmly attached to the Labour Party: a referendum held after the 1918 party conference rejected a proposal to withdraw by a majority of four to one, and this was overwhelmingly confirmed at the 1919 conference. It was this continued attachment of the BSP to the Second International which constituted the single biggest obstacle to unity.

The founding of the Third International strengthened the left in its struggle against opportunism and centrism. This was despite the fact that British communists learned of the founding congress only after it had closed and important documents did not appear until several months later. The invitation to the founding congress clearly set out the tactics to be adopted towards the centre parties: "splitting off the revolutionary elements, and unsparing criticism and exposure of the leaders." Separation from centrist organisations was, at a certain stage of development, "absolutely essential."[15]

Following the failure of the first official steps towards unity, the SLP directed its attacks against the leaderships of the ILP and BSP, that is:

...those socialists who acclaim the soviets without losing any of their reverence for parliament; who are equally ready to support the shop stewards' and workers' committees and at the same time the centralised bureaucratic trade union officialism; who cannot quite decide between Moscow and Berne; and who, while they denounce the murders of Liebknecht, Luxemburg and their colleagues, still sometimes refer to their murderers as a 'socialist government.'[16]

The SLP appealed to the members of both parties, who generally stood to the left of their leaders and were still strongly in favour of unity, to refuse to accept the breakdown of negotiations and to fight for a change of line.[17] Specifically targeting its propaganda at Maclean's tendency as the strongest opponent of opportunism, it called on the BSP to sever its links with the Labour Party: "Let the BSP stop playing at opportunist politics and join the ranks of revolutionary socialism or merge its identity in the constitutional ILP movement of parliamentarism. Which is it to be?"[18] The SLP's offensive against centrism began to show results, with militants splitting away from both the BSP and ILP to join the left.[19]

The WSF actually voted to adopt the name Communist Party at its 1919 conference, after hearing an intervention by a delegate of the Third International who delivered its recommendation that such a party be formed in Britain. This was premature; the Communist Party could not simply be summoned into being by a change of name, and in the end after criticisms from other groups the WSF postponed its decision.[20]

At two conferences held in June 1919, the WSF, BSP, SLP and the South Wales Socialist Society reached a high level of agreement. Differences remained between the BSP and the rest on the question of affiliation, but deadlock was avoided by the proposal of the SLP's unity committee that the united party should resolve this question by a ballot three months after its formation.

An anti-parliamentary communist party?

By recognising the need for a split with centrism and accepting into the ranks of the International those who were opposed to parliamentary action, the Bolsheviks showed that they were prepared if necessary to see an anti-parliamentary communist party in Britain. In July 1919 Sylvia Pankhurst wrote to Lenin, blaming parliamentary activity for ruining the revolutionary movement by focusing the attention of workers on electoral work, and hindering unity by alienating those like the revolutionary syndicalists, shop stewards and IWW who would never agree to join a party engaging in parliamentary activity. Pankhurst's own argument – which she obviously hoped Lenin would endorse – was for the revolutionary movement to devote all its energies to 'direct revolutionary action' instead.

Lenin's response was to agree that parliamentarism was "at present a partial, secondary question":

> There can be no doubt that the Communist International and the communist parties of individual countries would make an irreparable mistake if they were to antagonise the workers who are in favour of soviet authority but are opposed to participation in parliamentary work... Very many workers who are anarchists are now becoming sincere advocates of the power of the soviets, and this being so, it is clear that they are our best comrades and friends, that they are the best revolutionaries, who are enemies of Marxism through a misunderstanding, or, rather, in consequence of the fact that the predominant official socialism of the Second International...had betrayed Marxism, had fallen into opportunism...[21]

Even though Lenin's personal view was that it would be a mistake for British revolutionaries to reject participation in parliamentary elections, he argued strongly that it was "better to make that mistake than to delay the formation of a big workers' communist party in Britain out of all the trends and elements...which sympathise with Bolshevism..." Referring to the disagreements at the KPD's founding congress, he considered that while Luxemburg and Liebknecht had been correct to defend participation in the elections to the bourgeois parliament, "...they were still more correct when they preferred remaining with the communist party, which was making a partial mistake, to siding with the direct traitors to socialism."

Lenin's reply to Pankhurst has been used ever since it appeared as a defence of parliamentary action. He makes it very clear, however, that in the context of a struggle for a communist party in Britain, the onus was firmly on the supporters of parliamentary action to unite with its opponents, even if this resulted in a party defending an abstentionist position:

> If...among the BSP there were sincere Bolsheviks who refused, because of differences over participation in parliament, to merge at once in a communist party with [the anti-parliamentary elements], then these Bolsheviks, in my opinion, would be making a mistake a thousand times greater than the mistaken refusal to participate in elections to the British bourgeois parliament.[22]

If this did not prove possible, then, Lenin argued, disagreement over parliamentarism was so immaterial that the formation of two parties – one defending parliamentary action and the other rejecting it – would be a good step forward to complete unity in Britain. Although this was not the response that Pankhurst had hoped for, Lenin's reply convinced the WSF that it should not make abstention a question of principle in the unity negotiations but allow the new party work this out "as the situation developed."[23]

The British left and the international communist movement

In contrast to the parochialism of the centre and right, the left in Britain was the first to make effective contact with the Third International, Pankhurst personally playing a leading role. According to one unsympathetic historian: "During the first five months of the Comintern's existence, her interpretations of the British situation were accepted as authoritative by the ECCI and Lenin. Her articles appeared in four of the first five numbers of the communist International in its various language editions."[24] She also participated in several of the earliest meetings of the International in Western Europe, making important contacts with the revolutionary movement in Germany, Italy, and Holland.

In October 1919, Pankhurst attended the Bologna Congress of the Italian Socialist Party (PSI) where she met Bordiga and representatives of the Communist Abstentionist Fraction. She was also present at an international meeting organised by the PSI 'Maximalists' at Imola, along with delegates from Switzerland, Austria and France, where she called for a split from the Second International and adhesion to the Third. Her sympathies clearly lay with Bordiga's Fraction, whose abstentionist position she considered as a logical movement of the party towards the Russian revolution and the International.

She then travelled to Frankfurt for the conference that saw the setting up of the Western European Secretariat of the Third International in November 1919, which was attended by delegates from the Russian, Polish, Austrian and German Communist Parties and the Rumanian Socialist Party. Here Pankhurst was the only representative who could be considered of the left.[25] The WES, dominated by the right-wing leadership of the KPD, was soon to come into conflict with the left-wing communists who animated the other official centre of the International in Western Europe in Amsterdam.

In January she met again with the comrades of the WES in Berlin, before travelling on to Amsterdam for the conference of the newly-formed West European Bureau of the International. This opened on 3 February and lasted for four days before being broken up by the Dutch police. A 'rump' conference was held later with a small number of the participants. Despite its chaotic end – a result of the naiveté and inexperience of the Dutch communists in carrying out clandestine work – the Amsterdam conference was more representative of the communist movement in Western Europe and North America than the first congress of the Third International, with 16 officially mandated delegates from Britain, the USA, Holland, Belgium and Germany. It was also strongly representative of the left-wing of the communist movement. In addition to Pankhurst it included Pannekoek, Gorter and Roland-Holst as leaders of the Dutch Tribunists, Van Overstraeten from Belgium and Fraina from the USA (J.T. Murphy also attended for the shop stewards' movement and as unofficial observer for the SLP).[26]

The Amsterdam conference was a particularly important moment in the struggle for a communist party in Britain. It strengthened the left by giving the

International's backing to its positions on parliamentarism and the Labour Party, and provided an outline programme for regroupment based on a clean break with opportunism and centrism. The resolution on communist unity warned against the social patriots and opportunists, "particularly when catering to the 'left' tendency," as "a most dangerous enemy of the proletarian revolution." It was essential for communists to rigorously separate themselves from these elements:

> The toleration of opportunist or social patriotic elements in a communist party on the plea of unity, means violation of the only unity promoting the revolution-unity, consisting, not merely in formal acceptance of general principles, but agreement on fundamental action. It is necessary that communist groups still in the old reformist and opportunist parties (even if these repudiate the Second International) should sever their compromising relations and unite in the communist party (or form a communist party if necessary). Unity depends upon local conditions; but must be animated not alone by formal acceptance of communist theory, but uncompromising emphasis on the revolutionary practice developing out of that theory.[27]

The basis for communist unity was therefore "no compromise with the bourgeois or social patriotic parties, with parties affiliated with the Second International, or with the agents of capitalism in the labour movement..."[28]

This resolution was wholly in the spirit of the Third International, which had called for the splitting off of the revolutionary elements from the centrist parties. It immediately had the effect of throwing the BSP onto the defensive and its delegates objected strongly, fearing that "such a measure, by making it impossible for the English communist party now being formed, to affiliate with the Labour Party, would isolate it completely, and would prevent it becoming a living force in the political struggles of the country." These fears were not shared by the other British delegates who argued that, on the contrary, communist unity could only be achieved by a "complete rupture" with the Labour Party.[29] The resolution was adopted by 13 to 2, only the BSP voting against, but following protests from Clara Zetkin and the KPD delegation that the conference was unrepresentative, it was finally agreed that all resolutions would be accepted as "provisional" only, with a "relative value, as indicative of the tendency of the evolution of communist thought, particularly in the Anglo-Saxon countries..."[30] They would form the basis for a further conference to be organised within three months.

For the left, the Amsterdam conference meant that: "...if the international meeting can be held to speak for the Third International, the communists of Britain must either be out of the Labour Party or out of the Third International..."[34] Pankhurst's own conclusion, from an analysis of centrism in the German, Italian and French Socialist Parties, was that:

> We want no right wing compromises in the Third International; there must be a clean cut between the Second and Third Internationalists; no one can be permitted to have a foot in both camps. No party that is affiliated to the British Labour Party, and which thus belongs to the Second International, is free to join the Third International.[31]

The BSP leadership, faced with a membership which had just voted overwhelmingly for unity, was forced to call a further meeting with the SLP, WSF and SWSS. It dropped its insistence on a ballot of the new party's membership on the question of affiliation, and instead tried to reserve its right to work for affiliation inside the new party on condition that all branches would have complete autonomy to affiliate to local Labour Parties if they chose. This simply provided a cover for the BSP's continued attachment to social democracy and betrayed a completely federalist conception of the party.[32] The BSP's proposals were firmly rejected by both the SLP and WSF, Pankhurst reading out the Amsterdam resolution in support of her argument that the communist party must have a uniform policy based on no affiliation. The BSP responded that it would submit its case to the authority of the ECCI on the grounds that the Amsterdam conference was not representative, prompting the SLP to argue that the point was not who had passed the resolution, but whether it was "scientific"...[33] At a further unity conference in April, the BSP repeated its offer to drop the vote on affiliation and was again rejected. On Pankhurst's motion this meeting agreed to proceed to the formation of a communist party based on non-affiliation to the Labour Party. The BSP's further attempt to prevent the new party from committing itself in advance to any position on tactics was defeated and the meeting voted 8 to 3 for Pankhurst's motion, only the BSP voting against.[34] This was also one of the few occasions on which the question of parliamentary action was discussed. After a lengthy defence by the SLP delegates of the need for communists to make use of parliament, the meeting agreed: "That it be part of the work of the communist party to participate in parliamentary action in order to stimulate the revolutionary fervour of the working class, and to use it for agitational purposes."[35] This resolution was actually seconded by one of the BSP delegates, but the two others abstained because "they wanted complete freedom for the proposed new party to define its attitude on this question of tactics as on that of Labour Party affiliation".[36]

With hindsight we can see that this was closest the unity negotiations came to founding a communist party in Britain on the basis of a clean break with the Labour Party; with a position on parliamentary action at least approximating that of the Bolsheviks' 'revolutionary parliamentarism', and including an anti-parliamentary tendency prepared to work inside the new party for the adoption of an abstentionist position. At this crucial moment, however, the left failed to capitalise on its political victory and betrayed a centrist tendency to hesitate: a proposal by the SLP's William Paul to set up a joint committee to put the resolutions into effect was rejected, and in the end the conference simply adjourned. This represented the high point in the left's struggle against opportunism and centrism; from now on it was to find itself increasingly on the defensive.

Up until now the left had led the struggle against opportunism and centrism on the assumption that it had the full backing of the Third International; the resolutions of the Amsterdam conference only appeared to confirm this, despite their provisional status. But two key events in the spring of 1920 signaled a change of line by the Bolshevik leadership: the dissolution of the Amsterdam Sub-Bureau in early May; and the publication of Lenin's pamphlet *Left-Wing Communism, An Infantile Disorder* (written in late April but with excerpts on Britain first appearing in late July). On the eve of the CPGB's formation a letter from Lenin also confirmed his personal support for a communist party affiliated to the Labour Party and engaged in parliamentary activity.

Two developments in the British revolutionary movement itself in the first half of 1920 also had a negative effect on the struggle for a party based on left positions: the split between the 'realist' and sectarian wings of the SLP; and the formation of a rival anti-parliamentary 'communist party' by the WSF.

The split in the Socialist Labour Party

The tensions within the SLP, which had supposedly been resolved at the special conference of January 1919, soon reappeared over the actions of the unity committee. Although formally answerable to the national executive, in practice this operated as a faction inside the party, with its own political agenda, strategy and tactics. The crisis came to a head in the summer of 1919 after the committee, in a last ditch attempt to prevent the breakdown of negotiations, had proposed that the disputed question of affiliation be decided by a vote of the membership of the new party a year after its formation (in the end a period of three months was agreed). This was repudiated by the SLP executive, which promptly dissolved the committee, accusing it of plotting to hand the party over to the Labour Party.[37] The new executive, dominated by the orthodox De Leonists, then proceeded to carry out a referendum in such a way as to obtain a vote in favour of unity but against a vote on Labour Party affiliation, deciding on the basis of the result that it would take no further part in the unity negotiations despite the membership having voted overwhelmingly for unity. From this point the official SLP withdrew into sectarian isolation; a delegation was present at the unity conference convened following the Amsterdam conference, after the BSP had offered concessions, but decided that, "even if the BSP executive waived the question of affiliation to the Labour Party altogether, the SLP would not be willing to go forward, seeing that a majority of the BSP membership were in favour of affiliation."[38]

The former unity committee members continued to attend the negotiations in a personal capacity, maintaining close contacts with the BSP. Bell, MacManus and Paul also prepared a conference of the SLP to coincide with the party's official conference in April 1920, but this failed to attract wide support from the membership.[39] The unofficial SLP conference constituted itself as the Communist Unity Group (CUG). While supporting the use of parliamentary action for agitation purposes, the CUG strongly opposed affiliation to the Labour Party, quoting the Amsterdam conference resolution in its manifesto, which committed it to working for a communist party affiliated to the Third International.[40] The CUG's strategy – like that of the unity committee before it – was to try to isolate the BSP and force it to choose between the Labour Party and the Third International.

Given their sectarianism and strength within the party, a break with the orthodox De Leonists was a necessary step in the regroupment process. The task for revolutionaries in the SLP was to win as many militants as possible to the struggle for a class party inside the Third International. But when it came to a struggle for the organisation, the pro-unity faction revealed its immaturity, failing to undertake the necessary work to build support for their positions among the membership and then prematurely abandoning the organisation. As few as three SLP branches may have defected to the CUG.[41] More seriously, by demonstrating its willingness to compromise by proposing to form the communist party without a clear position on the Labour Party, the pro-unity faction undermined the CUG's subsequent ability to take a principled stand against opportunism. Its strategy of isolating the BSP and forcing it to choose between the Labour Party and the Third International was perfectly correct, but it was dependent on the International's full backing; having defined itself primarily as *for unity*, the CUG found itself poorly placed to go against the tide when the CI's policy changed.

The dissolution of the Amsterdam Bureau

Isolated by the Amsterdam conference resolutions, the BSP established its own contacts with the KPD-dominated West European Secretariat and launched a series of bitter and personal polemics against the positions of the left communists, aimed particularly at the WSF and Pankhurst.[42]

At a hurriedly called unity conference on 6 May, the BSP reached sudden agreement with the SLP, WSF and SWSS on the outstanding question of affiliation, which would now be settled at a specially convened meeting attended by delegates of all the participating groups. At this point the Amsterdam Bureau intervened to reiterate its view that:

> ...communists should not be affiliated, either directly or indirectly, to political organisations that accept the principles of the Second International (...) Since we agree with those communists in England [who] object to participation in the Labour Party, we are of opinion that they should not give up their attitude on the plea of unity. Much as we would like to see a united communist party in England, it may be better to postpone this ideal than to compromise on important issues.[43]

It rejected the BSP's previous plea for local autonomy as a "compromise [that] must lead to confusion when accepted by a united communist party." Despite later accusations of 'ultra-leftism', however, the Bureau did accept that groups like the BSP could affiliate to the Third International, but only "in so far as they accept communist principles and tactics, which involves a persistent struggle within the Labour Party against the policy and tactics of this body." The Bureau was convinced that any such work in the Labour Party would quickly lead to expulsion.

As part of this combat against centrism, the Bureau also denounced the attempts of the ILP's leadership to form a 'Two-and-a-Half' International,and intervened at the Strasbourg Congress of the French Socialist Party to press for the expulsion of its right wing.[44] Despite the fact that Germany was strictly outside its remit, it also protested on behalf of the KAPD in its conflict with the KPD and Western European Secretariat. The response of the ECCI was to withdraw the Bureau's mandate and hand over its functions to the Secretariat on the grounds that the Bureau had opposed the Executive Committee "on all questions." The only political positions cited were the rejection of parliamentary action and the abandonment of revolutionary work inside the trade unions, neither of which was an official position of the Bureau.[45]

By using organisational measures to deal with political disagreements on questions where there had hitherto been a degree of openness, the Bolshevik leadership of the International took a retrogressive step. By undermining the British left's efforts to isolate the BSP and force it to make a complete break with the Second International, the ECCI's dissolution of the Amsterdam Bureau had serious consequences for the struggle for a class party in Britain. The centrist leadership of the BSP now had the ECCI's approval in its political campaign against the left, and was able to avoid a split with the party's social democratic right wing on the vital question of the Labour Party.

The formation of the Communist Party (British Section of the Third International)

Despite its active participation in the unity negotiations, the WSF had always been reluctant to lose its organisational autonomy in a BSP-dominated united party, and never entirely abandoned its original plan to form an anti-parliamentary communist party. After the Amsterdam conference the WSF decided that it could not fuse with the BSP unless it left the Labour Party, but also saw difficulty in being in a united party which supported parliamentary action. If a merged party with the BSP fell through, the WSF decided it would immediately contact the SWSS, the Communist League and others willing to form a left-wing party.[46] In May, Pankhurst wrote to various left wing individuals and organisations including Gallacher, the SLP and the SWSS, seeking their views on the proposed rank and file conference to decide the question of Labour Party affiliation.[47] At this point Pankhurst still felt that, on balance, the left should participate, if only on the dubious grounds that the groups would not be bound by its decisions. However at the next meeting, with the SLP and SWSS absent, it was agreed against the WSF's vote that the conference's decisions would be binding. The SLP had already replied stating its refusal to support any further negotiations with the BSP and supporting unity on what it termed "strictly revolutionary lines." Encouraged, the WSF called its own conference of organisations that were anti-parliamentary and opposed to affiliation with the Labour Party. This was ostensibly to decide whether to take part in the proposed communist unity convention, but after hearing a report on the negotiations arguing that the new party would inevitably be dominated by the 'right wing' (i.e. the BSP and CUG), those attending decided to boycott any further unity negotiations and to immediately constitute themselves as the Communist Party (British Section of the Third International).[48]

The CP(BSTI)'s draft programme clearly explained the basis of its opposition to parliamentary action and the Labour Party in terms of the need to fight opportunism and centrism:

> The Communist Party refuses all compromise with right and centrist socialism. The British Labour Party is dominated by opportunist reformists, social patriots and trade union bureaucrats, who have already allied themselves with capitalism against the workers' revolution at home and abroad... The first essential of revolutionary propaganda and action is the existence of a party with clear and uncompromising doctrine and policy, which will persistently unmask and discredit the practice of opportunism and compromise.[49]

In an open letter to delegates at the communist unity convention on 31 July, the CP(BSTI) set out its basic principles, explaining the reasons for its refusal to run candidates for parliament and rejection of affiliation to the Labour Party, but avoiding any open criticism of the party to be formed or reference to international disagreements.[50]

Despite its formally correct positions, however, the CP(BSTI) was a voluntarist attempt to create a class party which avoided the difficult but necessary confrontation of positions within the revolutionary movement. Apart from the WSF, the new 'party' comprised only a few local groups and individuals. By making the rejection of parliamentary action one of the party's 'cardinal principles', the WSF also went back on its former acceptance that this was a secondary question which could be resolved within a united party, instead seeking support among those who were anti-parliamentary in principle. The alliance of the CUG with the BSP certainly isolated the WSF from its former supporters within the negotiations, and it was quite correct to criticise the CUG for its opportunism towards the BSP, but to justify the CP(BSTI)'s formation by characterising the whole of the BSP and the CUG as 'right wing' was both sterile and sectarian, while the WSF's search for allies led it into a futile flirtation with the sectarian leadership of the SLP, whose own suggested guest list for a 'strictly' revolutionary conference included the SPGB and the BSISLP, to whom Pankhurst made no objection, despite the fact that the former believed in a parliamentary road to socialism while the latter was a strictly orthodox De Leonist splinter opposed to all strike action as reformist![51] Despite its previously encouraging response, the SLP did not attend the WSF's conference and adopted a hostile attitude to Pankhurst's initiative.[52]

In deciding to proceed with the formation of an anti-parliamentary communist party, Pankhurst was undoubtedly influenced by the split in the German movement, which in April 1920 resulted in the formation of the Communist Workers' Party (KAPD).[53] At the KPD's second congress in October 1919 the new leadership had demanded agreement on work within parliament and the unions as a precondition of continued membership, closing the door on further debate on these crucial questions and then expelling all those in the party who disagreed, who included delegates of the numerically largest sections. While some elements immediately announced the formation of a new party, others like the Bremen Left worked as a fraction to try to preserve the unity of the party. The KPD itself was reduced a rump, having lost the majority of its membership; during the Kapp Putsch it offered to act as a 'loyal opposition' to the proposed 'socialist government' with the SPD of Scheidemann and Noske, for which it was criticised by Lenin and the ECCI. Faced with this blatant opportunism, the opposition was finally provoked into founding a new party, which immediately declared its adhesion to the Third International. Nevertheless, the formation of the KAPD was precipitate, and in reality the new party was a heterogeneous collection of opposition tendencies, including the anti-proletarian National Bolsheviks, the anti-partyists around Otto Rühle, and revolutionary syndicalists. The WSF's initiative displayed the same impatience and lack of organisational maturity and resulted in a similar lack of coherence. But whereas the KAPD was formed as a result of a split provoked by the right in the existing Communist Party, the CP(BSTI)'s voluntarist declaration only added confusion to an already difficult process to create a class party in Britain.

'Left-Wing' Communism, An Infantile Disorder

On the eve of the communist unity convention, extracts appeared from a new work by Lenin giving his personal support to parliamentary action and an electoral pact with the Labour Party, characterising the left's positions as a "childish sickness" of the communist movement.[54] The publication of what became known as *'Left-Wing' Communism: An Infantile Disorder* had a significant impact on the left's struggle against opportunism and centrism, and in view of the subsequent use of this work to dismiss the arguments of the communist left, and to justify all kinds of reactionary positions in the name of 'Leninism', its contents deserve closer examination.

Lenin's pamphlet was sub-titled 'an attempt at a popular discussion on

Marxist strategy and tactics', and if this was its only intention the whole British revolutionary movement would certainly have benefited. But first and foremost it was intended as a weapon in the ECCI's mounting campaign against the influence of the left wing in the Third International, and its publication was part of a drawing of battle lines for the CI's forthcoming second congress.

Lenin's basic premise was that the Russian revolution was, in its fundamental features, a model which would inevitably be followed by the proletarian revolution in Western Europe. After briefly describing some of the key reasons for the successful role played by the Bolshevik Party in the conquest of soviet power, including the class consciousness of the proletarian vanguard, its ability to link itself to the broad mass of the proletariat and the correctness of its political strategy and tactics, he then focused narrowly on the use made by the Bolsheviks of bourgeois parliaments in the years 1905 to 1908.

Similarly, although Lenin emphasised that the principal enemy of Bolshevism at that time was opportunism, and that this "*still remains the principal enemy on an international scale,*"[55] he then devoted the rest of his work to a polemic against "left doctrinairism" (Lenin did not at this or any other time use the derogatory and inaccurate term 'ultra-left'), which even on his own admission was a secondary error, and one "at present a thousand times less dangerous and less significant than that of right doctrinairism (i.e., social-chauvinism and Kautskyism)..."[56] With this highly significant (and often ignored) qualification, on the basis of the experience of Bolshevism in the period 1903 to 1917, Lenin then proceeded to criticise those communists in western Europe who rejected any compromise with the social patriots and opportunists, and who refused to participate in bourgeois parliaments or work in reactionary trade unions. His main targets were the German and Dutch lefts and Bordiga's Communist Abstentionist Fraction (which did not reject work in the trade unions), attacking their positions as 'naive', 'childish', 'ridiculous', 'stupid', etc. His criticisms of the British left were mild by comparison; he welcomed a letter by Gallacher defending anti-parliamentary views, which:

> expresses excellently the temper and point of view of the young communists, or of rank-and-file workers who are only beginning to accept communism. This temper is highly gratifying and valuable; we must learn to prize, appreciate and support it for, in its absence, it would be hopeless to expect the victory of the proletarian revolution in Great Britain, or in any other country for that matter.[57]

While he agreed that the leaders of the Labour Party were 'hopelessly reactionary', and would undoubtedly act as butchers of the revolution when they got into power, on the basis of a single speech by Lloyd George which called for a coalition between Liberals and Conservatives to prevent a Labour government, he argued that it was necessary for revolutionaries in Britain to give support to the Labour Party. Rejecting Sylvia Pankhurst's view that the communist party should not compromise with reformism, he argued that:

> On the contrary, the fact that most British workers still follow the lead of the British Kerenskys or Scheidemanns and have not yet had experience of a government composed of these people – an experience which was necessary in Russia and Germany so as to secure the mass transition of the workers to communism – undoubtedly indicates that the British communists should participate in parliamentary action..."[58]

Lenin admitted that he did not know enough about the question of affiliation, which in view of the Labour Party's "extremely unique character" was a "particularly complex" question. What he proposed went much further: instead of simply joining in order to carry out propaganda, the British communists should call for an electoral bloc to fight the Conservatives; then if the Labour leaders consented the communists would gain by helping the party to power and discrediting it all the more quickly in front of the masses, while if they refused, "we shall gain still more, for we shall at once have shown the masses...that the Hendersons prefer their close relations with the capitalists to the unity of all the workers."[59] This went far beyond the arguments of even the right wing of the BSP for affiliation. It was in effect the forerunner of the policy of 'united fronts' between the communists and the social democratic parties, which had hitherto been defined as parties of the bourgeoisie. This growing opportunist course in the Third International was shortly to become apparent at the CI's second congress.

By rigidly applying the 'model' of the Russian revolution to conditions in Western Europe, Lenin was led to conclude that the British working class had to go through the 'necessary' experience of a Labour government, and that communists should therefore actively help to bring the party to power. But by implying a parallel with pre-revolutionary Russia in February 1917 Lenin seriously *overestimated* the balance of class forces in Britain, and by arguing that Lloyd George's speech betrayed a weakening of the bourgeoisie as a whole he *underestimated* the relative strength and room for manoeuvre of the British bourgeoisie, whose strategy, as the left warned, was to use the trade unions to divert the threat of revolution while preparing if necessary to bring the Labour Party into government. For the newly-formed British communist party – a party of a few thousands, which had not yet clearly broken from either the right or the centre, and with a very weak left wing – to try to make an electoral bloc with the Labour Party in such conditions could only strengthen the influence of opportunism on the extremely limited forces of the proletarian vanguard in Britain.

Whatever its stated intentions, the effect of Lenin's characterisation of left communism as an "infantile disorder" was to isolate the Marxist left and provide a convenient 'Leninist' cloak for the opportunists and centrists to cover up their attachment to the institutions, methods and practices of social democracy. The BSP leadership was not slow to make full use of this new ammunition against its left wing opponents, sub-titling its own reprinted extracts "Lenin replies to our critics."

The left communists, however, did not allow themselves to be over-awed by the personal prestige of the pamphlet's author; after all, despite the excesses of Lenin's polemical style, this was still an open debate within the revolutionary movement. The *Dreadnought* printed in full the chapter on Britain, commenting that: "Comrade Lenin, more than once, found himself in a minority and opposed by comrades who are now his valued co-operators. He will not be surprised, therefore, if we adhere to our well-thought out opinions, and that we should defend our position."[60] In response to a further letter from Lenin condemning the WSF for refusing to take part in the communist unity convention, the *Dreadnought* warned explicitly against the opportunism inherent in Lenin's support for a communist party defending parliamentary action and affiliation to the Labour Party:

We believe that if Lenin were striving day by day with the actual situation in Britain that he would not give this advice... We are convinced that the party, whatever it may call itself, which is to be formed on July 31st, will have the virus of Second Internationalism in its arteries... The differences of tactics and of principles between the two parties which at present appear to be confined to the two questions of parliamentary action and affiliation to the Labour Party will be found in practice to cover a very much wider field... The party of the parliamentary communists is determined at all costs to secure a large membership; it has its eyes on every active socialist, whatever his or her views may be...[61]

Opportunism was indeed still the principal enemy. The struggle against it was to be taken up by the left at the CI's second congress.

The Communist Party of Great Britain: a partial regroupment

The communist unity convention held on 31 July and 1 August 1920 finally gave birth to the Communist Party of Great Britain.

The CPGB's founding congress was numerically dominated by the BSP but saw open and vigorous debate on the key questions of affiliation to the Labour Party and parliamentary action, with arguments against affiliation and calls for abstention from electoral activity put forward, amply testifying to the fact that this organisation was a political expression of the working class.[62] The debate on parliamentary action – originally only included because of the WSF – saw anti-parliamentary views expressed even by BSP delegates. Some showed the influence of the SLP in their emphasis on industrial organisation over political action, but others argued for an abstentionist position on the grounds that putting candidates forward at the present time was a diversion of the party's precious resources which far outweighed any possible gains, while others argued that a vote against parliamentary action would help to ensure that the party had in its ranks only "real revolutionary fighters" instead of opportunists and careerists.[63] Several BSP delegates also spoke against affiliation from their practical experience of working inside the Labour Party at a local level; of the vote catching opportunism and suppression of socialist views. In the end, affiliation was only accepted by 100 to 85 votes, highlighting both the strength of opposition within the new party and the irresponsibility of the CP(BSTI) in deciding not to participate.

But the convention also amply revealed the weight of opportunism and centrism in the new party, with openly opportunist positions being put forward, not only on major programmatic questions but also on equally important questions of internal functioning. Against accusations of authoritarianism and calls for local autonomy, the ex-SLP leaders in particular found themselves having to defend the need for strong party discipline and control of parliamentary candidates The resolution on the party's general policy, moved by A.A. Purcell, a prominent trade union leader, avoided any clear reference to the need to confront and destroy the capitalist state, merely referring to the need for communists to address the trade unionist slogan of 'control of industry.'[64] The resolution on parliamentary action provoked a reaction from several delegates who feared that its emphasis on the need for strong party control over parliamentary candidates would lead to "centralisation of the worst possible type, endangering local initiative and setting up a bureaucracy..."[65] An amendment from Purcell seeking relaxation of party control for those standing as trade union or Labour Party candidates received support from a third of the delegates; clear proof of the presence of a social democratic minority in the new party. In the end the resolution was overwhelmingly accepted, but an amendment ensuring party control of representatives was carried only by a narrow margin.[66] In the debate on affiliation to the Labour Party, Hodgson for the BSP made full use of Lenin's polemic against the left communists to remind those who opposed affiliation that "Lenin considers this kind of objection to Labour Party affiliation as one of the 'infantile disorders of the left communists.'"[67] In the end, the new party left the door firmly open to the entry of opportunist and centrist elements into its ranks, failing to agree any statutes or organisational rules for its functioning and merely adopting a very general proposal urging all members to "extend loyalty and fidelity to the Communist Party...and...subordinate themselves to the general will of the party."[68]

All this underlines the fact that the party formed on 1 August 1920 was only a partial regroupment. Significantly none of the organisations included in the Third International's original invitation were present at the unity convention. As a result, the left wing of the Communist Party of Great Britain was weak from the start. The responsibility for this certainly lies partly with the left, which amply demonstrated its political immaturity and organisational inexperience. But its failure to cleanly split the pro-Bolshevik elements in the BSP from the centrists and opportunists was ultimately due to the change of line by the leadership of the International. By trying to split the centrists, and regroup all those who were for the soviets but against parliamentary action, the left had only been putting into practice the International's original line; the switch by the ECCI from supporting the left to the much larger BSP alienated the anti-parliamentarians while strengthening the centre and the right.

The struggle of the left for a class party in Britain remained incomplete. Rather than being able to lead this struggle, however, the left now increasingly found itself forced to struggle as an opposition inside the International.

Notes

1 *Second Congress of the Communist International, Minutes of the Proceedings, vol. 1*, New Park, 1977, p.28.

2 *Workers' Dreadnought*, 11 December 1920.

3 *BSP Report of the Ninth Annual Conference, 1920*, p.3.

4 *Ibid.*, p.34.

5 *Ibid.*, pp.19-23.

6 Degras, *op. cit.*, p.4.

7 *The Call*, 11 December 1919.

8 Degras, *op. cit.*, p.3.

9 *Workers' Dreadnought*, 22 May 1920.

10 *Socialist*, 15 April 1920.

11 *Spur*, May 1920.

12 *Workers' Dreadnought*, 21 February 1920.

13 See *BSP Report of the Seventh Annual Conference, 1918*, pp.34-36.

14 *Socialist*, 2 January 1919.

15 Degras, *op. cit.*, p.3.

16 *Socialist*, 1 May 1919.

17 *Ibid.*, 27 March 1919.

18 *Ibid.*, May 22 1919.

19 See, for example, the correspondence from Eden and Cedar Paul in *Socialist*, 8 May 1919.

20 *Workers' Dreadnought*, 14 June 1919.

21 Pankhurst's letter appeared anonymously in *Communist International* no.5, 1919, and was reprinted along with Lenin's reply in *The Call*, 22 April 1920.

22 *The Call,* 22 April 1920.
23 WSF Committee Minutes, 3 February 1920 (Pankhurst Papers).
24 James Hulse, *The Forming of the Communist International,* Stanford, 1964, p.117.
25 *Workers' Dreadnought* supplement, 31 January 1920.
26 The only KPD delegate to arrive in time, Carl Stücke, was a leader of the Bremen Left and a representative of the KPD opposition. Herzog, the Swiss delegate, who arrived too late to take part in the proceedings, was also a left.
27 *Workers' Dreadnought,* 20 March 1920. See text selection no. 3.
28 *Ibid.*
29 *Ibid.,* 8 March 1920.
30 *Ibid.,* 20 March 1920.
31 *Ibid.,* 14 February 1920.
32 See *BSP Report of Ninth Annual Conference, 1920,* pp.34, 44.
33 *Workers' Dreadnought,* 20 March 1920.
34 *The Call,* 6 May 1920.
35 *Ibid.*
36 *Ibid.*
37 *Socialist,* 15 April 1920.
38 *The Call,* 1 April 1920.
39 14 of the 22 signatories of the CUG's Manifesto were SLP members. The official SLP claimed at the time only a third were SLP members (*Socialist,* 15 April 1920).
40 See 'Manifesto on Communist Unity' issued by the SLP unofficial conference, n.d. [April 1920].
41 See Kendall, *op. cit.,* n. p.435.
42 Inkpin probably visited Germany in early 1920 where he contacted members of the Western European Secretariat. His subsequent report in *The Call* smeared the KPD opposition with the positions of the National Bolsheviks, and as 'anti-parliamentarians of the syndicalist school' (see *The Call,* 6 May 1920).
43 Printed in *Socialist,* 6 May 1920, and *Workers' Dreadnought,* 8 May 1920.
44 See the communication from the Sub-Bureau published in *Workers' Dreadnought,* 17 April 1920.
45 *The Call,* 20 May 1920. The full text of the ECCI statement was sent out by radio on 4 May.
46 WSF Minutes, 3, 20 February 1920 (Pankhurst Papers).
47 Letter dated 19 May 1920 to Gallacher, Davies and Pritchard (SWSS), Mitchell (SLP), and local groups in Walthamstow and Hammersmith (Pankhurst Papers).
48 *Workers' Dreadnought,* 31 July 1920.
49 *Ibid.,* 3 July 1920.
50 *Ibid.,* 31 July 1920.
51 See Kendall, *op. cit.,* p.212.
52 *Socialist,* 1 July 1920.
53 The formation of the KAPD was mentioned in Inkpin's report from Germany in *The Call,* 6 May 1920.
54 Extracts from the chapter on Britain appeared in *The Call* (29 July), and the whole chapter in the *Workers' Dreadnought* (31 July).
55 Lenin, *Collected Works, vol. 31,* Progress, 1966, p.31, my emphasis.
56 *Ibid.,* p.103.
57 *Ibid.,* p.79.
58 *Ibid.,* p.84.
59 *Ibid.,* p.87.
60 *Workers' Dreadnought,* 31 July 1920.
61 *Ibid.,* 24 July 1920.
62 Some 160 delegates attended; of these 96 were from the BSP and 22 from the CUG. The rest were from miscellaneous groups and local socialist societies (*Report of the Communist Unity Convention,* CPGB, 1920, pp.71-72).
63 See the speeches by Gibbons (Ferndale Socialist Society), Hamilton (Liverpool CUG) and Webb (Littleboro CUG) (*Report of the Communist Unity Convention,* CPGB, 1920, pp.12, 15-16). Harry Webb spoke against both parliamentary action and affiliation to the Labour Party. He was elected to the CPGB Executive in 1921 but ceased any left wing activity.
64 *Report of the Communist Unity Convention,* CPGB, 1920, p.6.
65 *Ibid.,* p.23. This resolution was proposed by Tom Bell of the CUG.
66 84 to 54 votes (*ibid.,* p.29). Purcell became a member of the General Council of the TUC and deserted the CPGB in 1922, later playing an openly reactionary role in the General Strike.
67 *Ibid.,* p.33.
68 *Ibid.,* p.80.

Chapter 5

Opposition

Centrism was originally identified by the Third International as the most insidious danger facing the revolutionary movement, the struggle against which was "the indispensable premise for the successful struggle against imperialism."[1] This danger actually increased as a result of the International's success in establishing itself as a pole of regroupment, leading several of the largest and most influential parties of the centre, including the French Socialist Party, the Independent Socialist Party of Germany and the British Independent Labour Party, to withdraw from the Second International and, under strong pressure from their members, approach the Third. These parties were relatively big: the German USPD, for example, reached one million members during 1919; but they were still under the control of social patriotic leaders bitterly hostile to the proletarian revolution, with memberships that had not yet broken decisively from social democracy. Their approach to the Third International coincided with a downturn in the revolutionary wave and a growing realisation amongst the Bolsheviks that the proletarian revolution in western Europe was going to be a much more protracted process than they had expected. From this, the Bolsheviks began to theorise the need for the isolated Russian bastion to seek an accommodation,albeit temporary, with the major capitalist powers.[2] Such a policy implied a shift from support for the radical positions of the left towards compromises with the centre parties in the interests of winning over hundreds of thousands of supporters; from the creation of vanguard parties to lead an imminent revolution towards the building of mass parties engaged in the tactics of parliamentarism and work within the official trade unions. This policy shift had immediate implications for the International because of the Bolsheviks' authority and role in its leadership. From 1920 onwards the policies of the International became increasingly bound up with the needs of the Russian bastion.

The struggle against opportunism at the CI's second congress

While the CI's founding congress had in many ways expressed a high point of clarity about the meaning of the new epoch and the tasks of the proletariat, inevitably it had not been able to deal with many vital political and organisational questions. The stated objective of its second congress in the summer of 1920 was to turn the International from a "propaganda society" into a "fighting organisation"; by adopting positions on tactics such as parliamentarism and trade union action and the role to be played by the communist party, and, just as importantly, by agreeing statutes and conditions for admission to the International itself.

On all of these questions, the positions adopted by the Congress revealed the contradictory character of the strategy now pursued by the Bolsheviks. Essentially this was to try to capture the left wing of the centre parties like the USPD, while at the same time flattering the lefts (in particular the German KAPD and the British shop stewards), to bring them into the communist parties in order to act as a counterweight, but on the basis of support for parliamentarism and trade union action. In the case of Britain this policy meant accepting the left's criticisms of the BSP, which Lenin agreed was "too weak and incapable of properly carrying out agitation among the masses, while persuading the "younger revolutionary elements", like the supporters of Pankhurst and Gallacher, to join a communist party defending the standing of candidates for parliament and an electoral pact with the Labour Party.[3]

The left fought vigorously against these signs of a weakening in the CI's previously intransigent opposition to centrism. Bordiga, leader of the Communist Abstentionist Fraction of the PSI and the most prominent representative of the left at the Congress, warned that: "Opportunism must be fought everywhere. But we will find this task very difficult if, at the very moment that we are taking steps to purge the CI, the door is opened to let those who are standing outside come in."[4] Gallacher specifically warned the congress against the BSP, which had "not taken a decisive stand on the position of the Communist International", and still belonged to the Second.[5] It was Bordiga also who proposed the last and most rigorous condition of admission to the International, demanding that all party members who rejected the conditions laid down should be expelled.[6] The left's argument was essentially that the conditions for admission, far from being too rigorous, were not rigorous enough.

On parliamentarism, differences were focused on the opposing sets of theses presented by Bukharin, which advocated agitation and propaganda work within bourgeois parliaments; and Bordiga, which called for the complete rejection of parliament as an arena for communist work, active abstention and boycott of the ballot box. The debate revealed a high level of agreement on the implications of the new epoch of capitalist decadence in which, as Bukharin's theses stated, parliament had become a mere tool for "lies, deception, violence and enervating chatter."[7] There was no disagreement on this; nor was there any suggestion that parliament could be utilised as a step towards socialism. But despite this, the Bolsheviks still wanted communists to go back into bourgeois parliaments in order to destroy them. The left argued that this was at best futile, and at worst a compromise with reformism. This was also a debate about the applicability of the Russian experience as a 'universal model'; Bordiga argued that the historical conditions under which the Russian revolution developed were quite different from Western Europe and America:

The tactical experiences of the Russian revolution cannot be transferred to other countries where bourgeois democracy has already long since been introduced and where the revolutionary crisis will consist of a direct transition from this order to the dictatorship of the proletariat... The revolutionary problem demands, above all in western Europe, an abandonment of the ground of bourgeois democracy...the struggle for the conquest of power must be carried out in a new way, through direct revolutionary activity...[8]

The British left was well placed to contribute to this debate, pointing out how the bourgeoisie in Britain made use of parliamentarism as an ideological weapon against the revolution. In an intervention against the 'revolutionary' use of parliament, Gallacher warned that this was a dangerous diversion and waste of energy that only served to strengthen workers' illusions in democratic institutions:

There is now an alternative in front of the Communist International, as there is in front of the people of every country. There are two tactics; one that, through all kinds of democratic phrases, develops the feeling of submission in the people, and the other that consists in developing the revolutionary spirit in the masses.... Our energies must now be applied to sharpening the revolutionary struggle in the masses. The Communist International finds itself now faced with the alternative of taking either the road of submission or that of struggle.[9]

The debate on affiliation to the Labour Party saw a direct confrontation between the British left and the Bolshevik leadership. Lenin began by firmly rejecting the BSP's position that the Labour Party was nothing other than the political expression of the trade union organised workers: the Labour Party should be judged not by its membership but by its leadership and the political content of their actions, and on this basis he argued that the Labour Party was an organisation of the bourgeoisie.[10] But he then went on to accept the BSP's claim that communists would enjoy freedom of criticism inside the Labour Party, arguing that it would be "highly erroneous" not to do everything possible to remain in such a party.[11] Sylvia Pankhurst, drawing on her own bitter experience of trying to work within the Labour Party to change it, explicitly rejected the myth that communists could agitate freely inside it, emphasising its bureaucratisation and extremely ossified structure: "It is impossible to remain inside the party and change this organisation in any way."[12] Echoing Bordiga's warning against basing tactics in the advanced capitalist countries on the Russian experience, she stressed the depth of democratic and parliamentary illusions amongst the British workers and the contradictions involved in calling on them to participate in elections in order to 'destroy' the Labour Party.[13] The British left put up such strong opposition on this issue, winning the support of the Dutch and American lefts, that when the Congress eventually voted to support communists joining the Labour Party, it was by only 58 to 24 votes, with 2 abstentions.[14]

On the trade unions, the congress again adopted a contradictory position, recognising the counter-revolutionary role of the union bureaucracy, and supporting the creation of factory organisations such as the shop stewards' committees in Britain, while at the same time arguing that it was possible for communists to reform the unions from within and turn them into revolutionary organisations. Presenting the CI's position, Radek argued that: "If we wipe out the counter-revolutionary tendencies of the bureaucracy in...the trade unions...then these mass organisations of the working class are the organs best able to lead the struggle of the working class on a broad front."[15] The main opposition to this came from the American and British lefts who, while not rejecting communist work in the trade unions, argued that it was impossible to reform them, and that it was therefore necessary to create new factory organisations to wage the economic struggle against capitalism. Gallacher argued that, from the experience of the shop stewards' movement:

It is simply nonsense and ridiculous to talk of conquering the old trade unions with their ossified bureaucracy... We have been active in the British trades unions for 25 years without ever having succeeded in revolutionising the trades unions from inside. Every time we succeeded in making one of our own comrades an official of the trades unions, it turned out that then, instead of a change of tactics taking place, the trades unions corrupted our own comrades too.[16]

The Bolsheviks' response to this was to reject the conception that the unions had become part of the capitalist state, and simply to reaffirm the need for communists to go into the unions in order to provide them with a revolutionary leadership.[17] The Bolshevik leadership of the International certainly did its best to manage the congress in order to ensure its positions were adopted, but this was no sterile, stage-managed affair as later congresses were to become: charges of opportunism were laid directly at the International's leadership; alternative positions were vigorously proposed and, despite their enormous prestige, even Lenin and the Bolshevik leaders did not escape sharp criticism. Far from renouncing its criticisms, the British left led by Pankhurst and Gallacher put up vigorous opposition to affiliation to the Labour Party, and despite Lenin's personal backing it took all of his efforts, in private conversation, open session and the various working groups set up by the congress, to finally break down their resistance.

The impact of the CI's second congress on the struggle for the party

The CI's second congress clearly revealed a growing opportunist tendency within its leadership. A direct consequence of this was the formation of mass communist parties by centrist and even social patriotic tendencies: in Germany the Communist Party (KPD) merged with the left wing of the USPD in December 1920 to form the United Communist Party (VKPD) with 400,000 members; in France the leadership of the Communist Party created after the Congress of Tours in late 1920 was formed by the tendency around Cachin and Frossard, which had supported Allied imperialism in the war, while in Czechoslovakia the Communist Party – the largest in the CI with over 400,000 members – was formed in May 1921 by the social patriotic Smeral tendency.

In Britain, the Bolsheviks were forced to recognise that the party formed in August 1920 was only a partial regroupment; it was therefore necessary to re-start the unity negotiations in order to bring the left into the CPGB. So, while dismissing anti-parliamentarism as a "naive, childish doctrine which is beneath criticism,"[18] and characterising the views of the left generally as "not correct",[19] the ECCI called for further negotiations between all British communist organisations, based on the positions adopted at the congress.[20] Lenin personally had done everything in his power to persuade Pankhurst and Gallacher to encourage their supporters to go into the CPGB to fight for their positions, claiming that both parliamentarism and affiliation to the Labour Party were simply questions of tactics. According to Pankhurst:

> When, afterwards...I argued with Lenin privately that the disadvantages of affiliation outweighed those of dis-affiliation, he dismissed the subject as unimportant, saying that the Labour Party would probably refuse to accept the Communist Party's affiliation, and that, in any case, the decision could be altered next year. So too with parliamentarism; he dismissed it as unimportant, saying that if the decision to employ parliamentary action is a mistake, it can be altered at next year's Congress.[21]

Lenin urged her to join the united party and "Form a left block within it: work for the policy in which you believe, within the party." [22]

All this flattery aside, the decisions of the Congress presented the left with a difficult choice: either to accept the discipline of the International and fight for a reversal of policy at the next world congress; or to refuse to give up its positions and thus remain outside the International. Both Pankhurst and Gallacher, deeply affected by their experience in Russia, returned from Moscow committed to carrying out the ECCI's instructions, and Pankhurst even took the initiative in reconvening the unity negotiations. The CPGB itself was not so keen, even failing to publish details of the ECCI's resolution until directly challenged to do so by the *Dreadnought*, and then ominously warning the left that "If...they disobey the instructions of the International, or infringe the discipline of the new party...they will be breaking with the communist movement of the world with their eyes wide open," while at the same time pointing out that, given the system of proportional representation proposed by the ECCI, "we shall far and away outnumber any serious opposition...it is our platform that the new party is adopting, and...it is those who would not come to the unity convention that are now making concessions."[23] Given the hostility of the CPGB and the contradictions of the Congress decisions, it is not surprising that the autumn of 1920 saw a series of difficult debates on the left leading to tensions and splits.

On her return from Moscow Pankhurst set out to persuade the CP(BSTI) to accept the CI's conditions for unity. She minimised the party's differences with the International and emphasised the importance of accepting its discipline:

> We are part of the Third International, its decisions are of tremendous importance to us, especially as we must realise that an International can only be an International of action (just as a national party can only be a party of action) if its decisions are obeyed by its constituent parts. The fact that in some respects the tactical policy of the thesis (though not its essential object and theory), differs from what has been our own, lends great responsibility to our party's discussion of the thesis."[24]

At the CP(BSTI)'s national inaugural conference in September, Pankhurst was successful in obtaining the party's acceptance of the conditions for admission to the International. The CP(BSTI) agreed to attend the required unity conference but also decided to call a separate conference of left-wing organisations in order to maximise the left's negotiating strength.[25] In October, however, Pankhurst was arrested for "incitement to sedition" and sentenced to six months imprisonment: another shrewd act of repression by the British state which removed from the scene the most prominent left-wing communist and advocate of further communist unity. With Pankhurst in prison, tensions in the CP(BSTI) rapidly rose to the surface. Differences had already appeared on the party's attitude to industrial organisations, Pankhurst defending the CI's insistence on the leading role of the party.[26] Now further divisions emerged between those who favoured forming a 'left block' to work within the CPGB for a change of policy, and those who wanted to remain as a separate party defending anti-parliamentarism.

The left wing conference, held in Cardiff in December 1920, did not see the hoped-for strengthening of the CP(BSTI)'s ranks. A vote by 15 to 3 to recommend acceptance of the statutes and theses of the second congress cleared the way for the party's attendance at the forthcoming unity convention but provoked the secession of four Manchester branches (around 200 members). The party's executive, while insisting that it shared the seceders' views, refused to accept the split and reminded all branches of their duty to obey "the call of the executive of the world revolution...forming one united revolutionary party."[27] The Manchester opposition was essentially a syndicalist tendency which rejected political action in favour of an industrial struggle conducted through the trade unions, which were to be transformed by communists into "the machine which will emancipate the workers."[28]

Divisions also opened up over control of the party's press. This issue had always been an important one for the left (for example, in the struggle of the left wing of the pre-war SDF against Hyndman's flouting of party policy in the pages of *Justice*). On its formation, the CP(BSTI) had adopted the *Workers' Dreadnought* as its official organ, but Pankhurst, who was elected unopposed as editor, remained the paper's legal owner, and the party made little effort to exercise control. The Cardiff conference saw a call for party control over the paper as required by the CI's conditions for admission. In defiance of the executive, Pankhurst, in a statement from prison, announced that when the CP(BSTI) merged with the CPGB the *Dreadnought* would become "an independent organ, giving an independent support to the Communist Party from the left wing standpoint. The paper will be run by the comrades who are now responsible for it, until my release from prison."[29] The executive's response was to repudiate the *Dreadnought* as the party's official organ and institute a boycott of the paper.[30] This was a belated effort to redress organisational weaknesses resulting from Pankhurst's individualist attitude to party discipline, but the move against the *Dreadnought* should also be seen as part of a struggle between the executive, which was concerned to prevent any obstacles to unity, and Pankhurst's closest supporters, who were determined to continue oppositional activity in the CPGB. As a result, on the eve of its dissolution into the united party, the CP(BSTI) had effectively split into at least two factions. There were also tensions between London and the regions, with distrust expressed by some comrades of the control exercised by the party leadership in London.[31]

At the second congress, the ECCI had been particularly keen to see the shop stewards' committees enter the CPGB, seeing them as a "genuine proletarian mass movement", although by mid-1920 they had been reduced by unemployment to a propaganda group of only a few hundreds.[32] The shop stewards' delegates returned from Moscow as supporters of unity, in some cases having been personally convinced of the need for a political party, and at a specially convened meeting in September 1920 the movement's national administrative council declared its support for the formation of a united communist party. Since the committees themselves had no political conditions for membership, members were called upon to join the CPGB as individuals, while the committees – or what remained of them – would affiliate to the proposed Red International of Labour Unions, which was eventually set up after Murphy's return from Moscow at the end of 1920.

Although not uniformly against the use of parliamentary action, the shop stewards' movement was strongly opposed to the Labour Party, and the Congress decisions were therefore a major obstacle to further unity, especially in Scotland where, according to the Scottish Workers' Committee, communists were "nine-tenths anti-Labour Party."[33] This led some militants to call for a separate, anti-affiliation Scottish Communist Party within the International. Although this was formally ruled out by the CI's condition that there must be a single communist party in each country, it was not entirely unrealistic: after all, Lenin himself had referred in open session to the possibility of two parties in Britain; one pro- and the other anti-affiliation, and there was the precedent of the anti-parliamentary KAPD which had been given a consultative vote.[34] It was also argued on national grounds that the conditions for admission did not preclude the formation of a Scottish party because Scotland was a separate country.[35] But the proposal for a separate Scottish party also attracted sectarian elements: those who had either shunned or withdrawn from the unity negotiations, and had not joined in the struggle of the left at the Second Congress; in particular the SLP and the grouping around John Maclean.

The SLP was present at the second congress but only as an observer. For all its rhetoric, the SLP did not identify itself with the political struggle of the communist left against opportunism in the Third International, even claiming with typical parochialism that the theses and statutes adopted at the congress "fully vindicated" its own position.[36] It abstractly called for the formation of "a real left wing communist party" opposed to affiliation within the Third International,[37] but despite expressing support for the initiative to regroup what it called 'Left Marxist' forces in Scotland, the SLP treated this primarily as an opportunity to recruit Maclean and his supporters into its own ranks. At the same time it was pursuing unity with the ultra-orthodox De Leonist BSISLP.

John Maclean's support for a separate party was essentially a reaction to the downturn in the class struggle. After his break with the BSP in 1920 he began to call on Scottish workers to wage their own struggle separately from the working class in the rest of Britain, because the conditions for revolution were more advanced than in England, and to establish a "Scottish Communist Republic." Maclean had already been led into a dangerous flirtation with bourgeois Scottish nationalism, collaborating with the Honorable Stuart Erskine of Mar and joining his 'National Committee' in late 1919, and his arguments now became increasingly focused on the struggle for national independence, tainted with racial appeals for a common struggle with "our brother Celts of Erin" against "the English capitalists who are descended from the Germans".[38]

After the Labour Party rejected the CPGB's application for affiliation in September 1920 the case for a separate Scottish party was undermined. A conference in Glasgow in October decided to form the Communist Labour Party, but after the intervention of Gallacher the delegates agreed in the interests of unity that the new organisation should remain a 'provisional' body only, with the aim of regrouping the scattered forces of the left and ensuring a strong presence in the united party when it was finally formed.[39] Maclean was forced to abandon his own plan for a separate Scottish Communist Party after the SLP refused to support him. He then called on his supporters to join the SLP; Maclean himself became a member but resigned in 1921.[40]

In Wales the unofficial movement had already split; one section joined the CPGB while around a dozen ex-members of the SWSS formed an anti-parliamentary Communist Party of South Wales and the West of England in September 1920, on a platform identical to the CP(BSTI)'s. This ephemeral grouping displayed a localist vision of communist unity, arguing that this could only be achieved on the basis of "local autonomy in a given local area."[41]

The CP(BSTI), along with the Communist Labour Party and the shop stewards, fused with the CPGB at Leeds in January 1921.[42] The vote was unanimous and there was no political debate. On the eve of the Leeds convention Pankhurst wrote from prison, reiterating her support for the formation of a united party and setting out the conditions on which the CP(BSTI) should join: "That the left wing elements keep together and form a strong, compact left block within the party. Lenin advised this when I discussed the question with him in Moscow... The left block should have its own convenors, and its own special sittings, prior to party conferences, to decide its policy." Citing the example of the Italian Socialist Party, in which right, centre and left met to decide their policy during party conferences, she argued that the same procedure should be followed in the British party. The activities of the left block would not be confined to party conferences; every district would have its own block working to influence party policy and generally act as a 'ginger group' and give a lead: "The left elements should insist that the constitution of the party shall leave them free to propagate their policy in the party and in the Third International as a whole."[43]

Even if the British left had been as strong and well organised as its Italian counterpart, Pankhurst was in no position to ensure that these conditions were accepted and her supporters were unable to influence the unity negotiations; at Leeds the matter was not even discussed and the CP(BSTI) delegates appear to have made no effort to raise it. Nor did they use their presence on the CPGB's executive committee to fight for their positions, despite the fact that the new party's constitution granted the anti-affiliation left substantial representation.[44] Gallacher, who later as a Stalinist MP described how he recanted his left views personally to Lenin,[45] at this time also argued for the right of the anti-parliamentary left to defend its positions within the CPGB while respecting party discipline, and called on all its forces to enter the party in order to fight for a change of policy: "Those of us who disagree with any tactic already decided upon, must have the right to bring the others round to our point of view...and then, through the party, the world movement, by utilising the party to put the new point of view before the World Congress..."[46] But he also dropped his oppositional stance on joining the party. Only the group around Sylvia Pankhurst continued left wing oppositional activity within the CPGB.

The "Dreadnought" group: early left wing opposition in the CPGB

Disowned by the CP(BSTI), under the terms of Pankhurst's letter from prison the *Workers' Dreadnought* now became an "independent organ, giving an independent support to the Communist Party from the left wing standpoint." The *Dreadnought* welcomed the formation of the unified party at Leeds as a regroupment of revolutionary forces that were "not divided on any essential point of programme or tactics."[47] The group around the paper saw itself as a loyal opposition working to press the leadership to expel 'non-communist' elements and move the party leftwards: "By previously grouping together the left wing, and then going over in a body to the united party, a new force has been brought into the party, that whilst obeying the necessary discipline, will continue the necessary impulse to the left."[48]

The *Dreadnought* group's propaganda defended the general orientation of the CI's second congress, highlighting the revolutionary intent of its resolutions, and the failures of the British party to put them into effect. Even at this early stage it pointed out that:

> On the question of parliamentarism, even from the point of propaganda alone, destructive propaganda if you like, both the ex-CP of Great Britain and the new party, appear lukewarm, and to be marking time. Comrade Malone[49] is still an MP, elected on a Coalition ticket, and the party has not availed itself yet of the propaganda that might result from a by-election [which] could be forced now, and the question of unemployment brought forward, also the rights of political prisoners, and of communists generally.[50]

The *Dreadnought* also called for the full expression of the views of the rank and file and warned ominously against the imposition of formal discipline by the executive. To publicise political differences in the International and promote debate by party members it reprinted without criticism the chapter from Lenin's *Left Wing Communism, An Infantile Disorder* on working within reactionary trade unions, as well as the manifesto of the German KAPD and Gorter's 'Open letter to comrade Lenin', which was a full reply to his polemic against the left communists.[51] In April the paper briefly reported the Kronstadt uprising - but did not at this time express support for the rebels.[52]

Not surprisingly, the issue of party control over the *Dreadnought* soon reared its head. At Leeds there had been a lengthy discussion of the new party's attitude to communist papers other than its own official organ, the *Communist*, but the question of the *Dreadnought* was referred to the executive for a decision and left in 'abeyance'. Pankhurst's imprisonment was undoubtedly a mitigating factor in this; she was, after all, one of the best-known British communists and a victim of 'democratic' state repression. The paper itself called on branches to try to influence the forthcoming policy conference, to prevent a boycott of the paper and ensure tolerance of unofficial publications.[53]

With Pankhurst's release from prison in May 1921, the *Dreadnought* took a stronger line against the CPGB's opportunism. Under the heading "watch your leaders", it reported that the Labour-controlled Poplar Board of Guardians in East London was reducing outdoor poor law relief by 10 per cent and lowering the wages of municipal workers. The Board included CPGB members, one of them on the party's executive. Choosing her words carefully to avoid open confrontation, Pankhurst still argued forcefully that:

> For the Labour members of local governing bodies to join the employers' attacking party was what is ordinarily described as betrayal. For members of the Communist Party to take such action cannot fail to be regarded as a more serious dereliction of duty... The Communist Party is a party of revolution. It

declares that the capitalist machinery of parliament and local government cannot be used for reform, cannot be transformed, must be abolished. It declares that Communist Party members elected to parliament and the local bodies must use their positions thereon for obstructive, destructive revolutionary propaganda, and must act in harmony with the struggle of the communists and discontented masses outside. The action of the Communist Party members of the Poplar Board is in direct conflict with this declaration of the Third International. We do not wish wantonly to fling about the word 'betrayal'. As far as is possible, we prefer to regard the incident as evidence of a failure to grasp the realities of the situation; as a failure to comprehend the tactics of the Third International - the tactics of revolutionary communism.[54]

In publishing allegations against her own party's members, Pankhurst was flouting the basic rules of communist discipline; but so were the CPGB members she accused of participating in attacks on the working class as part of a Labour-controlled body. Yet it was Pankhurst who was condemned by the local CP branch. Once again Pankhurst was forced to point out that the British party was not carrying out CI policy:

The constitution of the Communist International precisely declares that the Communist Party representatives on elective bodies are responsible to the party. Why has the party left its representatives to do as they please, and only passed a vote of censure on those who, at long last, have called attention to the fact that these representatives are not moving in the path of the Communist tactics? What action is the branch now taking to construct, with its elected representatives, the policy they are to pursue on public bodies, and to see that the policy is applied?"[55]

These questions went unanswered. Instead, Pankhurst was summoned by the executive to give up control of the *Dreadnought* and, after refusing, she was expelled from the party in September 1921.

By continuing to publish the *Dreadnought* outside of party control Pankhurst was in breach of party discipline and the CI's '21 Points'. But the formal reasons for her expulsion should not be used to obscure the wider significance of the CPGB's suppression of the *Dreadnought* as a symptom of the growing rightward trend in the International; a trend already confirmed at its Third Congress in June with the expulsion of the German, Dutch and Bulgarian communist lefts. As Pankhurst wryly observed: "The executive of the Third International, after pleading with us to enter, now apparently encourages the excommunication of the left wing."[56] Essentially the *Dreadnought* group was warning against the very real danger of right opportunism and simply demanding the British party apply the decisions of the second congress:

...whereas we are face to face with an opportunist and reformist Labour Party, and since in the midst of capitalism, there is an ever-present tendency and temptation towards compromise with the existing order, it is essential for a Communist Party to be definite in excluding right tendencies. A Communist Party can only preserve its communist character by using its discipline to prevent right opportunism and laxity from entering the party; it must insist that acceptance of communist principles and avoidance of reformism be made a condition of membership...[57]

The reality was that the '21 Points' were now being used against the left in order to stifle dissent.

Following her expulsion Pankhurst set out a full summary of the main political differences between the left wing communists and the CPGB at this time. The British party, which had been formed from "groups of conflicting tendencies, brought together by outside pressure and largely composed of persons as yet untried in the political struggle", had as a result from the start shown a clear tendency towards opportunism. Furthermore, this tendency was inherent in the "illogical and unworkable" tactics adopted by the majority of the Third International at its second congress, which were intended to "secure numerous adherents, by striving to combine mutually conflicting policies."[58] This was revealed in the contradictory positions adopted on parliamentarism and trade unionism. On parliamentarism, Pankhurst observed:

When we, who are against the use of parliamentary action, argue that it is contradictory and confusing to declare on the one hand that parliament is useless and must be destroyed, and on the other hand to urge the workers to put us into parliament, those who have chosen the way of parliamentary action, reply that great masses of unconscious workers still have faith in parliament. Quite so, we answer, then we must undermine that faith: but appalled by the magnitude of the task of creating a body of conscious workers strong enough to effect any changes, the communist opportunists propose to accomplish the revolution with crowds of unconscious workers...the present policy of the majority of the Third International is to secure numerous adherents, by striving to combine mutually conflicting policies.[59]

The British party did not even operate this contradictory policy in the revolutionary or 'destructive' sense confusedly intended by the CI, as demonstrated by the actions of its representatives on the local bodies of the capitalist state up and down the country:

In our opinion, the use of parliamentary action by communists is illogical, contradictory and bound to lead to the lapses into rank reformism that we see wherever members of the Communist Party secure election to public bodies. These Communist Party members who have been elected to public bodies, are simply trying, like the Labour Party, to secure reforms: they are taking no step to unhinge the capitalist system.[60]

At root, parliamentarism, with all the bourgeois intrigue and petty routinism that went with it, was the politics of capitalism; the struggle for communism demanded new, revolutionary tactics.

On trade unionism, Pankhurst criticised the CI's contradictory decision to form a red trade union International as a hybrid body composed of the official trade unions, shop stewards and workshop committees and militant industrial organisations like the IWW. This displayed the same opportunist policy of roping in passive, unawakened masses, and failed to recognise the significance of the new forms of organisation created by militant workers to wage their struggles:

> These rebel organisms, at war with the old trade unionism, cannot be combined with it: to make them an official part of the unions is to destroy them: they exist as a protest against conservatism in the unions... They are the forerunners of what, some day, will break out spontaneously to form the soviets... The Third International was not content to make its industrial ally a relatively small, though intensely revolutionary body: it wanted something big and showy that could rival the Yellow Amsterdam International in actual numbers. Therefore it has built up a shapeless, incoherent body, decorated by the names of non-communist trade union 'big-wigs' with the paper backing of the unconscious memberships that do not know what trade unionism means...[61]

All these opportunist tactics were reflected in the CI's attempts to win over hundreds of thousands of supporters to create mass communist parties, against which the *Dreadnought* group defended its original view of the party as a disciplined vanguard of the class:

> It is essential that the Communist Party should not be a large confused mass of incoherent elements honeycombed by parliamentary and local government place-hunters, by people who believe that "parliamentary action will do it," and by those who have come into the party merely because they disliked the intervention against Soviet Russia. The Communist Party can only help to precipitate the revolution, and, more important, to make the revolution, when it comes at last a communist revolution, if it be a party of communists.[62]

The *Dreadnought* group was also the first tendency in the British party to alert workers to the degeneration of the Russian revolution, warning against the "tendency to slip to the right" and the "reintroduction" of certain features of capitalism in Russia. The cause of this was identified not as the backwardness of Russia or the intentions of the Bolsheviks but the pressure of encircling capitalism and the failure of the working class in the western democracies to make a revolution.[63] The *Dreadnought* reported news of the growing conflicts inside the Russian party leading to the formation of the Workers' Opposition.[64]

The small group around the *Workers' Dreadnought* was in effect the first left wing opposition to operate inside the British Communist Party, a full ten years before the emergence of the Trotskyist Left Opposition. Pankhurst's proposal for an organised 'left block' in the CPGB was stillborn due to weakness of the left in the party, as former allies drifted away or moved to the right, but the *Dreadnought* group's activity did have an echo in the party and the wider working class; Pankhurst's expulsion prompted protests from some branches and individual members, and expressions of solidarity and offers of financial support came from the South Wales miners and the international communist movement.[65] The group's main strength was its press; the *Workers' Dreadnought* was at this time a unique source of information for party militants on differences in the International and the positions of the communist left, and the executive's efforts to suppress the paper were motivated in part by concern at its influence among the rank and file.

The participation of the British communist left in the struggle against opportunism at the second congress was a vital experience for its main representatives in understanding the importance of fighting within the organisations of the proletariat. Ultimately for the left it was a matter of deciding as a fraction of a centralised International to accept its discipline and work within it for a change of line. While the deepening reflux in the revolutionary wave and the rightward shift of the CI made such a task increasingly impossible, this downturn did not yet appear irreversible. The clearest elements in the British revolutionary movement were those who belatedly decided to enter the CPGB and fight for their positions rather than those who stayed outside objecting to 'interference from Moscow' or trying to set up alternative parties or loose federations of anti-parliamentarians. As long as the International and its official parties remained proletarian political expressions, it was the duty of revolutionaries to fight within them to attempt to return them to a revolutionary course.

Notes

1 'Manifesto of the Communist International to the proletariat of the entire world', Degras, *op. cit.*, p.46.

2 The most important theorist of this new line was Radek who, from his vantage point as the CI's agent in Germany, in October 1919 observed that unless the world revolution happened soon, Soviet Russia would have to arrive at a *modus vivendi* with the capitalist world. Radek pursued this argument on his return to Russia as secretary of the CI (see E.H. Carr, *The Bolshevik Revolution, 1917-1923, vol. 3,* Pelican, 1966, pp.313-322).

3 *Second Congress of the Communist International, Minutes of the Proceedings, vol. 2,* New Park, 1977, p.184.

4 *Op. cit., vol. 1,* p.224.

5 *Ibid.,* p.134.

6 *Ibid.,* p.221-224.

7 *Op. cit., vol. 2,* p.3.

8 *Ibid.,* pp.16-18.

9 *Ibid,* pp.25-26.

10 *Ibid,* pp.183-4.

11 *Ibid.,* p.188.

12 *Ibid.,* p.180.

13 *Ibid.,* pp.179-180.

14 *Ibid.,* p.188.

15 *Ibid.,* p.66.

16 *Ibid.,* p.167.

17 *Ibid.,* pp.168-169.

18 'Theses on Parliamentarism', Degras, *op. cit.,* p.154.

19 'Theses on the Fundamental Tasks of the Communist International', Degras, *op. cit.,* p.126.

20 The resolution of the ECCI on the 'British Question' called for the convening of a conference to form a single communist party within four months of the return of the British delegates from Moscow. The original invite list named the CPGB, CP(BSTI), National Shop Stewards' and Workers' Committee Movement, Scottish Workers' Committee, the 'Welsh communists and industrial reform movement', SLP and the Left Wing of the ILP. The basis of agreement was to be the theses on the role of the Communist Party adopted at the second congress (*Workers' Dreadnought,* 25 September 1920).

21 Extract from *Soviet Russia As I Saw It,* in *Workers' Dreadnought,* 16 April 1921.

22 *Workers' Dreadnought,* 24 September 1921. Did Lenin really invite the left to form a block in the CPGB? It has been denied by 'Leninists'. There is no direct evidence in the proceedings of the second congress, but it is consistent with Lenin's line of argument, and there is no evidence that it was denied

at the time. Corroborating evidence comes from Gallacher, who, having been similarly convinced personally by Lenin to join the CPGB, argued along exactly the same lines (see n.46).

23 *Communist*, 25 November 1920.

24 *Workers' Dreadnought*, 2 October 1920. The conference also considered sending a delegate to represent the CP(BSTI) on the ECCI.

25 *Ibid.* Representatives were invited from the English Shop Stewards' and Workers' Committee Movement, Scottish Communist Labour Party, Scottish Workers' Committee and Glasgow Communist Group.

26 *Workers' Dreadnought*, 25 September 1920.

27 *Ibid.*, 8 January 1921.

28 *Ibid.*

29 *Ibid.*, 15 January 1921.

30 Letter to Pankhurst from Edgar Whitehead, the CP(BSTI) secretary, dated 16 January 1921 (Pankhurst papers).

31 See the letter of 'A.T.' to *Workers' Dreadnought*, 15 January 1921.

32 'Theses on the fundamental tasks of the Communist International', *Second Congress of the Communist International, Minutes of the Proceedings, Vol. 2*, New Park, 1977, p.271.

33 *Worker*, 14 August 1920, cited in Kendall, *op. cit.*, p.259.

34 In December 1920 the KAPD was recognised as a sympathising party of the International. The Bolsheviks were willing to offer the KAPD a place on the ECCI but were prevented from doing so by bitter personal opposition from KPD leader Paul Levi.

35 *Vanguard*, December 1920, reprinted in Nan Milton (Ed.) *John MacLean, In the Rapids of Revolution, Essays, articles and letters 1902-23*, Allison & Busby, 1978, p. 225.

36 *Socialist*, 16 December 1920.

37 *Ibid.*

38 *Vanguard,* August 1920, in Milton (Ed.), *op. cit.*, p.219; and July 1920, in Nan Milton, *John Maclean*, Pluto Press, 1973, p.238.

39 See *Worker*, 20 November 1920. The conference was attended by representatives of the Scottish Workers' Committee, SLP and CP(BSTI), along with several local communist groups. Maclean's grouping was represented by James MacDougall but Maclean himself was not present. Both the SLP and CP(BSTI) called on the conference to join their respective parties because their programmes were the same.

40 After two further terms of imprisonment, in 1923 Maclean set up his own group, the Scottish Workers' Republican Party. He died in 1923, his physical and mental health finally destroyed by the British state. His political heritage has been claimed by everyone from the Stalinists, the Labour Party and of course the Scottish nationalists, but John Maclean, for all his errors, died an implacable enemy of the capitalist system.

41 'Report on Revolutionary Organisations in the United Kingdom', 9 December 1920, CAB24/116/CP2273, cited in R. Pitt, *John Maclean and the CPGB,* second edition, 1996, p.31.

42 170 delegates attended from the CPGB, CLP, CP(BSTI) and various independent groups, with Jack Tanner of the NSS&WCM in the chair. The ILP Left Wing sent a fraternal delegate and Murphy spoke as fraternal delegate of the RILU.

43 *Workers' Dreadnought*, 15 January 1921.

44 See reports of the conference in the *Communist* and *Workers' Dreadnought,* 5 February 1921. Seven members were appointed by each of the main component parties (2 each from the CLP and CP(BSTI) and 3 from CPGB), plus ten members elected by region, a number of whom were also from the left.

45 See his highly unreliable memoir, *Revolt on the Clyde*, Lawrence and Wishart, 1936, p.253.

46 Letter to Pankhurst, n.d. [December 1920] (Pankhurst Papers).

47 *Workers' Dreadnought*, 5 February 1921.

48 *Ibid.*

49 The CPGB's only MP at its formation, Colonel Cecil L'Estrange Malone had been elected as a Coalition Liberal in the 1918 general election and was a leading member of the anti-socialist Reconstruction Society before undergoing a startling conversion to socialism after a visit to Russia in September 1919, joining the BSP and attending the CPGB's founding congress in July 1920. Not surprisingly, doubts were cast on his credibility and John Maclean suggested that Malone could be a government agent. At best, Malone was a political adventurer and his acceptance into the CPGB, let alone as its sole parliamentary representative, is evidence that the party fell far short of the discipline demanded by the CI's conditions for admission.

50 *Workers' Dreadnought*, 5 February 1921.

51 The KAPD's manifesto appeared in the *Workers' Dreadnought* on 29 January 1921; Gorter's 'Open

letter' appeared in ten instalments from 25 September 1920 to 11 June 1921.

52 *Workers' Dreadnought*, 16 April, 7 May 1921.
53 *Ibid.*, 12 February 1921.
54 *Ibid.*, 30 July 1921.
55 *Ibid.*
56 *Ibid.*, 24 September 1921.
57 *Ibid.*, 17 September 1921.
58 *Ibid.*, 24 September 1921.
59 *Ibid.*
60 *Ibid.*
61 *Ibid.*
62 *Ibid.*
63 *Ibid.*, 17 September 1921.
64 *Ibid.*, 3 September 1921.
65 *Ibid.*, 24 September, 8 and 15 October 1921.

Chapter 6

Defeat

1921 saw a series of significant setbacks for the world revolution: in Germany a poorly prepared armed uprising ended in failure and further repression, while in Russia the isolated proletarian bastion was forced to seek an accommodation with world capitalism, entering into secret military deals and trade agreements with the major imperialist powers, and re-introducing elements of the capitalist market to try to re-stabilise the war-ravaged economy. The Bolshevik Party found itself inextricably enmeshed in the state apparatus, and the growing conflict between the interests of this state and the working class soon came to a head in the bloody crushing of the uprising at Kronstadt.

Reassured by the quarantining of the revolution in Russia, the bourgeoisie began to go onto the offensive. In Britain, having isolated the workers' struggles through the manoeuvres of the unions, it commenced a well-prepared strategy of picking off each sector of workers one by one, inflicting a major defeat on the miners in the Spring. Hit by growing unemployment and unable to break out of trade union control, the working class continued to show huge reserves of militancy but was unable to reverse the rising tide of defeat.

The attempt by the Third International to create mass communist parties in such conditions through compromises with social democracy only hastened their degeneration. From 1921 onwards, revolutionaries were forced increasingly to swim against this tide.

The early degeneration of the Communist Party of Great Britain

The policies and tactics pursued by the British Communist Party in the first three years of its existence amply confirmed the left communists' critique of opportunism in the International and the contradictory nature of the positions adopted at its second congress. The effect of these positions; on affiliation to the Labour Party, support for work inside parliament and the trade unions, and the subsequent imposition of the united front tactic, was to strengthen social democratic tendencies in the CP and move the party further to the right.

The CPGB's first application to join the Labour Party in August 1920 simply quoted verbatim the resolutions of its founding congress, which repudiated the reformist view that revolution could be achieved by parliamentary methods. Not surprisingly, the Labour Party's national executive rejected this on the grounds that the CP's objects "did not appear to be in accord with the party's constitution, principles and programme", to which the CP retorted: "So be it. It is their funeral, not ours."[1] It has since been suggested that this was a symptom of sectarianism in the party, the application being deliberately couched in terms designed to invite rejection.[2] In fact, it reveals the contradiction inherent in the CI's policy: was affiliation intended to be a way of demonstrating to the workers the capitalist nature of the Labour Party, or a serious attempt to work within it to win over its members, for which, as the CI's theses argued, certain compromises may be necessary? At this time, there were still grounds for believing the former: after all, Lenin himself had argued in *Left-Wing Communism* that "If the Hendersons and the Snowdens reject a bloc with us on these terms we shall gain still more, for we shall have at once shown the masses that [they] prefer their close relations to the capitalists to the unity of all the workers."[3] And at the second congress, he had claimed that if, having joined the Labour Party, the communists were expelled, then this also would be a "great victory."[4] Recognising the dangers involved in communists joining what Lenin called a 'thoroughly bourgeois' party, the CI's theses were conditional on the Labour Party allowing the CPGB "freedom of criticism and freedom of propaganda, and organisational activity."[5] The refusal of the CPGB's application was proof that this so-called freedom did not exist; a possibility the CI had at least considered:

Were this tendency to succeed [for the Labour Party to become a mass opportunist party], the Labour Party would never afford the socialist organisations which form part of it the right to an individual communist policy, nor to the propagation of the revolutionary struggle. It would bind their freedom of action hand and foot. It is thus evident that no kind of organisation seeking to carry out a communist policy could possibly belong to the Labour Party.[6]

For the left communists of the *Workers' Dreadnought* group, the conclusion was clear:

Now that everyone, including comrades Zinoviev and Lenin, must finally admit that the Labour Party is a political party with all the attributes of a political party, we again submit, that for the Communist Party to affiliate to the Labour Party, striving to capture it from within, is the same as for communists to remain a part of the Scheidemann party in Germany, striving to capture it also from inside.[7]

But instead of dropping the tactic, the ECCI instructed the CPGB to renew its efforts, which it did by refuting the charge that it intended to disrupt the Labour Party and protesting that it accepted its constitution.[8]

The refusal of its first application left the CPGB temporarily free to oppose Labour candidates, and at the Caerphilly by-election in August 1921 it stood its own candidate against Labour, polling only 2,500 votes.[9] At Woolwich in March, where Labour lost a previously safe seat to the Conservatives, it even called on workers to abstain because Tories and Labour were "two of a kind."[10] This was clearly in conflict with the continued pursuit of affiliation. The third CI congress was forced to note the failure of the communist movement in Britain to develop into a mass party, and because it believed that that "new revolutionary perspectives" were about to open up, it now made this the CPGB's most important task.[11] In December 1921, this was refined as the tactic of the united front, which specifically

directed the British Communists "to begin a vigorous campaign for their acceptance by the Labour Party."[12]

The opportunist logic inherent in the united front tactic set the CPGB on an
even more slippery slope. At a closed meeting in late December 1921, the CP
leadership, acting on the CI's instructions, went so far as to deny that it adhered
to the programme of the Third International, or that it repudiated the achievement
of revolution by parliamentary methods, or defended the necessity of a violent
revolution. Gallacher, the former anti-parliamentarian, went even further: "What
the Labour Party and the members of the Labour Party are fighting for and
subscribing to is the overthrow of capitalism and the institution of socialism.
That is what the Communist Party is fighting for. Fundamentally we are agreed."[13]
By the time the CP formally adopted the policy at its 1922 party conference, the
Labour Party was characterised as "the organised political party of the working
class", whose present policy and leadership needed changing in order to
"transform [it] into an instrument of revolutionary progress."[14] In August 1922 the
CPGB withdrew all further electoral opposition, and in the general election that
year called on workers to vote for the Labour Party.[15] The election of two Communist
MPs (one endorsed by the Labour Party) only worsened the CP's opportunism,
to the extent that the CI had to intervene; the CPGB was forced to admit that its
actions had led to the weakening of any independent role for the party and the
suppression of communist positions.[16] The British party certainly stood to the
right of the CI leadership at this time, but when the first minority Labour government
was formed in early 1924, the ECCI offered the CPGB's support and spread
illusions in Labour's ability to defend the working class and oppose war.[17]

At the local level also, the CPGB acted as the left wing of the Labour Party. As
we have already seen, in the East End of London its elected representatives
participated in Labour-led attacks on workers' living conditions. Even in the well-
known case of Poplar, where in September 1921 Labour councillors were
imprisoned for refusing to collect the rates, the CP (which had two members on
the council) failed to criticise the limitations of Labour's campaign – which was
essentially an argument within the local state about spreading the burden of
providing poor relief – and hailed it as "a lesson in communist action."[18] It was
left to the *Dreadnought* group to point out that "To the unemployed, half-starved
on the paltry pittances doled out to them, the equalisation of rates is rather a
remote question... The borough councillors are in a difficulty; but the workers
beneath struggle with cold and merciless poverty: it is to them we must address
ourselves..."[19] The depths of the CPGB's opportunism were starkly demonstrated
in September 1923, when the Poplar Board of Guardians, which included two
prominent members of the CPGB, called in the police to break up a peaceful
demonstration by unemployed workers against cuts in relief. The police fell
upon the unarmed workers, men and women, viciously beating them and causing
many casualties. The *Dreadnought* group vigorously exposed this attack on the
working class by the CI's British party.[20]

This opportunism was mirrored in the CPGB's attitude towards the trade
unions. The CP's interventions in the class struggle failed to warn the workers
against the unions' counter-revolutionary role: in the miners' strike of October
1920, for example, it referred to the Miners' Federation as the "vanguard of British
trade unionism" and warned the workers against the government but not the
Triple Alliance, criticising the latter only for its "weakness" and the failures of its
"reformist leaders" rather than for its active sabotage.[21] After the capitalist state
had prepared all its weapons and set the miners up for defeat, the CPGB blamed

the strike's subsequent failure on right-wing union leaders like J.R. Thomas, drawing the lesson merely that the leadership of the unions needed to be changed.[22] Under the CI's direction, the CPGB abandoned any call for the formation of independent forms of struggle against the unions and actively opposed any tendency within the workers' struggles to break from union control, raising the slogan "back to the unions" and calling for their reorganisation based on local trades councils under the control of the TUC.[23] This paved the way for the defeat of the 1926 general strike when, having spread illusions in the so-called left-wing trade union leaders of the Comintern-backed Anglo-Russian Committee, the CP raised the infamous slogan "All Power to the General Council [of the TUC]."[24] The roots of this betrayal were already well established in the practices of the CPGB from 1921 onwards, and in the policies imposed upon it by the International.

The rearguard fight of the left in the CPGB, 1921-1922

The CPGB's early degeneration did not go wholly unopposed within the party. Aside from the *Dreadnought* group, and even after Pankhurst's expulsion, opposition was expressed at both local and national levels; through speeches, amendments and votes at party conferences, individual and group protests and refusals to carry out directives, resulting in disciplinary action and the expulsion of whole branches. All this has been dismissed – as it was at the time by supporters of CI policy – merely as the persistence of 'left sectarianism', or the resistance of 'old-fashioned' social democratic branches to the reorganisation of the party along Bolshevik lines. In fact, this early left-wing opposition in the CPGB was in political continuity with the struggle of the left to form a vanguard party based on a clean break with the Second International. The first CP congresses saw renewed efforts to reverse support for official policy on the Labour Party, parliamentarism and the trade unions, with amendments to the party's constitution put forward to curb opportunist tendencies in the spirit of the CI's '21 Points.'[25]

The CI's united front policy came as a shock to the party, which, according to the leadership's own official report, led to a "considerable" loss of membership.[26] There was resistance to its adoption at the party's special policy conference in March 1922, which debated two separate resolutions: one on the united front, which was carried "practically unanimously"; and one on the party's electoral policy, which saw an amendment put forward opposing affiliation to the Labour Party.[27] This was lost by 31 votes to 112, indicating opposition by a fifth of the party to official CI policy. Clearly this was contradictory as in practice the two issues were inextricably linked; since the ECCI's united front directive specifically ordered the British communists to campaign for affiliation, the vote was in effect a rejection of the united front. In her own observations on the conference, Sylvia Pankhurst reported a speech by one delegate opposed to the united front, George Garrett of Liverpool, who argued for a "clean" party, "absolutely a working class party, with a revolutionary outlook."[28] In response to a questionnaire sent out before the CI's fourth congress, the ECCI reported that a quarter of the British party was opposed to the united front.[29] In September 1922, the party's executive heard reports of protests from 'certain branches' including Aberdeen, Bradford and Hull, after members had refused to carry out its direction to join their local

Labour Party. The Pendleton branch was reportedly also having problems carrying out the united front policy, while Bridgeton had already "placed itself outside the party."[30] The detailed reports of party officials in response to the ECCI questionnaire provide further evidence of the state of the branches at this time; some reported no disagreements while others, for example in Glasgow, Liverpool, Leeds and Bradford, described varying degrees of dissent.[31] Contrary to the leadership's claim that all this opposition had ended by the time of the October 1922 party conference, 10 per cent of delegates still voted against affiliation.[32] In November, the Barrow branch did not distribute the party's election manifesto.[33] Many others with dissident views undoubtedly voted with their feet; active membership of the party, which was around 3,000 in January 1921, had by 1922 dropped to no more than 2,000.[34] As late as August 1923, individual CPGB members were still being expelled for publicly opposing Labour Party and united front policy, but by the end of 1922 the so-called 'Bolshevisation' of the party had effectively stifled this opposition.[35]

The CPGB inherited many organisational weaknesses; it had a federal constitution, which led to a lack of centralised functioning and ineffective leadership, and very loose rules which did not effectively exclude opportunist and reformist elements as required by the '21 Points'. It was also hemorrhaging members and real sales of its paper, the *Communist,* were very low. Some basic steps were taken to tighten up internal functioning, with the adoption of a new constitution and rules, but the problems came to a head at the 1922 policy conference where a special organisation commission was set up composed of elements outside the existing leadership. As a result, a new model of organisation was adopted based on the theses of the third CI congress, with a complex, top-heavy structure of departments and special committees at national, district and local level.[36] Factory groups or 'cells' replaced the branches, where much of the remaining proletarian life in the party was expressed.[37] In the context of the decline of the revolutionary wave and the CI's degeneration, 'Bolshevisation' was a major step in the bureaucratising of the British party and the suppression of internal dissent. It also formed part of the political struggle of the ECCI to install a leadership that would loyally implement the policy of the united front and defend the interests of the Russian state; the commission was assisted in its work by the CI's special representative, Borodin, and the entire CPGB central committee was invited to Moscow for consultations in order to break down resistance to the changes. The replacement of the old executive by the new leadership faction led by Palme Dutt and Pollitt not only signified a defeat for the old right-wing BSP-dominated leadership but also for ex-SLP leaders like Murphy, MacManus and Bell, who were eased out of their prominent roles in the party's industrial organisation.

The left in the CPGB proved far too weak and fragmented to resist this degeneration. Its opposition in the early years of the party represented a rearguard fight by elements of the original left wing against the influence of reformism, and to try to ensure that the party was based on clear revolutionary principles. The most serious weakness of this left was not so much the extent of its support or lack of organisation, but its fatal tendency to try to conciliate with the CPGB's opportunism, and its avoidance of a political confrontation with the leadership of the International. But it did ring the alarm bells against the drift to the right in the International and its British party, and at least tried to resist the onset of the bourgeois counter-revolution.

The existence of this opposition, almost ten years before the emergence of a

British section of the Trotskyist Left Opposition, is further proof that the CPGB cannot be written off as a bourgeois organisation from birth.

The early degeneration of the Communist International and the exclusion of the communist left represented a significant defeat for the world revolution. It left surviving revolutionary minorities, in conditions of increasing isolation and demoralisation, with the task of trying to understand the reasons for the defeats suffered by the proletariat. This posed some very difficult questions: were the International and its official parties still proletarian or had they definitively betrayed and passed over to the enemy camp? And if they were now lost to the working class, was it necessary or even possible to call for the formation of new parties and a new International? In answering these questions, revolutionaries faced the danger, on the one hand, of prematurely abandoning organisations which, although in an advanced state of decay, had still not definitively passed over into the camp of capital; and on the other, out of sentiment or a desire to retain some influence among the working class, of remaining attached to organisations which had ceased to defend the interests of the proletariat. At the heart of the debates which took place from the early 1920s into the 1930s was the question of the class nature of the Russian revolution: had this indeed been the world's first successful seizure of political power by the proletariat led by the Bolshevik Party, as the left had originally proclaimed, and if so, what had happened to it? Here also, there was a real danger of clinging to the defence of what had become a definitely counter-revolutionary regime and to all of the opportunist positions enshrined as 'Leninism' that flowed from this; or, alternatively, of throwing into question the whole experience of the proletariat and falling prey to nihilism or despair.

The "Workers' Dreadnought" group after 1921: the dangers of not understanding the conditions for a new party and International

Outside of the CPGB after 1921, the small group around Sylvia Pankhurst continued to act as a rallying point for left-wing opposition, denouncing the betrayals of the CPGB and the CI and alerting the working class to the degeneration of the Russian revolution. The *Workers' Dreadnought* became the most important English language journal of the international communist left, publicising the emergence of left-wing opposition within the Bolshevik Party itself and reprinting key texts of the German, Dutch and Russian left communist oppositions.

The main political influence on the *Dreadnought* group at this time was the German-Dutch left, or more specifically the tendency around Gorter. At the third CI congress, the KAPD had rejected the CI's ultimatum to merge with the VKPD within three months, provoking a major debate in the party about whether it should try to remain in the International to fight for revolutionary positions or abandon it and form a new one. A minority in the KAPD's Berlin district influenced by Gorter began to theorise that the Russian revolution from the very beginning had had a 'dual' character: proletarian in the cities and bourgeois in the country; and that both the Bolshevik Party and the Third International shared this character, acting partly in the interests of the proletariat and partly in the interests of Russian capitalism. For this minority, the International and *all of its sections* had become subordinated to the Russian bourgeois state and definitively lost to the proletariat. It therefore called for the immediate formation of a new International to replace the Third. The majority of the KAPD opposed this as premature, and the minority, which also rejected the party's participation in struggles for immediate demands as 'reformist', was excluded from the Berlin district, transferring itself to the Essen district where in April 1922 it founded the Communist Workers' International, or KAI (*Kommunistische Arbeiter-Internationale*).[38]

The *Workers' Dreadnought* immediately welcomed the proclamation of the Communist Workers' International and published its manifesto, announcing that: "Since the Third International is firmly bound to the soviet government and the Russian party: since a Moscow executive wholly dominated by Russian policy controls the action of all the national parties affiliated to the Third International, since every day this policy becomes less revolutionary, the rise of a Fourth International has become inevitable."[39] It also announced its intention to form a new party in Britain, the 'Communist Workers' Party'. Despite the publication of a statement of principles and repeated appeals, however, this was never formed, although there were local groups in London, Sheffield, Portsmouth, and Plymouth.[40] Similarly, sympathising parties of the KAI were reported to be in existence in Bulgaria, Yugoslavia and South Africa, as well as Russia, Germany and Holland, and later Austria, but few of these had any substantial strength.[41]

By adopting the KAI's programme, the *Dreadnought* group was accepting without criticism Gorter's contention that by the summer of 1921 the Bolshevik Party and the Third International had become 'completely bourgeois and capitalist', throwing into question the whole history of its previous support for the Bolsheviks and the Russian revolution. The positions defended by the KAI were also regression from the group's earlier clarity on the trade unions: Pankhurst had always criticised the industrial unionists for trying to build new, 'revolutionary' unions, yet now she advocated the formation of "One Revolutionary Union of Workers in all industries" along the lines of the German *Unionen*, as a means of "preparing the machinery of the soviets."[42] The proposed 'All-Workers Revolutionary Union of Workshop Committees' also remained stillborn. By announcing its intention to create a new party and new unitary organisations in a period of a capitalist counter-offensive and mass unemployment, the *Dreadnought* group showed its failure to understand the balance of class forces and the most basic conditions for creating such organisations. In a period of deepening defeat, this could only add to the disorientation and demoralisation of revolutionaries.

The most valuable contribution of the *Dreadnought* group in the early 1920s was in developing an understanding of the degeneration of the Russian revolution and the nature of the soviet state. The *Dreadnought* group still believed that capitalism had actually been abolished in Russia in 1917, and saw the introduction of the New Economic Policy in 1921 as a "reversion to capitalism." It also made concessions to the idea that in Russia conditions were not ready for proletarian revolution, referring to its "special difficulties" in applying the soviet system due to the backwardness of the country, which had "only partially progressed from feudalism into capitalism."[43] But it was able to avoid the most fatalistic conclusions of Gorter about the 'double' or reactionary character of the Russian revolution, instead correctly posing the root of the problem as the isolation of the proletarian bastion in Russia and its encirclement by the hostile forces of world capitalism. The group even accepted, albeit reluctantly, that from the Russian state's point of view it may have been necessary to enter into compromises with the imperialist powers, but it implacably opposed the surrender of communist principles involved in concessions like the trade agreement signed with Britain in October 1921, which was accompanied by a promise to cease any anti-British activity by the International, and it highlighted the growing conflict between the interests of the soviet state and the international communist movement: "the soviet government now concentrates on the capitalist development of Soviet Russia... We cannot follow them into that morass, but continue to keep to the communist path."[44] It identified the adoption of the united front with the objective need of the Russian state to abandon the struggle for world revolution and make an accommodation with capitalism, and with some foresight described the trade deals made with the major capitalist states as a potential step on the road to a new inter-imperialist war. By December 1922 the group had also reversed its position on the Kronstadt uprising, concluding that:

...the Kronstadt rebellion against the Russian soviet government was by no means a White Guard insurrection but an uprising of sailors, workers and peasants against the Bolshevik bureaucracy...it was not a fully conscious communist [movement]: it was a movement of the poor oppressed against their oppressors...unfortunately in this case the soviet government and the soviet bourgeoisie...[45]

A key influence on this evolution was the left communist opposition in Russia. In 1922 the *Dreadnought* reprinted texts of the Workers' Opposition; the Group of Revolutionary Left Communists (Communist Workers' Party) of Russia (which in reality was a small group of exiles in Berlin linked to the KAI), and later of the Workers' Group of the Russian Communist Party (Bolshevik). The latter was a strictly clandestine grouping animated by the metalworker and old Bolshevik Gabriel Miasnikov, which in its manifesto declared its aim to act as an internal fraction to exert pressure on the party leadership. Far from abandoning the Russian revolution, this group, as its name suggests, saw itself in continuity with the programme and statutes of the Bolshevik party, and appealed for a struggle for its regeneration.[46] By opening itself up to the positions and analyses of the Russian communist left, the *Dreadnought* group was to a certain extent able to overcome its theoretical weaknesses,. Its experience of active involvement in the struggle against opportunism in the Third International also gave its analyses a broad historical perspective, which traced the degeneration of the Russian revolution to the first appearance of an opportunist course before the second CI congress in the policies advocated by Lenin in *Left-Wing Communism*. In January 1922, for example, reporting news that the KPD had made a proposal for unity with the Second and 'Two and a Half' Internationals, Pankhurst surveyed the Third International's regression thus:

We have noticed, with deep regret, the withdrawal of the Third International from its original bold position, and its steady reversion to the compromising policy which led to the downfall of the Second International. The original policy of the Third International, the slogans raised at its inception as a natural sequel to the great uprising in Russia caused the Second International to collapse. The Third International was left triumphant whilst only a few fragments of once large parties remained to dispute with it in the field of international socialism. Since that victory the Third International has steadily surrendered, one by one, its original principles and what at first appeared to be its essential characteristics. Lenin's "Infantile Sickness of Leftism" was not the first sign of this deterioration. It marked, however, very forcibly, the unfortunate break which the Executive in Moscow was making with the elements in the movement which are striving for international revolution, in the way the October revolution taught us to believe to be the Bolshevist way. Those who have not seen, or have refused to see, the retrogression which has been taking place in the Third International will not believe that the Moscow Executive will agree to the German Communist Party's proposal. Those, on the other hand, who have been watching the trend of events, both carefully and impartially, have been for some time expecting reconciliation either open or secret, between the official elements of the Third and Second Internationals. The policy of the Moscow Executive has for some time been heading strongly in that direction.[47]

Pankhurst's conclusion was that the Third International had fallen into "premature decay." Ultimately, the failure of the *Dreadnought* group was in not being able to build on these valuable insights as part of the work of a solidly organised fraction linked to those sections of the communist left, notably the Italian left around Bordiga, which continued to wage a political struggle inside the International. This failure was compounded by its inability to fully confront the implications of the defeats suffered by the working class, which could only add to its demoralisation and hasten the group's disappearance. The *Workers' Dreadnought* ceased publication without explanation in 1924 and Pankhurst subsequently abandoned revolutionary politics.[48] With the disappearance of the *Worker's Dreadnought* group, a vital link was lost with the original British communist left which had actively participated in the struggle for a class party inside the Third International.

'Anti-parliamentary' and 'council' communists: the dangers of rejecting the Russian revolution

The only other group in Britain to sympathise with the positions of the communist left during the 1920s and 30s was the Anti-Parliamentary Communist Federation. This was a regroupment of the anarchist-communist current around Guy Aldred in early 1921. Aldred's paper the *Spur* published extracts from the KAPD's manifesto as "a call to arms to all British anti-parliamentarians",[49] and the APCF sent a delegate to the third CI congress, where they made contact with the German, Bulgarian and other lefts. Politically however, as we have seen, this current identified with Bakunin as much as Marx, and was strongly influenced by anarchism especially on questions of organisation.

By mid-1922 the APCF had effectively broken with the Third International, but it continued to defend the contribution of the Bolsheviks to the world revolution, keeping an open mind on accusations of repression and rebuking those anarchists like Emma Goldman who denounced the soviet government for pandering to the capitalist press.[50] It was only in late 1925 that the APCF finally dropped its uncritical attitude, concluding that "Whatever Lenin achieved for the revolution in Russia, Leninism has merely betrayed and corrupted communism or socialism outside Russia."[51] On the eighth anniversary of the October revolution, responding to news of the persecution of the Communist Workers' Groups and the imprisonment of Miasnikov, it announced that the Bolsheviks were counter-revolutionary, and that capitalism and militarism now existed in Russia.[52]

As with the *Dreadnought* group, the experience of the Russian communist left was a key influence on the APCF's developmen. Aldred was particularly impressed by Miasnikov's "magnificent career of struggle", reprinting extracts from his prison manifesto and publicising the positions of the Communist Workers' Groups in the pages of the APCF paper, the *Commune*.[53] Through the small group of exiled Russian left communists in Berlin, the APCF established contacts with surviving sections of the German, Dutch and Russian left communist oppositions in the late 1920s, which helped the group to break out of its isolation and deepen its understanding of the degeneration of the Russian revolution. As a result, the APCF moved closer to the positions of the 'council communist' or 'councilist' movement.[54]

'Council communism' emerged from the disintegration of the German and Dutch lefts in the 1920s. Increasingly influenced by the anti-party theories of Otto Rûhle, 'councilism' represented a regression from the clarity of the communist left, theorising the degeneration of the Bolshevik Party and the counter-revolutionary role of social democracy as nothing less than proof of the bourgeois nature of all parties. This denial of the need for a separate political organisation went hand in hand with a rejection of the Russian revolutionary experience of 1917, which brought councilism close to the positions of the anarchist movement. Despite this, the council communist current in the 1930s and 40s, animated by former left communists like Pannekoek in Holland and Mattick in the USA, kept alive the experience of the workers' councils in the German revolution and continued to defend internationalism.[55]

In Britain, the APCF was alone in identifying with the struggle of the communist left and against the Trotskyist Opposition, which it denounced as a "worthless sham" after it declared its support for the defence of the Soviet Union under the existing leadership of the CPSU.[56] The APCF reprinted texts by the Dutch-based Group of International Communists (GIC), agreeing with its arguments that Russia was now a capitalist state acting in its own imperialist interests, and that the Third International was a weapon in the hands of "the new Russian capitalist class."[57] Aldred also denounced what he termed 'Leninism', which had 'negated' communism and played an active counter-revolutionary role in Russia and abroad.[58] These were distinctive positions of council communism, although the APCF used them in an eclectic way without taking a position on the political differences between the groups of the Dutch-German left. Its various contacts, although valuable in opening up the British movement to the history and positions of left and council communism, did not lead to closer collaboration or joint work, and Aldred obstinately resisted proposals even for an international conference of left groups.[59]

Aldred altered his own political perspectives after concluding from the rise of fascism that parliamentarism as a force had collapsed, and that therefore anti-parliamentarism was no longer relevant. He now called for the formation of unitary organisations, similar to the German *Unionen*, which would pave the way for workers' councils.[60] He left the APCF in 1933, for no clear political reasons, and after a brief flirtation with the ILP formed his own group, the United Socialist

Movement. In his 1935 pamphlet *For Communism,* influenced by both American Trotskyism and council communism, Aldred elaborated a distinctive analysis of the defeat of the revolutionary wave and the degeneration of the Communist International.[61] Although now more sympathetic to Trotsky's struggle against Stalinism, Aldred demonstrated that communist opposition to the counter-revolution had not begun with him, and that the reactionary course of the CI's official parties started much earlier: "It was left to the anti-parliamentary elements to proclaim correctly, years before, the death of the Third International and the necessity either of a fourth or a new International, or else of no formal International at all."[62] He also criticised the fallacy of continuing to regard Russia as the 'workers' fatherland': "fundamentally [Russia] is a capitalist country, and she grows daily more capitalistic, and more imperialistic... Only the world revolution can arrest the march of reaction in Russia."[63]

Written in the depths of the counter-revolution, at a time described by the Russian communist writer Victor Serge as 'midnight in the century,' Aldred's writings represent a rare attempt by revolutionaries in Britain to try to go to the roots of the defeats suffered by the proletariat, and to re-appropriate the contribution of the communist left. But in drawing out the implications of his analysis, Aldred, echoing the earlier views of Gorter and the KAI, began to call into question the whole experience of the Russian revolution, claiming that "the triumph of Leninism in Russia contained in itself the seeds of Stalinism and of later degeneration", and that:

> ...the Communist International enjoyed only a feverish existence as the afterbirth of the Russian revolution. It was doomed to disaster for its very organisation made it impossible for it to function except as the ramification of the Russian revolution. The pet fallacy of Stalinism, 'socialism in one country', meaning literally, 'capitalism and dictatorship in Russia', was foreshadowed in every thesis of the Communist International.[64]

Following this line of logic, Aldred argued that if the basic conflict was not as the Trotskyists claimed between Stalinism and Leninism but as the council communists argued between Bolshevism and communism, then the workers could not defend Bolshevism but should bury it as a "social democratic negation of communism": "The question of Marxism even arises and we are compelled to consider, whether, in certain phases, Stalinism is not the logical development of Marxism and whether even Marxism itself, is not, in certain phases, a negation of communism."[65] Although he denied it, by rejecting the Russian revolution Aldred was throwing into question all the historic gains of the workers' movement and giving way to what the Italian left at that time called "proletarian nihilism." The views expressed in *For Communism* reveal just how close he had come to the positions of the anarchist movement.

The APCF after Aldred's departure identified itself more explicitly with council communist positions. In 1935 it published two pamphlets, significantly titled *Leninism or Marxism,* which included two texts by Rosa Luxemburg allegedly revealing her opposition to the "bourgeois prejudices" of Lenin and of "Leninist ideology"; and *The Bourgeois Role of Bolshevism,* which was a translation from Mattick's *International Council Correspondence* of the 'Theses on Bolshevism' issued by the GIC. The 'Theses' were a key statement of the theory of the international council communist movement, explicitly rejecting the proletarian experience of the Russian revolution and affirming the bourgeois character of the Bolshevik Party, which had 'tricked' the workers into believing it was interested in world revolution.[66] In its own introduction to the 'Theses', the APCF argued that the Bolshevik Party had been "called upon to complete the task of the bourgeois revolution", although it still acknowledged that it had originally been the "spearhead of the revolution." The APCF's rather weak conclusion that Bolshevism was "incapable of assuming the leadership of the working class movement for emancipation" suggests that it did not rigorously defend the GIC's conclusions.[67]

Like the council communist movement internationally, the 'anti-parliamentary communist' current in Britain represented a regression on the clarity of the communist left in the early Third International, but it continued to defend basic class positions in the depths of the counter-revolution, opposing Stalinism, the Labour Party and trade unions, and keeping alive the essential idea of revolution as the self-emancipation of the workers. By identifying with the council communists' rejection of the Russian revolution, however, the APCF proved again the strength of anarchist influences on the British revolutionary movement.

The emergence of the Trotskyist Left Opposition: the dangers of not breaking with opportunism

As has often been pointed out, the CPGB, unlike other communist parties in the 1920s, did not give rise to any significant opposition to Stalinism; there was no British counterpart to Bordiga in the Italian party or Karl Korsch in the KPD, for example. This is largely due to the original weakness of the left wing in the CPGB and its early suppression by the CI. However, despite the expulsion of the *Workers' Dreadnought* group and the 'Bolshevisation' of the party after 1922, dissent in the CPGB was not completely crushed. From the mid-1920s, the focus for this dissent was the struggle of the Stalinist bureaucracy to destroy all remaining left-wing opposition to its rule. Initially the CP leadership did not realise the significance of the struggle within the Russian party, and expressed some support for Trotsky's criticisms of the Russian party; the ex-SLPer Tom Bell even wrote openly in the party journal about the defeat of the world revolution and the tendency for the Russian party to transform itself into a bureaucratic state apparatus...[68] Very quickly, however, it lined up with the CI leadership and blocked any wider debate in the party. A small section of the CPGB membership attempted to oppose the leadership's unquestioning obedience to the CI and expressed support for the views of Trotsky and the Left Opposition. A few branches, including Dundee and the London District Committee, protested the leadership's denunciation of Trotsky without any discussion by the membership, and in January 1925 at a meeting of 200 London party members summoned to endorse the leadership's line, a minority challenged the party's hasty condemnation of Trotsky without full information. 15 members backed an amendment expressing 'emphatic support' for the "left wing minority's fight in the Russian party against bureaucracy, and equally of the Comintern's struggle against all right-wing divergences from Leninism..."[69] This was one of the very few attempts to openly express support for the Left Opposition. In 1928 there was an attempt to demand a discussion of the defeat of the Chinese revolution, and the London membership again challenged the leadership's support for Bukharin's expulsion from the Russian party in 1929.[70]

What finally crystallised opposition in the CPGB was the new line in CI policy known as the 'third period', which began in 1927 with a warning by Stalin of the threat to the USSR from a new imperialist war of intervention led by Britain. This demanded the abandonment of the previous emphasis on a united front with the social democrats in favour of 'class against class' slogans, accompanied by outright denunciations of the social democrats as 'social fascists' and preparations for a supposed new 'revolutionary upswing' in Europe. In Britain this meant dropping the campaign for a Labour government in favour of the slogan "For a revolutionary workers' government." This violent swing to ultra-leftism with its use of radical-sounding phraseology in a period of deepening defeat was entirely dictated by the foreign and domestic policy of the Russian state and had nothing to do with the communist left's principled opposition to social democracy.

Given the depth of its attachment to the Labour Party and the trade unions, not surprisingly this new line threw the CPGB into some disarray. Although it 'unanimously' endorsed the 'third period' policy at the Ninth ECCI Plenum in February 1928, the party leadership retained deep reservations. The CPGB formally adopted the new line at its tenth congress in January 1929, but the re-election of the old leadership forced the ECCI to intervene, and it was only after a ruthless organisational struggle that it was finally able, at a specially called party congress in November 1929, to install a leadership faction which would unquestioningly implement the new line. This internal struggle signified the final Stalinisation of the British party. While much of the resistance to the new line came from elements too deeply embedded in social democracy to embrace the slogans of the 'third period' policy, in a very weak and confused way it also expressed the last gasp of proletarian life in the party, and finally gave birth to an organised opposition identifying with the positions of Trotsky and the International Left Opposition.

At this time there were several groupings and individuals inside and around the party defending oppositional views, some of whom had connections with the earlier left communist opposition in the International, including Jack Tanner, Ned MacAlpin and Dick Beech.[71] The discussion circle in London animated by Beech[72] was in contact with another opposition grouping known as the 'Balham Group', which moved closer to Trotsky's positions and, following discussions with the Left Opposition, finally established its British Section in late 1931.[73]

The appearance of the British Left Opposition was a basic proletarian reaction to the final Stalinisation of the CPGB. The group defended the need for international revolution and denounced the Stalinist policy of 'socialism in one country' as "national socialism." But by adopting the programme of the Left Opposition it was accepting all the opportunist positions adopted at the first four congresses of the CI and defending Trotsky's view that Russia was still a workers' state. The group supported Trotsky's call for a united front of the KPD with the social democrats in Germany as the only way to defeat fascism, while at home it defended the need for a 'real' united front.[74] On the vital question of war or revolution, the group shared Trotsky's view that the world situation remained

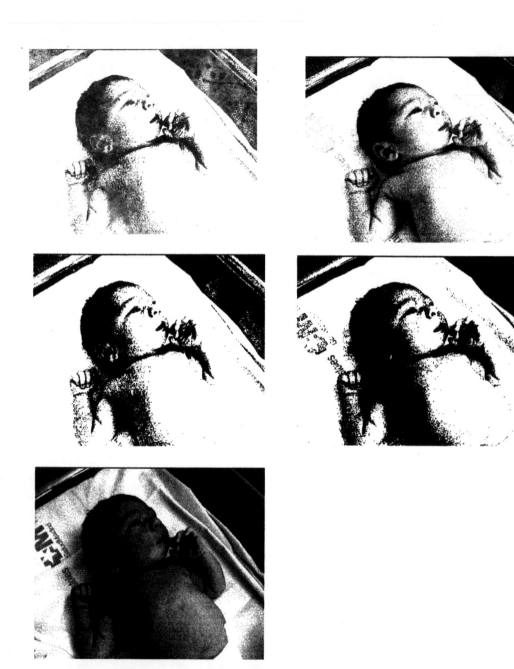

favourable to world revolution and that the British situation was 'pre-revolution-ary'.

To begin with, the British Left Opposition saw itself as an expelled fraction working to reform the party and the International, and even after the Balham Group's 'liquidation' in August-September 1932 it stated its intention to return to the party. This proved futile and in 1933 the British Trotskyists finally formed an open organisation, the Communist League. In line with the orientation of the Left Opposition at this time, their aim was still to reform the International, and the first issue of their paper, *The Red Flag*, declared that "We are a group of revolutionaries who have been expelled from the Communist Party for advocating the policy and principles upon which the Communist International was founded. Our object is to win the Communists back to that policy..."[75]

After Hitler's final seizure of power in Germany, Trotsky concluded that the CI was dead, and its parties were no longer capable of reform, the decisive factor in his view being the refusal of the KPD to enter into a united front with the social democrats. He now proclaimed the immediate necessity of building new parties and a new International, arguing that this was possible by linking up with the 'left socialist' (i.e. centrist) parties. In view of the weaknesses of the Left Opposition's forces, Trotsky called for the merger of its sections into the parties of the so-called 'London Bureau' (the 'Two-and-Three-Quarters' International). In Britain, where the Independent Labour Party had recently voted to disaffiliate from the Labour Party and was flirting with the Stalinist CP, he proposed that the Communist League dissolve and its members enter the ILP; not to split it but in order to help "transform it into a truly Marxist party."[76]

This threw the young British Section into confusion. The priority of the International Secretariat had been to set up a sympathising group without any rigorous clarification of programmatic positions, and differences had quickly opened up: on Trotsky's analysis of the death of the Communist Parties; the role and functioning of the group, and the focus of its activity. There was strong opposition from the majority of the group to entry into the ILP, the outcome of which was an acrimonious split in the British Section, with the active encouragement of Trotsky and the International Secretariat: the minority abandoned independent activity to set up the 'Marxist Group' inside the ILP, while the majority continued an open existence as a sympathising section of the Left Opposition. The majority, however, rapidly became demoralised at the Opposition's failure to strengthen its forces, and finally stated its intention to work "loyally as an integral part of the Labour Party."[77] In this they anticipated the minority by less than a year; having spread illusions in centrism, by 1936 Trotsky was arguing that the British Trotskyists should enter the Labour Party as individuals, where they should form a secret faction and avoid any criticisms of the leadership or open defence of their political positions.[78]

This whole strategy of the Trotskyist movement was fundamentally opportunist. The victory of fascism in Germany signified that the road was open not to world revolution but a new imperialist world war, and Trotsky's argument for the liquidation of the tiny minorities of the Left Opposition into the mass social democratic parties (the so-called 'French Turn') was tantamount to abandoning the whole struggle of Bolshevism and the European revolutionary movement to form a new revolutionary international against the reactionary Second International. The 'French turn' not surprisingly provoked convulsions in the Trotskyist movement and in Britain it led to the dissolution of the meagre forces of the Left Opposition into the organisations of centrism and social democracy.[79]

By contrast, the Italian communist left, which had also concluded that 1933 marked the CI's death, recognised that, given the incapacity of the proletariat to oppose the capitalist crisis, the foundation of new parties was not on the agenda; the role of the surviving fractions of the old parties was the work of theoretical reflection which would provide a solid basis for reconstructing the parties of tomorrow, in preparation for a new revolutionary situation. Despite for a time entering into close relations with the International Left Opposition, the Italian left remained completely opposed to Trotsky's attempts to artificially create a Fourth International out of a bloc with the centrist parties, and for this reason was eventually excluded from contact with the groups of the Opposition through a series of opportunistic manoeuvres.[80]

The Third International died in 1928 when it adopted the thesis of 'socialism in one country' at its Sixth World Congress. This was its 'August 1914', signifying its definitive betrayal of proletarian internationalism and the final victory of opportunism. However, as the Italian left understood, individual parties do not die, they betray.[81] The circumstances of the old parties' betrayal and the actual process of their integration into the capitalist camp varied in each national capital. Mainly this took place through the CPs' adoption of policies of support for the national defence of their respective bourgeoisies in 1933-35, which was intimately linked to their support for the foreign policy of the Stalinist state; Russia's entry into the League of Nations in 1934 signified its integration into the system of imperialist blocs in preparation for the next world war. In France, for example, the CP endorsed the Laval government's rearmament proposals after Stalin had recognised this as a 'positive' step. In Britain, there was no such single event to mark the CPGB's definitive betrayal until its spectacular support for British imperialism in the second world war, but by 1935 through its support for a 'Popular Front' with the Liberal and Tory Parties it had become an active factor in the war preparations of the British bourgeoisie.

One sign of the fact that a party is still in the process of degeneration but is not yet completely dead for the proletariat is its ability to give rise to proletarian expressions of opposition. Although the degeneration of the CPGB began very early on, with the expulsion of the *Dreadnought* group and the suppression of left wing opposition in 1922, the appearance of very weak opposition to Stalinism as late as 1932-33 confirms that there was still proletarian life in the party. Only through the expulsion of these groupings could Stalinism totally consolidate its grip on the CPGB, after which the party became completely unsalvageable for the working class.

Following the example of the left fractions which broke from the Second International in 1914, but which continued to wage an organisational struggle within the social democratic parties, the task of revolutionaries towards the degenerating communist parties in the 1920s and 1930s was to engage in a determined struggle to try to return them to a revolutionary course; or when it became clear that this was no longer possible, to detach themselves in order to establish the organised fractions which would, once the conditions for revolution returned, form the nucleii of future parties and a new revolutionary International.

The defeat of the world revolution and the passage into the camp of capital of the parties thrown up by the working class in the post-war revolutionary wave was a tragedy for the proletariat. Within this greater tragedy of defeat, we must note the failure of the revolutionary movement in Britain to establish a strong left opposition; first within the CPGB in order to combat its degeneration, and then, following the definitive passage of the party into the camp of capital, by maintaining an organised left fraction linked at the international level to other surviving fractions of the communist left. The disappearance of the *Workers' Dreadnought* group in 1924 shows the relative weakness of the revolutionary Marxist current in this country. However, the efforts of the *Dreadnought* group in the early 1920s, and of the anti-parliamentary or council communists in the late 1920s and 30s, to try to go to the roots of the defeats suffered by the proletariat, and to understand what had happened to the Russian revolution, testify to the stubborn strength of revolutionary ideas in Britain even in the worst depths of the counter-revolution. The struggle of the left communists and of the council communists in Britain provides a vital link between the old workers' movement in the last revolutionary wave and the revolutionary minorities of the working class which emerged from the resurgence of workers' struggles in the 1960s.

Notes

1 See letter from CPGB to Labour Party Executive dated 10 August 1920, and reply dated 11 September 1920, in *The Communist Party and the Labour Party. All the Facts and All the Correspondence*, CPGB, London, n.d. [1921]), pp.5-6.

2 Brian Pearce, 'Early Years of the CPGB', in M. Woodhouse & B. Pearce, *Essays on the History of Communism in Britain*, New Park, 1975, p.153.

3 Lenin, *Collected Works, vol. 31*, Progress, 1966, p.31.

4 *Second Congress of the Communist International, Minutes of the Proceedings, vol. 2*, New Park, 1977, p.188.

5 *Ibid.*, p.270.

6 *Moscow's Reply to the ILP*, Left Wing Group of the ILP, 1920.

7 *Workers' Dreadnought*, 13 August 1921.

8 *Communist*, 16 September 1920.

9 See *Ibid.*, 13, 20 August 1921.

10 *Ibid.*, 19 February 1921.

11 'Theses on tactics', in Degras (Ed.), *op. cit.*, pp.244-5.

12 Extract from the 'Directives on the United Front' adopted by the ECCI, 18 December 1921, in Degras, *op. cit.*, p.313.

13 'Communist Party affiliation to the Labour Party: transcript of the meeting of 29 December 1921', Society for the Study of Labour History, *Bulletin*, no. 29, Autumn 1974, p.31.

14 CPGB, *Communist Parliamentary Policy and Electoral Programme*, pamphlet produced for the policy conference, 1922, pp.6-7.

15 L.J. Macfarlane, *The British Communist Party, its Origin and Development Until 1929*, MacGibbon and Kee, 1966, p.101.

16 *Workers Weekly*, 17 February 1922, quoted in Macfarlane, *op. cit.*, p102.

17 *Ibid.*, 22 February 1924, quoted in James Klugmann, *History of the Communist Party of Great Britain, vol. 1, Formation and Early Years, 1919-1924*, Lawrence and Wishart, 1968, p.253.

18 *Communist*, 22 Ocober 1921, quoted in Klugmann, *op. cit.*, p.123.

19 *Workers' Dreadnought*, 10 September 1921.

20 *Ibid.*, 6 October 1923. The demonstration was called by the Unemployed Workers' Organisation, a local group formed as a militant alternative to the CPGB-dominated NUWM.

21 *Communist,* 7 October 1920.

22 *Ibid.*, 23 April 1921.

23 *Worker*, 18 November 1922, quoted in James Hinton and Richard Hyman, *Trade Unions and Revolution: the Industrial Politics of the Early British Communist Party*, Pluto Press, 1975, pp.25-26.

24 *Workers' Weekly*, 8 January 1926, cited in Hugo Dewar, *Communist Politics in Britain: the CPGB from its Origins to the Second World War*, Pluto Press, 1976, n.p.148.

25 *Draft Constitution and Rules*, CPGB, 1921.

26 ECCI, *Fourth Congress Report*, p.61, quoted in Henry Pelling, *The British Communist Party*, 1958, p.25.

27 CPGB, *Report of the Policy Conference*, 1922.

28 *Workers' Dreadnought*, 1 April 1922. For the official report of the conference, see *Communist,* 25 March 1922.

29 Degras, *op. cit*, p.417. This recorded all levels of disagreement, passive as well as active, but its results are consistent with the scale of opposition to affiliation.

30 Minutes of the Executive Committee meetings, 16-18, 22 September 1922, File 495/100/58 on microfilm, CPGB archive.

31 File 495/33/239a, CPGB archive.

32 *International Press Correspondence*, 17 October 1922 Supplement.

33 Minutes of Central Executive meeting, 21 November 1922, File 495/100/58, CPGB archive.

34 Klugmann, *op. cit.,* pp.197-198.

35 *Workers' Weekly*, 11 August 1923.

36 'Theses on the structure of communist parties and the method and content of their work'. These were hastily drafted and passed unanimously without discussion (Degras, *op. cit.*, pp.256-271).

37 *Report on Organisation presented by the Party's Commission to the Annual Conference of the CPGB, October 7, 1922*, CPGB, 1922.

38 For a more thorough critique of these theories see the ICC, *The Dutch and German Communist Left*, 2001, pp.180-182.

39 *Workers' Dreadnought*, 8 October 1921. Pankhurst had referred to the possibility of a new left-wing international around the KAPD back in August. Her knowledge of the KAPD minority's breakaway move may well have influenced her own personal confrontation with the CPGB leadership.

40 *Workers' Dreadnought*, 11 February 1922.

41 *Ibid.*, 29 July 1922, 27 October 1923.

42 *Ibid.*, 11 February 1922.

43 *Ibid.*, 24 December 1921.

44 *Ibid.*, 22 April 1922.

45 *Ibid.*, 10 December 1922.

46 The group was suppressed by the Cheka and Miasnikov imprisoned in 1924. See the protest in *Workers' Dreadnought*, 31 May 1924.

47 *Ibid.*, 7 January 1922.

48 Pankhurst left the East End of London and retired from politics, her interests turning to feminism, world language and poetry, but she later became an active anti-fascist campaigner, founding a Womens' International Matteotti Committee in 1932, and was a strong supporter of Abyssinia and the League of Nations after the Italian invasion in 1935. She went to live in Ethiopia becoming a friend of the emperor Haile Sellassie and died there in 1960.

49 *Spur*, February 1921.

50 *Commune*, December 1924. Goldman for her part accused the APCF of being in the pay of Moscow and Aldred a blackmailer employed by the CP!

51 *Ibid.*, October 1924.

52 *Ibid.*, November 1925.

53 *Ibid.*, February 1926, November 1927.

54 *Ibid.*, March to August 1927. The APCF published correspondence from Heinrich Berges of the 'INO', which appears to have been a loose grouping of Otto Rühle's AAUD-E; Karl Porth of the *Entscheidene Linke* ('Resolute Left'), the opposition group around Karl Korsch which had been expelled from the KPD in 1926; and Henk Canne Meijer on behalf of the International Bureau of the GIC. Further letters came from Canne Meijer and from Lopez Cardoza in the name of a a surviving fragment of the KAI in Amsterdam. Aldred's contact was 'Kate Rumonova', who played an active role in the international work of the KAI. See ICC, *The Dutch and German Communist Left*, 2001, n.p.196.

55 For an in-depth study of the origins and positions of council communism, see *The Dutch and German Communist Left.*

56 *Commune*, September-October 1927. This did not prevent the APCF from expressing solidarity with Trotsky when he was sent into internal exile in 1928.

57 *Commune*, May 1927.

58 *Ibid.*, November 1927.

59 *Ibid.*, July-August 1927.

60 *Council*, February 1933. See Shipway, *op. cit.*, pp.129-131.

61 Aldred was in contact with the Communist League of Struggle around Albert Weisbord and Vera Busch, which was close to the Left Opposition but not a member; and the United Workers' Party around Paul Mattick in Chicago. He was also in contact with Andre Prudhommeaux, animator of the council communist *Spartacus* group in France.

62 *For Communism*, p.38.

63 *Ibid.*, p.39.

64 *Ibid.*, p.8.

65 *Ibid.*, p.9.

66 See *The Dutch and German Communist Left*, pp.236-241.

67 *The Bourgeois Role of Bolshevism*, APCF, Glasgow, 1935.

68 *Communist Review*, February 1924, cited in Macfarlane, *op. cit.*, p.92.

69 *Workers' Weekly*, 23 January 1925, quoted in John McIlroy, 'New light on Arthur Reade: Tracking down Britain's First Trotskyist', *Revolutionary History*, vol. 8, no.1, 2001, p. 42.

70 See S. Bornstein & A. Richardson, *Against the Stream. A history of the Trotskyist Movement in Britain, 1924-38*, Socialist Platform, 1986, p.27. A Trotskyist history of the movement.

71 All three had defended left positions at the second CI congress in 1920; Jack Tanner as a delegate of the shop stewards' movement ; MacAlpin as a leader of the American Communist Labor Party, and Dick Beech as delegate of the IWW. See Albert Glotzer's account of 'British Trotskyism in 1931', in *Revolutionary History*, Spring 1988, and S. Bornstein & A. Richardson, *op. cit.*

72 Beech became a member of the CP (BSTI) and was elected as its representative on the CPGB's provisional executive committee in January 1921. He remained in the CPGB, becoming active in the unemployed movement and apparently acting as a courier and maritime specialist for the CI. He had extensive contacts with the international opposition, corresponding with Trotsky and contributing articles to the American opposition paper *Militant*. His political orientation at this time was essentially syndicalist, attempting to form an independent left-wing movement in the trade unions and criticising the 'sectarianism' of the CPGB Minority Movement for refusing to support workers' struggles. Beech quit the CPGB by 1930, but remained outside the official Trotskyist movement. In the early 1930s he joined the ILP and later became an active trade union official and a member of the Labour Party (see Ken Weller, *'Don't Be A Soldier' - The radical anti-war movement in North London 1914-1918*, Journeyman, 1985, pp.64-65).

73 A key contact was Henry Sara, a pre-war revolutionary syndicalist, anti-war agitator and collaborator of Guy Aldred's. He was imprisoned during the war for opposing conscription, released only in 1919, and connected for a time with Pankhurst's group. In 1921 he traveled illegally to Russia, joining the CPGB on his return despite misgivings about the crushing of the Kronstadt uprising, Although aware of the Stalin-Trotsky struggle he publicly defended the party line and stood as a CPGB parliamentary candidate in 1928.

74 See the documents of the Balham Group included in Reg Groves, *The Balham Group, How British Trotskyism Began*, Pluto, 1974, pp. 81-107.

75 *Red Flag*, May 1933.

76 Letter to the British Section, 16 September 1933, in *Trotsky's Writings on Britain vol.3*, New Park, 1974, p.89.

77 'Aims and Objects of the Marxist League', quoted in S. Bornstein & A. Richardson, *op. cit.*, p.196.

78 "It is very important that we do not lay ourselves open at the beginning to attacks from the Labour Party bureaucracy, which will result in our expulsion without having gained any appreciable strength... Obviously, we will not be able to raise the issue of the Fourth International immediately." (Interview with Collins, *Internal Bulletin* of the Marxist Group, Summer 1936, in *Trotsky's Writings on Britain, vol. 3.*, New Park, 1974, p.138.)

79 In the USA Hugo Oehler and a group of supporters expelled from the Trotskyist Workers' Party for opposing the 'French turn' formed the Revolutionary Workers League in 1935. The RWL called for a 'New Communist (4th) International' and set up an 'International Contact Commission' with sympathising sections in Austria, Britain and Germany. The British affiliate, the Leninist League, had been formed in 1932-33 by a small group of workers in Glasgow including a CPGB founding member (Hugh Esson or 'Hugh Morrison'). To begin with the Leninist League was politically close to the Left Opposition; it sold the American Trotskyist paper *Militant* and was in contact with the Balham Group. But increasingly it took an independent line, criticising Trotsky's opportunist call for a Fourth International based on alliances with

centrist organisations as a betrayal of the Left Opposition's original principles. By 1934 the League had broken with Trotskyism and adhered to the 'Oehlerite' current. Politically 'Oehlerism' did not make a clear break with the opportunist positions of the second CI congress and represented a 'half way house' between Trotskyism and the Communist Left.

80 See ICC, *The Italian Communist Left, 1926-45*, 1992, pp. 57-73.

81 *Bilan*, no. 1, quoted in ICC, *International Review*, no.51, 1987.

Conclusions

The communist left's struggle for an intransigent class party in Britain in the early 1920s ended in failure. The question is why did it fail? And what lessons can we draw for today?

First, as the most intransigently revolutionary tendency of the proletariat, which attempted to build a party capable of leading the struggle for a successful world communist revolution, the British communist left inevitably shared in the defeat of this struggle. With the disappearance of the practical possibilities for revolution, the left was rapidly forced to retreat, trying to hold onto the proletariat's revolutionary programme against the tide of reaction, excluded from the International and its official parties and, in the midst of deepening poverty and unemployment, increasingly isolated from the class as a whole. While the left in Britain can be criticised for failing to remain in the CPGB until the last possible moment to regroup the forces of opposition, its refusal to compromise its principles for the sake of temporary and illusory influence within the masses was a sign of political strength rather than weakness.

An 'un-British' tradition?

With hindsight, does the defeat of the revolutionary wave prove that the left's efforts to build a revolutionary party in Britain were wrong? Were they based on an over-optimistic view of the revolutionary possibilities that existed in a country with such deeply ingrained traditions of peaceful and gradualist struggle?

Even at its high point in early 1919, the class struggle in Britain failed to develop into a direct revolutionary threat, due partly to the bourgeoisie's decisive action against the slightest sign of insurrection, but more fundamentally to its relative strength and room for manoeuvre: in particular the ruling class was able to exploit Britain's status as 'victor' in the imperialist war to drive a wedge between the British and German workers, while deploying the trade unions to prevent any generalisation of their struggles. But the question of whether revolution was on the agenda in Britain was determined primarily by the international balance of class forces rather than any national specificities, and this balance of forces was dynamic rather than static. The repression of the December 1918 Berlin uprising gave the world bourgeoisie a vital breathing space, but the German working class as a whole was still far from defeated and the road remained open to a return of mass strikes and the reappearance of the workers' councils. A renewed revolutionary offensive in Germany could have opened a breach in the bourgeoisie's defences and given a vital impulse to the revival of struggles in Britain and western Europe. This in turn could have created practical opportunities for the workers to unmask the counter-revolutionary role of the trade unions and social democratic parties. Faced with such a perspective there was a need for a vanguard party in Britain regrouping the most advanced workers, armed with a clear programme, strategy and tactics, to provide a lead to the workers' struggles and to clarify their revolutionary goals; but also to warn against the manoeuvrings of the most experienced and cunning bourgeoisie in the world. The absence of such a party at the height of the revolutionary wave in Britain proved to be a source of serious weakness.

The real lesson therefore is not that the formation of a communist party in Britain was premature, but that it was *too late*.

And if the left was wrong to struggle to form a revolutionary party, who was right? The centrists, who hesitated to break decisively from social democracy, the Labour Party, the trade unions and the Second International? Or the right, which essentially saw itself as the left wing of the Labour Party? These elements, far from expressing a superior understanding of 'British conditions' or the interests of the British working class, at best expressed the enormous difficulty the whole working class faced in breaking from weight of bourgeois democratic and reformist mystifications; and at worst the outright counter-revolutionary nature of the British Labour Movement. The need for new parties and a new revolutionary International was determined by the entry of capitalism into its epoch of decadence and the definitive betrayal of the social democratic parties. It was the left that, albeit in a fragmentary way, most clearly understood this change in historical period and the consequent need for a clean break with the obsolete programme of the Second International.

Bolshevik dupes?

Again with hindsight, even though the left was essentially correct in trying to build a revolutionary party in Britain, perhaps it was mistaken in adhering to the Bolshevik-dominated Third International? Was the left, in effect, duped by Lenin and the Bolsheviks, whose objective interest was not to spread world revolution but, as the council communists of the 1920s and 1930s argued, to hold onto state power and advance the interests of Russian capitalism? Should the left instead have gone ahead to form a genuine, 'home grown', anti-parliamentary communist party, without interference from Moscow?

The myth of an indigenous anti-parliamentary communist movement, embracing both anarchists and Marxists, which was opposed to and destroyed by alien 'Leninism', is a popular one amongst anarchists and 'councilists' in Britain precisely because it provides an alibi for their anti-Leninism, and because it papers over the differences between the Marxist and anarchist wings of the workers' movement.[1] But it is based more on prejudice than an honest appreciation of the history of the revolutionary movement. The fact is that the left in Britain, including the best elements of the anarchist movement at the time, defined itself by enthusiastic support for the Russian revolution in October 1917 and practical solidarity with Lenin and the Bolshevik Party against all the bourgeoisie's lies about a Bolshevik 'coup d'etat'. For the Marxist left, adherence to the Third International was a necessary and logical step in the struggle to regroup revolutionaries internationally after the collapse of the Second. Those lefts like Pankhurst and Gallacher who returned from the CI's second congress and their encounter with Lenin as converts to the need to join the CPGB have been patronisingly lambasted by anti-Leninist writers as "brainwashed" and suffering from "double-think."[2] Such insults not only unconsciously echo the Stalinists' attacks on their left opponents, but also fail to consider seriously the actual positions and perspectives defended by the communist left at this time. The struggle against opportunism within the International was a struggle between different wings of the same movement, agreed on the same programme and goals. For the left it was ultimately a question, not of renouncing its criticisms, but of deciding as a fraction of the centralised International to accept collective discipline and to work within it for a change of line. This did not prevent it from waging an open political struggle inside the International against the opportunist positions adopted by its leadership. Far from being 'duped', the left developed a serious critique of the Bolsheviks' errors, and openly warned against the betrayal of the Bolshevism's original principles and the Russian bastion's growing accommodation with capitalism, while at the same time avoiding the worst errors and fatalistic conclusions of the council communists. Others on the anti-parliamentary left, however, rejected the whole concept of centralised organisation and objected to the 'interference of Moscow' in the affairs of the British socialist movement. The real issue here was the influence of anarchism on questions of organisation and the prevalence of parochial 'Little England' attitudes, against which the Marxist left had to fight.

Whether consciously or not, by denying the proletarian nature of the Bolshevik Party and the early years of the Third International, the effect of the anarchist or 'anarcho-Marxist' version of history is to reject not only the struggle of the communist left for a class party in Britain, but also the struggle of the left fractions inside the Second International against opportunism and centrism before the first world war. As we have seen, those revolutionaries who defended proletarian internationalism against the imperialist war emerged from within the social democratic parties themselves, where before the final betrayal of social democracy in 1914 they had been the best and most intransigent defenders of internationalism, and were in effect putting into practice the official position of the International itself against militarism. It was precisely these left fractions – including the Bolsheviks in Russia – that formed the original nucleus of the new revolutionary International and of the new class parties. The wholesale rejection of social democracy, and of the whole painful process of constructing mass parties and trade unions to wage a struggle for reforms within capitalism during its ascendant phase, remains a heavy weight on the development of the revolutionary movement today. In this sense, it is perhaps not surprising that Guy Aldred has become an attractive figure for the anarchist milieu in Britain; with his pre-1914 rejection of social democracy as 'capitalist'; his later repudiation of Bolshevism as a 'social democratic negation of communism', and his questioning of Marxism itself as developing 'logically' into Stalinism, Aldred foreshadowed many of the prejudices of today's 'anarcho-Marxists'.

An infantile disorder?

Did the failure of the British communist left, on the other hand, prove the correctness of Lenin's characterisation of its positions as 'abstract', 'purist, 'sectarian' – in other words was left communism indeed an 'infantile disorder' which simply needed to be overcome as quickly and as painlessly as possible, as Lenin argued?

Firstly, this study has shown that, far from being 'ultra-left', as many subsequent writers have tried to smear it, the communist left was fundamentally the left wing of the Third International, and as such the most intransigent defender of its principles based on the experience of the Russian Bolsheviks in 1917 and the German Spartacists in 1918-19. Ultra-leftism was a separate and distinct phenomenon that emerged within the International, expressing itself in a tendency towards adventurism and attempts to artificially provoke revolutionary situations. It was particularly strong in Germany, where with the support of elements in the CI's leadership it led to the failed armed uprising of March 1921 and further splits in the Communist Party. In this proper sense, it should be noted that ultra-leftism was never a very influential tendency within the British revolutionary movement, only flowering inside the CPGB during the 'third period' of Stalinism, with its calls for revolutionary preparations and denunciations of the Labour Party as 'social fascist'.

Secondly it is a myth that the left was somehow opposed to 'dirtying its hands' in the class struggle. The organisations of the left actively intervened in all the significant workers' struggles of the period, taking a lead role, for example, in organising mass anti-war demonstrations in London and in the workers' protests against British military intervention against Russia, as well as taking leading positions in the unofficial shop stewards' and workers' committee movement. Nor did the left reject intervention in the trade unions where, as Pankhurst argued, in the absence of the workers' councils it was necessary to develop revolutionary alternatives. Despite its confusions about the actual potential for such work (for example, seeing rank and file control as a way of transforming the unions from within), the left cannot be accused of abstention from the class struggle. Here we must distinguish the Marxist left current from both the genuine 'left doctrinaires' (SPGB, De Leonists) for whom any strike was a diversion from their own obsolete programme (parliamentarism, industrial unionism); and also the 'anarchist communist' current around Aldred, which in common with much of the British socialist movement tended to limit itself to abstract propaganda for socialism. Ultimately, the left was not able to clarify the question of the exact relationship between the new 'minimum programme' of socialism, as Luxemburg expressed it, and the proletariat's struggle for immediate demands in this period. As we have seen, the left itself shared the characteristic weaknesses of the socialist movement in Britain: a spontaneist view of the class struggle and a tendency towards abstract propaganda rather than determining demands and tactics from a concrete analysis of the situation. But it was the left, due to its theoretical insights into the change in period and its practical grasp of the need for a decisive break with reformism, which best understood that fundamentally the role of revolutionaries in the epoch of imperialism was, as the Third International proclaimed at its founding congress, to develop the mass action of the proletariat into open confrontation with the capitalist state.

The change in period also implied a change in the nature and role of the class party itself. Again, the left did not defend a coherent, thought-out position on this vital question, and still shared the dominant view in the socialist movement, that the ultimate role of the party was to take power on behalf of the class: even after her break with the CPGB and the Third International, Pankhurst, for example, continued to defend a vision of revolution as a *coup d'etat* by a small determined force of revolutionaries.[3] But with the opportunist attempt of the CI to build mass parties, important differences were brought out into the open; it was the left which best understood that in the new epoch, in which permanent reforms were no longer possible, the party could no longer hope to regroup the great mass of the proletariat in its ranks around a minimum programme of demands. Instead, the role of the party was to act as a vanguard, regrouping the most advanced elements of the class around the defence of a clear revolutionary programme. Inevitably, except in periods of open confrontation with the capitalist state, revolutionaries would form only a tiny minority of the class. The merit of the left in this period was precisely to warn against attempts to build a party with a large membership through political compromises with centrism, and in view of Lenin's later attacks on it the irony is that the left's view on this question was based firmly on the experience of the Bolshevik Party itself in 1917; of a small party at first but one which refused to compromise its programme with other parties, forming the core – in Gorter's words "hard as steel, clear as glass"[4] – around which the masses could regroup in a revolutionary crisis. It was precisely this model on which the CI leadership turned its back in its pursuit of mass communist parties; the left faithfully held to it.

Fundamentally then, far from being an 'infantile disorder', the communist left represented the political response of the most advanced fraction of the proletariat to the new conditions of capitalist decadence. In the midst of the turbulent events of the revolutionary wave and faced with the practical needs of the struggle for a communist party, the left inevitably revealed its immaturity, and this was particularly true in Britain, where its forces were relatively weak and fragmented, and where the reformist past weighed particularly heavily on the working class. The left's premature abandonment of the Third International and the mistaken attempt to create a new party in a period of deepening defeat were clear symptoms of this immaturity, which contributed to the disappearance of the left communist current into the night of the counter-revolution. But if this undoubtedly constituted a failure, what about the alternative? The opportunist tactics of the Communist International and the effort to build a mass party in Britain were not only singularly unsuccessful but more importantly involved capitulations to the capitalist Labour Party and trade union bureaucracy, which ultimately disarmed the CPGB and, thoroughly Stalinised, handed it over to the class enemy to use as a weapon against the working class in the preparations for a new imperialist world war.

Lessons for today: the importance of the struggle for a revolutionary organisation

The struggle of the British communist left for a class party remains to be completed anew. While an examination of all the changes in the conditions for the party is beyond the scope of an historical study, what, finally, can we say are the lessons of the period 1914-1921 for today?

The struggle of the left wing of the Third International was the highest expression of the working class's struggle to create a world communist party on the basis of the new conditions of capitalism and their meaning for the class struggle. The basic positions adopted by the International on its formation, and more specifically the orientation defended by the left in the debates on the questions of tactics towards parliament and the trade unions, while by no means complete, are still a crucial reference point for the revolutionary movement of today in defining the programme of the party of tomorrow.

Beyond the question of the party's programme, this study has highlighted the importance for Marxists of translating their struggle for correct political positions into an intransigent organisational struggle, to ensure that, in their methods and tactics, their day to day functioning and activities, the organisations so painfully created by the class to give expression to its historic goals and interests become practical weapons in its struggle to emancipate itself: from the fraction around Marx and Engels in the First International which fought against both reformism and the anti-organisational tactics of the anarchists; to the internationalist left in the Second International around Lenin, Luxemburg and Pannekoek which led the fight against the open revisionism of the right and the veiled opportunism of the centre; to the Zimmerwald Left which regrouped those tiny minorities defending a clear revolutionary defeatist position against both chauvinism and social pacifism; to the left wing in the Third International which resisted the leadership's opportunist tactics towards centrism – historically it has always been the left in the workers' movement which has best expressed the need for an intransigent struggle for the organisation; against both the open opportunism of the right and the conciliations of the centre. Or rather, more correctly, the left *is* the organisational expression of the most intransigent trend in the workers' movement; composed of the clearest-eyed and most resolute, far-thinking elements, linked solidly to the class's previous experience but capable of making the necessary theoretical breaks with the outmoded past and embracing the new conditions of the struggle.

The struggle of the left for a class party was above all a struggle against the ever present influence of bourgeois ideology within the working class; a struggle principally against opportunism, which expressed the enormous weight of the past on the class, and its immense difficulties in breaking with the organisations, methods and tactics which it had so painfully built up and utilised in the previous period of capitalism's ascendance, but which now stood as a reactionary barrier to the revolutionary future. This opportunism expressed itself not only in open political positions but also in attitudes towards organisation: fear of centralised control; support for 'local autonomy', for 'freedom of opinion' in the name of 'unity'... In this sense, centrism served as a cover for open opportunism, revealing itself in a fear of open confrontation of positions and attempts to conciliate between mutually exclusive positions, but also in hesitations in the face of the need to pursue an organisational struggle; a reluctance to match the opportunist right in ruthlessness; to act on a majority, to follow through on political victories. Although these tendencies revealed themselves in specific forms, around particular political positions, they are ever present enemies of revolutionary action and must be recognised; their features, their behaviour and even psychological forms, identified, given their proper names, and fought.

Today, at the beginning of the 21st Century, we are in the midst of an extremely difficult and dangerous period, in which, however, the proletariat remains undefeated. For those political minorities of the class that have emerged from the revival of the class struggle in the late 1960s, the immediate task is not the declaration of the party but the regroupment of revolutionaries at an international level around a common platform of basic political positions. These basic positions, while clarifying the lessons of all the experiences of the working class throughout its history, must of necessity take as a reference point the contribution of the left fractions in the degenerating Third International. The organisation of revolutionaries itself will only exist and evolve through a continual struggle against the influence of bourgeois ideology within the workers' movement; principally against opportunism and centrism, but also against the prevalent ideas in decomposing capitalist society, of anarchist and anti-organisational prejudices, nihilism and despair. The whole experience of the proletariat in western Europe in the last revolutionary wave, including Britain, has emphasised both the crucial role of the proletariat's class party in its revolutionary struggles and catastrophic consequences of its absence or late formation; if today is not the same world as in the last revolutionary wave of 1917-21; if we have not yet reached the moment where the formation of the international communist party is even possible, we can certainly say we have reached the equivalent of Zimmerwald; the moment when it is necessary for the left to regroup its forces and send out a united message of internationalism; to demonstrate the need for the proletarian revolution as the only way to end the threat of war and avert the final descent of humanity into barbarism. The political heritage of the left's struggle for a class party not only remains as a vital source of lessons for today's revolutionaries; it also serves as an imperative for action.

Notes

1 A good example is Bob Jones' pamphlet *Left-Wing Communism in Britain 1917-21...An Infantile Disorder?* (Pirate Press, 1991), which argues that the formation of the CPGB was an "unnatural development for Britain." Jones' version of history is so selective that it avoids entirely the embarrassing fact that the main representative of left-wing communism in Britain, Pankhurst's *Workers' Dreadnought* group, was a strong and enthusiastic supporter of Bolshevism.
2 Jones' treatment is peppered with references to "Comintern trickery" and its "willing accomplices" (i.e. Pankhurst and Gallacher), while the left's acceptance of collective discipline in agreeing to unity on the basis of the '21 Points' is dismissed as a "collective delusion", a "mind block"...
3 *Workers' Dreadnought*, 24 September 1921.
4 *Ibid.*, 26 June 1920.

Epilogue

Revolutionaries in Britain and the second world war

By the outbreak of the second world war there were very few proletarian political groups in Britain which had managed to survive the counter-revolution without betraying or succumbing to the effects of defeat and demoralisation. In addition to the council communists around the Anti-Parliamentary Communist Federation and Guy Aldred's United Socialist Movement, those groups and elements remaining either on a proletarian terrain, or in the more ambiguous swamp between the proletariat and the bourgeoisie, were:
- the Socialist Party of Great Britain
- some elements in the anarchist movement
- the Trotskyists, mainly in the Revolutionary Socialist League and the Workers' International League.

In the face of a threatened second worldwide massacre, the slogan raised by internationalists in 1914 was even more relevant: "Turn the imperialist war into a civil war!" (Lenin, 1914). In the face of the very real brutalities of the fascist regimes, and the insidious use of anti-fascism as an ideology to mobilise workers for war, it was all the more vital for revolutionaries to warn the class against the no less vicious nature of bourgeois democracy, and to affirm, in words of Karl Liebknecht, that: "The enemy is in your own country!"

The example of the *Vanguard* group around John Maclean in the first world war was still a valid model for revolutionaries in Britain: refusal to support the bourgeoisie's war effort; calls for class war against British capitalism through anti-war propaganda among the workers; and intervention in every struggle for immediate demands to develop a mass movement against the war.

For the Italian communist left around the journal *Bilan* the victory of fascism in Germany marked a break in the revolutionary course which had appeared in 1917, and a decisive turn towards the only capitalist outcome of its historic crisis: world war.[1] The late 1930s saw a build up of military preparations and an extension of imperialist conflicts: the Italian invasion of Abyssinia; the war in Spain, and the war between China and Japan. In this situation the watchword of *Bilan* was: "No betrayal!"

Trotsky, on the other hand, while defending the correct position that capitalism was in its death throes, drew the opposite conclusion; that the situation was pre-revolutionary, requiring only the necessary leadership, which the Fourth International – founded on the very eve of the world war – would provide. As we will see, this led his supporters to depart from the principle of internationalism and to participate in the war.

Other proletarian political groups, while clinging to the principle of internationalism at least in words, did not defend it in practice, or found it very difficult to go beyond abstract slogans. The two questions which proved to be a 'litmus test' for these groups' ability to defend internationalism were: whether democracy was in any way to be supported against fascism; and whether all states were equally reactionary and therefore to be opposed.

The Socialist Party of Great Britain

In response to the war in Spain and the rise of fascism, one part of the SPGB called for the defence of democracy, basing itself on the party's own position that the revolution would be won through the democratic process, although the SPGB took the position that "Democracy cannot be defended by fighting for it."[2] The SPGB's 1936 pamphlet *War and the Working Class* declared war to be an inevitable product of capitalism and opposed any participation by the working class: "War...solves no problem of the working class. Victory and defeat alike leave them in the same position... They have no interest at stake which justifies giving support to war."[3]

In the issue of its paper *Socialist Standard* following the declaration of war in 1939, the party's executive committee printed a statement reiterating this position and denouncing both sides in the war. It expressed its concern at the "sufferings of the German workers under Nazi rule", declared its wholehearted support for "the efforts of workers everywhere to secure democratic rights", but repeated its position on "the futility of war as a means of safeguarding democracy". It called on workers to refuse to accept the prospect of war and "to recognise that only socialism will end war", concluding by repeating the expression of "goodwill and socialist fraternity" to all workers that it had made in 1914.

In practice the SPGB made no attempt to oppose the war. From July 1940 onwards, in order to avoid being suppressed by the state its paper carried no openly anti-war propaganda, apologising to its readers that "While we deeply regret having to adopt this course, we cannot see any workable alternative to it."[4] As a consequence the *Socialist Standard* continued to appear throughout the war, filled with 'historical' and 'theoretical' articles, and the party continued to hold public meetings. It was left to individual members whether to accept conscription or become a conscientious objector.

The anarchists

In the war in Spain, the *Freedom* group and anarchists generally gave uncritical support to the Spanish anarcho-syndicalists of the CNT-FAI and their call for a united anti-fascist struggle, but at least one section took a more critical stance. In 1936 the journal *Spain and the World*, started by the Italian anarchist Vero Recchioni ('Vernon Richards') later joined by Marie Louise Berneri, published criticisms of the CNT-FAI's collaboration with the bourgeois Popular Front government.[5]

On the outbreak of the second world war this same grouping started the journal *War Commentary*, which strongly denounced the pretence that the war was an ideological struggle between democracy and fascism, and the hypocrisy of the democratic allies' denunciations of Nazi atrocities after their tacit support for the fascist regimes and for Stalin's terror during the 1930s. Highlighting the real nature of the war as a power struggle between British, German, Russian and American imperialist interests, *War Commentary* also denounced the use of fascist methods by the 'liberating' allies and their totalitarian measures against the working class at home. In 1942,for example, after a sordid deal by Churchill and Roosevelt with the 'French Quisling' Admiral Darlan, the paper ruthlessly exposed the democratic illusions of the bourgeois left:

> ...it should be obvious to the *Tribune* that capitalists, politicians, generals and diplomats...have gone to war to defend the British Empire, 'to hold our own' as Churchill put it: they have gone to war to defend Christianity, that is to say the principles upheld by Franco and Co; they have gone to war to reinforce their position... If the allies' victories continue, many more fascist rats will leave the Axis' sinking ship, and be welcomed by the democratic camp. And that is as it should be. The rats who helped Mussolini to conquer Abyssinia, who helped Franco to crush the Spanish revolution [sic], who armed Japan against China, who bombed the Arabs and the Indians, come together when it suits them... Everywhere workers will understand that it is not through military or diplomatic victories that fascism will be crushed.[6]

But the group's perspectives for the working class remained abstract. It called for international working class solidarity and the class struggle "as the only means for the workers to achieve control over their destiny",[7] but despite its sharp exposés of democratic hypocrisy and analyses of international events, *War Commentary* explicitly avoided any "slogans, manifestos and programmes", claiming merely that: "Our policy consists in educating [the working class], in stimulating its class instinct, and teaching methods of struggle."[8] In this, it revealed its anarchist prejudices against centralised political organisation and intervention in the class struggle.

The council communists

The Anti-Parliamentary Communist Federation welcomed the election of the Spanish Popular Front government in 1936 and threw itself enthusiastically into support for the 'Spanish struggle', supporting the legal government against the flouting of 'international law' and urging protest strikes to pressure the British government into lifting its arms embargo, thus effectively taking sides in what was in reality an inter-imperialist struggle. The group also gave uncritical support to the CNT-FAI and cooperated with the *Freedom* group to publish a bulletin, *Fighting Call*, which reprinted without comment articles by the CNT-FAI and speeches by anarchist ministers in the bourgeois government. However, some militants who went to Spain were more critical of the CNT-FAI leadership, rejecting the idea the 'democratic' capitalism was preferable to 'fascist' capitalism and warning that anti-fascism was the "new slogan by which the working class is being betrayed."[9] Before the war in Spain ended, the anarchists in the group broke away and the APCF managed to avoid making the same errors at the outbreak of the second world war. It denounced the British democratic capitalists who used fascist methods against colonial workers and peasants, and warned against driving the Italian and German workers into the arms of their rulers by supporting British imperialism. Rejecting the slogan of 'Victory for the Allied nations' raised by a group of Indian nationalists, the APCF stated:

> We stand for the victory over Hitlerism and Mikadoism - by the German and Japanese workers, and the simultaneous overthrow of all the Allied

imperialists by the workers in Britain and America. We also wish to see the reinstitution of the workers' soviets in Russia and the demolition of the Stalinist bureaucracy. In a word, we fight for the destruction of all imperialism by the proletarian world revolution.[10]

The APCF thus remained faithful to the watchword of internationalism, although its practical slogans remained abstract; for example calling on workers to demand that their 'spokesmen' organise a general strike against conscription on the eve of war.[11] Still heavily influenced by anarchism, the group did not engage in any practical anti-war activity, although *Solidarity* provided informative coverage of the class struggle against the war abroad, via correspondents like the ex-Spartacist Ernst Schneider ('Icarus') who was a regular contributor.[12] Later in the war, commenting on the trend for democratic capitalism to use totalitarian methods, the APCF did try to give a more practical perspective to the growing workers' struggles:

The only answer to fascism is the workers' social revolution, by workers' control, by immediately fighting conscription in all its phases, by building up workers' committees in opposition to the boss and the trade unions; by building workers' open forums, where the workers themselves can discuss and decide. By that method we can stem fascism and open up the road to workers' power.[13]

Solidarity also provided a forum for diverse anti-war elements. For example, in the middle of the war its pages carried a debate on the relationship between party and class, with contributions from Pannekoek and Paul Mattick. While remaining a heterogeneous grouping which was unable to decisively break from the influence of anarchism. the APCF, unlike Guy Aldred's grouping,[14] was able to make a contribution to the understanding of the Marxist movement in Britain on a number of important questions, including the change in period from ascendant to decadent capitalism and its implications for the proletariat's struggle, and the capitalist and imperialist nature of the Russian state.[15]

The Trotskyists

As the historic course opened towards generalised imperialist war, Trotsky's mistaken understanding of the balance of class forces led him to defend increasingly dangerous opportunist positions, including support for bourgeois democracy as a 'lesser evil' against fascism, 'unconditional defence of the Soviet Union', and support for 'national liberation.' Even before the second world war these positions led the Trotskyists to take sides in inter-imperialist wars: for example, with the democratic imperialisms against fascism in Spain; Stalinist Russia against Poland and Finland, and China against Japan. These positions were enshrined in the 'Transitional Programme'; a series of demands supposed to be impossible for capitalism to grant, therefore demonstrating the system's bankruptcy and pushing the working class to struggle for its destruction. At the beginning of the second world war, Trotsky set out the main lines of a 'proletarian military policy', which was essentially an application of the transitional programme to a period of universal war and militarism, centred on the demand for compulsory military training under the control of the trade unions.[16]

Trotsky himself remained faithful to internationalism, affirming in his manifesto on the war that: "...the Fourth International builds its policy not on the military fortunes of the capitalist states but on the transformation of the imperialist war into a war of the workers against the capitalists..."[17] He strongly attacked the idea that the democratic imperialisms were in any way worth defending against fascism:

> The victory of the imperialists of Great Britain and France would be not less frightful for the ultimate fate of mankind than that of Hitler and Mussolini. Bourgeois democracy cannot be saved. By helping their bourgeoisie against foreign fascism, the workers would only accelerate the victory of fascism in their own country. The task posed by history is not to support one part of the imperialist system against another but to make an end of the system as a whole.[18]

But at the same time, the policies he outlined, particularly for the Trotskyists in the democratic states, put the Fourth International on an extremely steep, slippery slope towards abandoning an internationalist position and supporting the participation of the workers in an imperialist war in the name of defending democracy against fascism. Addressing members of the American Socialist Workers' Party, Trotsky argued that:

> We cannot escape from the militarisation, but inside the machine we can observe the class line. The American workers do not want to be conquered by Hitler, and to those who say 'Let us have a peace program', the worker will reply, 'But Hitler does not want a peace program.' Therefore we say: We will defend the United States with a workers' army, with workers' officers, with a workers' government... 'Roosevelt (or Wilkie) says it is necessary to defend the country – Good! Only it must be our country, not that of the Sixty Families and their Wall Street. The army must be under our command; we must have our own officers, who will be loyal to us.' In this way we can find an approach to the masses that will not push them away from us, and thus prepare for the second step – a more revolutionary one.[19]

The role of the Trotskyists was to actively participate in this war for democracy as "the best soldiers and the best officers and at the same time [sic] the best class militants" with the stated aim of making propaganda inside the bourgeois army and winning it over to the proletariat.For the same reason Trotsky was in favour of conscription.[20] In his zeal to distance himself from pacifists and liberals, he even went as far as advocating American military intervention in Europe as the best way to defend democracy in America.[21] After Trotsky's murder by the Stalinists in August 1940, it was left to the members of the Fourth International, led by its largest section the American SWP, to turn his proposals into a practical intervention.

In Britain in 1939 the two main Trotskyist groups were the Revolutionary Socialist League (RSL), which was the official section of the Fourth International; and the Workers' International League (WIL), formed from a split in 1937. Both groups denounced the British bourgeoisie's war preparations and raised internationalist slogans: "Turn the imperialist war into a civil war", "The enemy is in your own country."[22] However, other aspects of the Trotskyist programme undermined this opposition: both groups spread illusions in the Labour Party and the trade unions as mass bodies belonging to the working class. Far from warning workers against the dangers of these capitalist organs, which were essential to the bourgeoisie for mobilising workers behind a war to defend democracy, they called for the election of a Labour government with a full 'socialist' (i.e. state capitalist) programme, supposedly to "expose it in front of the masses."[23] Both groups also clung to the un-Marxist idea that Russia was still a 'workers' state' because 'collectivised property relations' and a 'planned economy' existed there, which must therefore be defended. Even after the Hitler-Stalin pact and the Red Army's invasion of Finland and Poland, they denied that the Stalinist regime had any imperialist designs of its own, and even saw a 'progressive side' to Stalin's occupation of eastern Poland because he had taken measures like expropriating private landlords.[24]

The RSL and the WIL both raised transitional demands before the war, but it was the WIL which enthusiastically took up what became known as the Proletarian Military Policy (PMP), thus solving the problem for the Trotskyists of raising such demands inside the capitalist war machine during wartime; the RSL, an unstable regroupment of mutually hostile factions, began to break up and became increasingly inactive. Differences between the two groups opened up after the German invasion of France in 1940. The WIL explained the victory of fascism as due to the French bourgeoisie's reluctance to fight for fear of provoking an uprising by the workers. To prevent an invasion of Britain the WIL raised the slogan, "Arm the workers", and criticised the British capitalist class for "...refusing to take the one course which would doom any invasion, however formidable, to inevitable futility and defeat: the arming, mobilising and organising of the entire working class for resistance, factory by factory, street by street, house by house."[25] The WIL posed the problem as one of transforming the imperialist war, not into a civil war, but "a genuine revolutionary war against Hitlerism", thus crossing the line from internationalism to national defence. The call to 'Arm the workers' at the height of a patriotic invasion scare could only mean the British working class defending their 'own' capitalist state against a German assault.

This was not just a matter of abstract propaganda; in practice it led the Trotskyists to support the increased exploitation of the working class in order to produce guns and material for the imperialist war. The WIL was activist and gained some influence among industrial workers as the war went on and strikes grew. While it opposed the Stalinist-controlled Joint Production Committees, which tied workers to ferocious levels of exploitation in the cause of anti-fascism, the WIL argued that production *could* be increased as long as it was under 'workers' control', and it gave uncritical support to the Trotskyist-led shop stewards' committee in the Nottingham Royal Ordnance Factory, which was briefly granted control by the management over production and pay, and where output of guns duly rose. An additional justification for this support was that the guns were intended to aid the Russian war effort. In reality of course the workers had no control whatsoever over how the British bourgeoisie directed its war material; and even if the guns did get to Russia they were to be used as weapons in the struggle of the democratic gangsters – with their new ally, the butcher Stalin – against their fascist rivals.

The WIL's active support for the war effort was no aberration but the logical consequence of its enthusiastic adoption of the Proletarian Military Policy developed by the American SWP, which had avoided organising any opposition to America's entry into the war and publicly declared that it had no intention of sabotaging the war or obstructing America's military forces in any way.[26] Put on trial for conspiracy in 1941, the SWP's leaders, far from denouncing the war or calling for the overthrow of the capitalist state, publicly declared their support for a war against Hitler as long as it was under the leadership of a "workers' and farmers' government."[27]

This open defence of social patriotic views provoked a reaction from some in the Trotskyist movement, particularly Grandizo Munis and the exiled Spanish section, the Revolutionary Communists of Germany (RKD), and the tendency around the Greek Trotskyist Agis Stinas.[28] At first, a minority in the WIL also opposed the new line, criticising it as a concession to defencism, but they soon gave in and the policy was confirmed. The centre and left factions of the RSL opposed it, while the right, which was closely allied to the WIL, supported it. The RSL criticised the WIL for pandering to chauvinism in the working class, and identified the PMP as a symptom of the degeneration of the Fourth International towards the bourgeoisie.[29] But when the RSL and the WIL merged in March 1944 it was on the basis of the latter's positions, and the new organisation, the Revolutionary Communist Party, overwhelmingly adopted the PMP with the full backing of the International Secretariat of the Fourth International.

Trotskyist historians have since tried to play down the significance of these betrayals, claiming that the PMP was merely a tactic, applicable only in certain circumstances and later dropped; any errors committed by the WIL or other groups were similarly tactical or the result of polemical excess.[30] In fact, as we have seen, what became the PMP was devised by Trotsky himself as the specific means of applying the Trotskyist transitional programme in wartime. It became the official position of the Fourth International and was promoted as such by its central organs. Far from being in any way repudiated, the FI's abandonment of internationalism was confirmed at its first post-war congress in 1948. By this point, revolutionaries who had remained faithful to internationalism like Munis, Stinas and the RKD (and later Natalia Trotsky), were forced to break definitively with the Trotskyist movement.[31] Nor was the PMP the only means by which the Trotskyists betrayed internationalism. As we have seen, the slogan of 'unconditional defence of the Soviet Union' also led them to give practical support for the war. Only those revolutionaries who were able to recognise that proletarian internationalism was their primary duty in an imperialist war, and who rejected any support for the counter-revolutionary Russian state, were able to avoid passing over into the bourgeois camp.[32]

Conclusions

The response of proletarian political groups in Britain to the second world war highlights the crucial importance for revolutionaries in this country of opposing any support whatsoever for bourgeois democracy. Any concession to the idea that the workers should fight to defend democracy against fascism led straight into the arms of the democratic capitalist gangsters, who did not hesitate to use the horrors of Nazism as an alibi for their own sordid imperialist interests. This is precisely the trap that the Trotskyists plunged headlong into with their call to "arm the workers" for "a revolutionary war against Hitler."

For the anarchists of the *Freedom* group, the trap was sprung earlier, in Spain, where their uncritical support for the capitalist Popular Front government led them to take sides under the reactionary banner of anti-fascism, thus passing over to the enemy camp. The heavy influence of anarchism also led the weak council communist current to take sides in this war, and only the split of the anarchist faction, together with the albeit weak influence of the communist left, allowed the APCF to climb out of this trap and defend a basic internationalist position in the second world war.

In between these two currents, the grouping around *Spain and the World* and *War Commentary* avoided the trap of anti-fascism to a certain extent, but did not break with other aspects of anarchism. As with the Friends of Durruti group in Spain, rather than demonstrating the vitality of the anarchist movement, it proved more the resistance by proletarian elements to anarchism's betrayals, and this grouping's inability to break clearly from anarchist positions weakened its ability to make an organised intervention with clear political perspectives for the class struggle.

The SPGB meanwhile, in splendid isolation from events, showed its unhealthy respect for the niceties of bourgeois legality by giving up any anti-war activity in the face of the threat of suppression by the democratic state; which at the very least makes it guilty of 'cowardice in the face of the enemy' and demonstrates its total irrelevance to the proletariat as a political group.

The profound defeats suffered by the proletariat after 1921 meant that it entered the second world war with a much more unfavourable balance of forces than the first. Does this mean that the defence of internationalism was of symbolic value only? Not at all; the class struggle did not stop during wartime and there were important strikes in Britain towards the end, in which it was important for a revolutionary voice to be heard; against the reactionary slogans of the Trotskyists and the vague educational efforts of the anarchists. The strike waves in Italy and Germany and elsewhere testify to the combativity of the proletariat even in the most difficult conditions, and it was the duty of revolutionaries to be present in all these struggles to provide a clear communist intervention.

In the period of counter-revolution, of which the world war was the ultimate expression, the watchword, as the Italian left understood, was "No betrayal!" The surviving minorities of revolutionaries in Britain, very weak and confused, nevertheless represented the political continuity between the 'old' workers' movement and the proletarian party of the future. Internationalism was part of the unbroken thread; an essential position in the communist programme of humanity. Even in the extremely hazardous conditions of occupied Europe, under threat from the Gestapo, local police and Stalinist assassins, elements of the surviving communist left undertook anti-war activity, issuing leaflets calling on soldiers to fraternise, etc. This is an example of internationalism in action that today provides an inspiration: internationalism, expressed in the old slogan of the workers' movement, "workers' of the world unite!", is still the first duty of revolutionaries.

Notes

1 See ICC, *The Italian Communist Left 1926-45*, 1992, p.69

2 Robert Barltrop, *The Monument: The story of the Socialist Party of Great Britain*, Pluto Press, 1975, p.99.

3 Quoted in *War and Capitalism*, SPGB, 1996.

4 David Perrin, *The Socialist Party of Great Britain*, Bridge Books, 2000, p.115.

5 These criticisms were by Camillo Berneri, Marie Louise's father, who was editor of the Italian revolutionary anarchist paper *Guerra di Classe* and fought in Spain. In Barcelona, he discussed with delegates of the majority of *Bilan* – the only one of their contacts to have any positive results – before

being murdered by the Stalinists during the May events of 1937 (see *The Italian Communist Left*, p.98). Vero Recchioni, later Vernon Richards, was a collaborator of Berneri.

6   *War Commentary*, December 1942, quoted in *Neither East Nor West, Selected Writings by Marie Louise Berneri*, Freedom Press, 1952, p.49.

7   *War Commentary*, August 1941, *Ibid.*, p32.

8   *War Commentary*, December 1940, *Ibid.*, p.19.

9   *Workers' Free Press*, October 1937, quoted in Wildcat, *Class War on the Home Front*, 1986, p.29. The APCF also reprinted a denunciation of the counter-revolutionary actions of the CNT-FAI from *International Council Correspondence*, journal of the American council communist group around Paul Mattick ("'Tear Down the Barricades'", *Workers' Free Press*, September 1937, reprinted in *Revolutionary Perspectives*, no.1).

10   *Solidarity*, October-November l942, Wildcat, *op.cit.*, p.51. At the same time this article did express support for the nationalists in their "fight for liberation from British imperialism."

11   *Solidarity*, May 1939, in Wildcat, *op. cit.*, p.40.

12   As a revolutionary sailor in the first world war, Schneider had taken part in the armed uprising in the German Navy, later writing an account of these events (*The Wilhelmshaven Revolt by 'Icarus'*, first published by Freedom Press, 1944; Simian Press edition, 1975).

13   *Solidarity*, May 1944, Wildcat, *op. cit.*, p.57.

14   Guy Aldred's United Socialist Movement, which was formed after an obscure split in the APCF in 1933, opposed the second world war but lapsed into bourgeois pacifism, collaborating with dubious elements like the Duke of Bedford, an apologist for Nazism who advocated a negotiated peace with Hitler.

15   *Solidarity* ceased publication in 1945 after it became clear that there would be no repeat of the revolutionary upsurge at the end of the first world war, although William MacDougall continued to animate a 'Workers' Open Forum' and remained politically active until his death in 1981. For more details of the history of council communism in Britain see Shipway, *op. cit.*, and the pamphlet *Class War on the Home Front*, Wildcat, 1986.

16   See in particular 'American Problems', *Discussion Bulletin*, Socialist Workers' Party, September 1940, in *Writings of Leon Trotsky (1939-40)*, Pathfinder, 1969, p.333.

17   *Manifesto of the Fourth International on the Imperialist War and the Proletarian World Revolution*, May 1940, in *Writings of Leon Trotsky (1939-40)*, Pathfinder, 1969, p.222. For more on Trotsky's position on the second world war, see 'Trotsky fell as a symbol for the working class', *International Review*, no. 103.

18   *Ibid.*, p.221.

19   'American Problems', *Discussion Bulletin*, Socialist Workers' Party, September 1940, in *Writings of Leon Trotsky (1939-40)*, Pathfinder, 1969, p.333.

20   'On conscription', *ibid.*, p.321.

21   'How to really defend democracy', *Fourth International*, October 1940, in *Writings of Leon Trotsky (1939-40)*, Pathfinder, 1969, p.344.

22   See, for example, *Militant*, September 1939 (RSL), and *Youth for Socialism*, July 1939 (WIL).

23   See, for example, *Militant*, May 1939, and *Workers' International News*, December 1938.

24   *Youth for Socialism*, April 1940.

25   *Workers' International News*, February 1941.

26   *Statement on the US Entry into World War II*, Socialist Workers' Party, 1941.

27   'A criticism of the Minneapolis Trial' by Grandizo Munis, in *International Bulletin*, Pioneer, New York, June 1942.

28   Opposition to the PMP was also voiced by the Fourth International's Indian section, and some French and Belgian Trotskyists. For more on Stinas' defence of internationalism, see ICC, *International Review*, no.73.

29   A majority of the RSL – both the pacifist leadership and the left, which was the most dogmatically attached to work in the Labour Party – rejected the PMP at the 1941 party conference, and this even became a condition of membership in 1942 (see S. Bornstein & A. Richardson, *War and the International. A History of the Trotskyist Movement in Britain, 1937-1949*, Socialist Platform, 1986, p.41). The Left Fraction of the RSL defended a caricature of Lenin's revolutionary defeatism, even going as far as preferring military occupation in order to help create a revolutionary situation.

30   See, for example, the article by former WIL member Sam Levy, in *Revolutionary History*, vol. 1, no.3, Autumn 1988.

31   The RKD had broken with official Trotskyism on the outbreak of war and affiliated to the 'International Contact Commission' of the Oehlerites. Stinas broke with the FI in 1947 and the exiled Spanish section a year later. In Britain, the Left Fraction of the old RSL, the most persistent critic of the PMP and the leadership of the Fourth International, did not make this break and vainly attempted to recreate a British

section within it. The Left Fraction lingered until 1967, remaining attached to work inside the Labour Party ('the Tactic') with all the fervour of a religious sect (see 'Brief notes on the history of the Left Fraction', *Revolutionary History*, vol.1, no.1, Spring 1988).

32 The Greek revolutionary Agis Stinas, for example, refused to defend the Soviet Union even though he still believed Russia to be a degenerated workers' state, and argued that there was nothing progressive in any national struggle.

Appendix

Introduction

The following texts have been selected to illustrate the evolution of the positions defended by the British communist left: from its origins in the left internationalist trend of the workers' movement in 1914 up to the disappearance of the original left communist current in the 1920s.[1]

Each text relates broadly to a key stage in this evolution:

1. The defence of internationalism on the outbreak of war and the struggle of the Zimmerwald Left against chauvinism and social pacifism;

2. The vital split between the revolutionary and reformist wings of the workers' movement based on the experience of the October 1917 revolution;

3. The development of anti-parliamentary and anti-trade union positions in the early Third International, and the influence of the western European left on the struggle for a break with the social democratic parties;

4. The political struggle of the left against opportunism and centrism in the negotiations to form a communist party in Britain;

5. The struggle of the communist left to oppose the growth of opportunism inside the Third International and its official parties;

6. The efforts of the British communist left to highlight the degeneration of the International and to analyse the reasons for the defeat of the revolutionary wave.

Very few of these texts have ever been reprinted and almost all are made available for the first time in over eighty years.

1. Rebuilding of the International by Peter Petroff

(from *Vanguard*, December 1915)

Peter Petroff was a member of the Russian Social Democratic Labour Party who fought in the 1905 revolution. He escaped from exile in Siberia and reached London where he became a prominent member of the opposition in the SDF before moving to Glasgow to join the struggle of Maclean and the BSP's Glasgow District Council against the war. He maintained links with the revolutionary movement abroad, particularly with the Nashe Slovo group in Paris, and knew both Lenin and Trotsky personally.

Only five issues of the Vanguard *were published before the government suppressed it in January 1915. Despite this it was the most important expression of the revolutionary left in Britain during the early years of the first world war. Due to its émigré Marxist contacts it was also an invaluable source of information on the socialist anti-war movement abroad.*

In November's Vanguard *Petroff contributed a long article on the causes of the Second International's breakdown, in which he highlighted the uneven development of its constituent parties and the lack of awareness of its positions among the mass of organised workers; questions he was to return to in the following issue. In the article which appears here, Petroff makes a critical analysis of the Zimmerwald conference and the centrist limitations evident in its manifesto, but he still clearly sees the conference as a key moment in the regroupment of revolutionaries internationally and crucially makes a link with the need for a struggle at home to 'purify' the British Socialist Party of both chauvinism and centrism. Also of particular importance for the British socialist milieu is his argument that revolutionaries should participate in all the struggles of the workers, in order to sharpen the class struggle and prepare for revolutionary action.*

The Vanguard's *suppression denied Petroff the opportunity to develop these arguments in greater depth. His emphasis on a struggle for peace and democracy shows that revolutionaries had not yet fully grasped the realities of the new epoch of capitalism opened up by the war; the 1917 Russian revolution was to prove in practice that the seizure of political power was now on the historic agenda, not a struggle for reforms.*

Some of Petroff's other comments reveal him to be closer to Trotsky than to the Bolsheviks at this time; for example, his criticisms of those who called for the formation of a 'central committee' to direct the imminent social revolution, which is presumably a reference to the Bolsheviks, while his implicit rejection of a 'right of nations to self determination' suggests that he sided with Luxemburg rather than Lenin on this particular question.

The outbreak of the war has brought in its train the disorganisation, and in some countries the demoralisation, of the socialist and other working class organisations.

The progress of the war is bringing about a gradual awakening of the organised workers in almost all the belligerent countries. The illusions as to the 'war of liberation', the fight against Prussian militarism, the restoration of small nationalities, all are disappearing before the driving wind of reaction.

"Words and illusions vanish; facts remain."

The realities of the war are being understood, the glamour and romance is passing away. Events are teaching the people in a few months more than they could have learned from years of propaganda. How weak and pitiful are now the words of those labour and socialist 'leaders' who, at the very outbreak of war, deserted the socialist and labour banner and rushed to the assistance of the enemy. While these wretched creatures were talking about national unity, national defence, the capitalist class and their governments have been riveting more securely the chains of slavery upon the working class.

In republican France all liberties are suppressed, and the spirit of the government is shown in the appointment of the strikebreaker, Briand, as premier.

Great Britain, which, in the past, has so boasted of its political freedom, has become the domain of a few influential financiers and armament manufacturers who dictate to the government, through the agency of the Northcliffe press, the foreign and domestic policy of the country. Parliament has become emasculated: liberty is personified by Lord Kitchener of Khartoum, and justice by F.E. Smith, the Ulster dispatch rider.[2] The workers are smarting under the tyrannical Munitions Act, and the campaign for the destruction of trade unionism continues under government patronage.

In Russia, wholesale theft and bribery have reached unheard-of dimensions even for that country. The illusions of the Liberals have faded. Their candidates for the ministry remain unfledged. The immoral monk, Rasputin, and the bandit, Khyostov (Minister of the Interior) are ruling supreme.

In Germany the well-known Prussian methods of rule have been accentuated.

Under these circumstances it is natural that signs should begin to appear, in all the countries, of a desire for the reconstruction of the international organisation of the proletariat. Those sections of the working class who maintained the honour of the International, are growing in numbers and influence. Resolute attempts are being made by them, to cleanse the Augean stables of jingoism in the working class movement, and to prepare for serious national and international action against the war.

The International Conference at Zimmerwald is a tentative step towards that end. In the manifesto issued by that Conference they rightly state that:

> Under these unendurable conditions, we, the representatives of the socialist parties, trade unions, or minorities of these; we, Germans, Frenchmen, Italians, Russians, Poles, Letts, Rumanians, Bulgars, Swedes, Norwegians, Dutch and Swiss; we, who do not believe in national solidarity with the plundering class, but who stand for the international solidarity of the proletariat and the fight against the capitalist class, have met here to knit together the broken ties of international relationship, and to call upon the workers to bethink themselves and fight for peace.[3]

The manifesto truly declares that the war is the outcome of capitalism and imperialism:

> The ruling powers of capitalist society, who dominate the lives of the people – the monarchical as well as the republican governments, the diplomats, the mighty employers' federations, the bourgeois parties, the capitalist press, the church – all of them responsible for the war, which is only a result of the capitalist system of society, and is carried on solely in the interests of the capitalists.

The manifesto concludes with a strong appeal to the workers of all countries:

Workers! Since the very outbreak of the war you have placed your energy, courage and endurance at the disposal of the governing classes. This must cease. Fight for your own cause, for your ideal – for socialism, for the liberation of the oppressed peoples and enslaved classes by means of determined class struggle.

It is the duty of the socialists in the belligerent countries to carry on that fight vigorously. It is the duty of the socialists in the neutral countries to assist their comrades in this struggle against bloody barbarism, with all the means at their disposal.

Never in the history of humanity was there a more urgent or noble task than that which falls to us to perform. No sacrifice is too great to be made for the fulfilment of this object: the attainment of peace among the nations.

A committee has been elected at this Conference in order to facilitate communication between the internationalists of the various countries. A number of organisations have declared their adherence to the decisions of the Conference.

All this is, however, to use a Liberal phrase, but one step in the right direction. The manifesto does not call for definite revolutionary action. It simply invites the socialists of the various countries to carry on a campaign for peace. In its positive demands it includes only a miserable Liberal phrase about 'small nationalities' and a statement in general terms against annexations. The authors of the manifesto have not even attempted to analyse the actual state of affairs and the apparent tendencies in order to derive therefrom a programme and policy for the proletariat.

Unfortunately, in this respect the manifesto bears a strong resemblance to the platitudes of which many of the leaders of the old International were so enamoured.

It could scarcely be otherwise. It has long been said that a conference or a congress does not create anything new. It only can give coherent expression to what is actually prevailing in the elements of which it is composed.

In the international socialist literature great chaos seems to prevail as to the ways and means of rebuilding the International. Some socialist organs seem to treat the war and the demoralisation of the International as mere incidents. They think, evidently, that when the fighting is done and peace negotiations are commenced, Jules Guesde, Vandervelde, Hyndman, Henderson and Südekum will meet each other, forgive and forget their common patriotic blackguardism, and as a sign of truce accept some of the panaceas of the Union of Democratic Control guaranteed to cure the world of all its ills.[4]

These organs and their parties are talking about the sanctity of human life, the horrors of war, but do not show any desire to desert their quietism and to combat vigorously the militarist and reactionary forces.

Others are talking about the social revolution as the immediate step. They do not trouble as to whether this can be accomplished without the necessary forces, but rest content so long as it is stated in resolutions. These people, who are more revolutionary than reason permits, suggest the formation of an omnipotent central committee to control the whole world. Just in the same way as the Hegelian 'idea' was considered the driving force of history, so, in the mind of socialists, this 'committee' will become the driving force of the revolution irrespective of the balance of power in the various countries. Yet, a glance at the history of the International Workingmen's Association and the development of the Second International, would show that the power and growth of the International depended on the relative strength of its composite parts in the various countries.

The foreign policies of the great powers are determined by the relationship of forces within each country. How can the foreign policy, say, of this country, be transformed either by confessions of socialist faith or the establishment of a central committee independent of national frontiers, when the power of government and all the institutions are controlled by the reactionary Liberal and Tory organisations? As a matter of fact, many socialist organisations have not yet managed to get rid of the patriotic, reactionary elements in their midst, which evidently must be the preliminary to any action that will affect the policy of the country.

The German anti-war socialists have struck the right note when they declared in their manifesto that "the enemy is within our own gates." The enemy – the capitalist class and its government, or the despotic government of Russia – must be crushed by the people, each people against its own government. The working class with a common programme must fight in their respective countries for the termination of the war and the sweeping out of power of those responsible for it. That means also the restoration of the political liberties possessed by the workers before the war, and their extension in such a way as to assist the working class in its struggle for emancipation.

With the exception of one or two countries where the workers are actually carrying on a revolutionary struggle, the socialist and labour organisations are busy expressing platitudes or striving for small increases of wages or similar issues.

This explains the nebulous nature of the Conference decisions. In order to make international conferences really successful, delegates must be properly elected by the membership of their respective organisations. The agenda ought to be carefully considered by the constituent parties before the conference takes place. The decisions arrived at by the international congresses should be submitted for the approval of the members of the organisations in each country, and ought to be acted upon in the same way as would any resolution on important internal affairs. Only under these circumstances will the decisions of the international congresses be effective.

The Zimmerwald Conference did not lose anything, for instance, by the absence of the 'delegate' of the BSP, of whose appointment the members got to know only after a passport had been refused.

As to the programme and policy of the proletariat at the present moment, we shall now only indicate its general outlines, leaving its detailed consideration for a future issue.

Peace must be obtained by the pressure of the mass movements of the people who, in such case alone, would be able to dictate the terms of peace. We are not interested in fostering nationalism or regenerating small nationalities. Our business is the destruction of the monarchies and complete democratisation of the states, and the gaining of liberties by the proletariat no matter to which nationality they may belong. We must rather destroy the barriers separating the various nations, and on the basis of the economic evolution that binds nations together endeavour to erect a political system corresponding to the actual needs of the day.

The prolongation of the war with all that that means will inevitably revolutionise the masses of the people and make drastic action not only possible, but imperative. And the step taken at Zimmerwald, we hope, will prove to be the commencement of steady progress towards the realisation of our objects.

We must, therefore, purify our parties and immediately proceed to gather our forces, participate in all the chance encounters between the workers and the capitalists, sharpen the class struggle and make ourselves ready for drastic, revolutionary action.

We call upon our comrades in the various branches to affiliate with the Committee of the Zimmerwald Conference. The EC of the British Socialist Party adopted a resolution expressing pious approval of the Conference, and then, almost in the same breath, announced that the Belgian Minister of State, Vandervelde, required money, which will undoubtedly be used by him for the further demoralisation of the International. We would suggest to those members of the EC, who pose as the opposition in the BSP, to sit down fast on one of the two stools between which they are wavering. It is clearly impossible to support the manifesto of the Zimmerwald Conference and at the same time Vandervelde, Hyndman and company. The majority of the EC are so international that they did not even reprint and circulate the very mild manifesto issued by the Conference. Yet they are appealing for £200 for the 'reconstruction' of the International with Vandervelde sitting at its head.

2. What is our position?
by 'John Bryan' (Theodore Rothstein)
(from *The Call*, 3 April 1919)

Theodore Rothstein was one of the most articulate representatives of the revolutionary wing of the BSP in 1918-1919, leading the debate in the party press on the basic issues of reformism versus revolution and soviet versus parliamentary democracy. 'What is our position?', written under the pseudonym 'John Bryan', appeared in the run up to the BSP's 1919 annual conference, which saw the final showdown between the reformist and revolutionary wings of the party.

Politically the article expresses the strengths but also some of the limitations of the majority of the left wing in the BSP. It is clear evidence of the movement towards revolutionary positions by a significant section of the party's membership under the influence of the class struggle. In a frontal attack on both social pacifism and reformism Rothstein uses concrete historical examples to expose the flaws in the arguments of all those who believed in peaceful revolution by parliamentary methods; in the BSP but also in the wider British socialist movement. In his depiction of the alternative to such obsolete and reactionary methods, however, in comparison with the statements of Pankhurst and others at this time Rothstein is less clear about the nature and role of the soviets or workers' councils, envisaging the formation of a 'Labour Convention' which establishes a situation of dual power. In his description of a 'congress of delegates from the rank and file' he leaves the door open to the idea that such a body could emerge from within the institutions of the 'Labour movement' itself, without a struggle against it.

This equivocal attitude in the face of the need for clear revolutionary positions is reflected in Rothstein's own political itinerary. Unlike Petroff and Maclean, he did not take up a clear internationalist stance against the war and was hesitant in his support for the Zimmerwald movement and for a break with the Second International; for which he earned Lenin's criticism. He also supported a negotiated peace and the entry of the Mensheviks into the provisional government in Russia, before he finally endorsed the soviets' seizure of power in October 1917.

In fact, Rothstein is a figure of some controversy in the revolutionary movement, ever since John Maclean accused him of being a British government agent. An émigré from Lithuania, he had been active in the pre-war opposition to Hyndman's chauvinist leadership but resigned from the BSP following the outbreak of war and found work with the War Office; the source of later suspicions about his role. The exact nature of his work is not clear, but included contact with Military Intelligence and Foreign Office officials. From 1919 Rothstein acted as the Third International's main agent in Britain, controlling funds from Russia to support the revolutionary movement in Britain. As such he played an influential role in the formation of the Communist Party of Great Britain. He left for Moscow in September 1920 and took up a position in the soviet government, later becoming a loyal servant of the Stalinist state until his death in 1953.

The time, it seems to me, has arrived when we, of the British Socialist Party, must make up our minds where we stand. We are constantly proclaiming our complete sympathy with the revolutionary doctrines of the Russian Bolsheviks and German Spartacists, and I gather that a resolution is to be submitted on behalf of the EC to the conference at Sheffield, sending our greetings to the Hungarian and

Bavarian proletariats, who have seized the reins of power and have established or are about to establish a communist regime. At the same time, only a few months ago, we were anxious to send delegates to the anti-Bolshevik, anti-Spartacist, and anti-revolutionary conference at Berne, and were very angry with the wirepullers of the Labour Party when we found ourselves excluded from the delegation. Are we with the Russian Bolsheviks and German-Hungarian communists or not? If we are, why did we want to go to Berne? If we are not, what are we? These questions have been occupying my mind ever since my return home, and now they have been put to us as a party fairly and squarely by the resolution establishing a Communist International, which was adopted at the communist congress in Moscow, and which, I learn, is to be published in the present issue of the paper. Obviously we cannot belong to both Internationals at one and the same time. Are we to join the Moscow International or shall we remain in the fold of the Berne one? In other words, are we prepared to take our share, in this country, in *making* the social revolution by calling upon the working class to rise, and help it to do so, or shall we go on preaching the social revolution, in common with the anti-revolutionary 'patriotic', opportunist, and pacifist socialists of all hues and shades?

To my mind – and I have made it up long ago – the choice is quite simple. We all from the most moderate to the most revolutionary, are agreed that the social revolution, that is, the conquest of power by the working class and the subsequent transformation of our capitalist into a socialist society, is inevitable. If we did not believe in its coming, we should not be socialists. But there are some who do not believe in revolutionary methods at all, and there are others who believe them to be practicable in other countries, but utopian and unnecessary in ours. Britain, they say, is different from the continent. Britain has a 600-year old parliament, its people have been wedded for centuries almost to parliamentary methods of political warfare, and last but not least, our ruling classes are differently constituted, mentally and morally, from the ruling classes abroad, inasmuch as they have learnt the wisdom of yielding and compromising to a degree unknown elsewhere. Should they, it is argued, find themselves one day confronted with the determined will of the people in the shape of a Labour or socialist majority in parliament, they 'will be off and say no more.'

I, for one, do not agree with this anti-revolutionary optimism. That Britain is different from other countries I agree. Only the other day I read quotations from a leading article in the Vienna *Arbeiterzeitung*, the organ of the Austrian socialists, setting out in very eloquent language how and why Austria is so totally different from Russia as to make Bolshevism out of place and out of tune there. Similar articles, no doubt, were appearing before in the Hungarian socialist press, and I well remember reading them many months ago in the *Vorwärts*.[5] Why, I remember reading a celebrated article in the last-named paper some twelve months ago, at the height of the German offensive, in which the writer, the editor himself, argued in a most convincing manner that even the idea of a republic was totally foreign to Germany, which 'traditionally' was wedded to a centralised monarchy! And in Russia herself, as students of her political history well know, had not the so-called *Narodniki*, the precursors of modern Socialist-Revolutionists, argued, since the days of Alexander Herzen, that capitalism and its offspring, the proletariat, could never strike root in Russia's soil, and that, in consequence, socialism could never be brought about there by class war? The truth is, every country can claim exemption from the operation of social and historical forces on the plea of 'peculiarities', since every country is 'peculiar', but underlying all peculiarities are the same social factors – modern industry, capitalism, proletariat, and, now, the world war – which are bound to produce the same effects.

Britain has an old parliament, and its people has [sic] become accustomed to the parliamentary forms of political warfare? So had Russia, so had France before 1792, so had Germany till yesterday: all had century-old monarchies and were used to be governed [sic] by an irresponsible bureaucracy from above. But now they are all republics; Russia, Holy Russia, Russia of the Tsars. Russia of the peasantry, with its superstitious awe before the 'Little Father', having become a socialist republic, and Germany, Germany of the Hohenzollerns and Junkers, Germany of the most marvellously organised bureaucracy, hovering over the brink of the communist abyss. Our ruling class knows how to yield and compromise? Look at Ireland, look at Egypt, and calculate how much our ruling classes would be prepared to 'be off and say no more', when it should come to the fundamental issues of power and property. Is it not plain to every student of our history that the 'wisdom' of yielding and compromise, with which our ruling classes are generally credited, was but the fruit of their lack of sheer physical power in the shape of a large standing and well-drilled army such as was placed in the hands of their brethren on the continent by the geographical situation and consequent military requirements of their respective countries? With a small army such as they have hitherto had what more could they than keep in subjection Ireland, which was conveniently close at hand, and backward, disorganised countries like India, Egypt, and tropical colonies? The attempts to apply this insufficient force in dealing with their own people at home or in America and Canada necessarily failed each time, and taught them that 'wisdom' which is now trotted out by the anti-revolutionary socialists. But surely the times are changing? Surely the governing classes are perceiving the dangers which have arisen to them from the war and revolution, and are arming in advance, by continuing conscription and by raising volunteer forces, to meet them when they come too close? Those who cannot read these plain signs of the times are blind. Our ruling classes are no more willing to yield and compromise on the fundamental questions mentioned above than any other ruling classes in our, or before our, times, and they will resist by force as others did.

And how, speaking concretely, are we going to get a socialist majority in parliament? Is it to come gradually, in the course of five or ten general elections – that is, in about twenty five or fifty years? The socialists who reason so are obviously not young men in a hurry and the ruling classes will gladly agree to such a 'compromise' with Bolshevism, and go peacefully to bed. Or is the majority to burst out overnight? But how will you adjust it precisely for the time of the general election? Suppose the working class suddenly feels a desire to upset the precious capitalist society, but find that the general election to parliament is only due three years hence. Will they, remembering that they are 'traditionally' wedded to parliamentary methods, pickle their revolutionary ardour as careful German housewives pickle cabbage, and produce it when the government issues the order for the elections? Or is it not more likely that they will forget their parliamentary 'traditions', and confront both parliament and the government with some such tangible expression and embodiment of their will as a Labour Convention, a congress of delegates from the rank and file, call it soviet or by any other name? I think that the latter course is more likely – especially as we have had interesting precedents in other countries; and what will parliament and the government do then? Will they dissolve themselves and invite the workers to take their seats? Or will they start parleying with them, thereby themselves making the Convention or the soviet a permanent institution, rivalling in authority and disputing power with parliament?

One need only put these concrete questions in order to perceive that they admit of one reply only: a revolution, just because it is a revolution, breaks with all traditions and establishes its own practice. Such was the case even in this parliamentary country in 1649-1659, and such will be the case when the next revolution is made by the proletariat. It will make its revolution outside parliament and parliamentary forms of warfare, and we shall see essentially the same phenomena in other countries.

Are we 'in' for such a revolution? Is it our mission to agitate and work for it? Then our place is in the Third International. If not, then the sooner we recognise our mistake in identifying ourselves with the Russian and other communists and in sending greetings to the revolutionary proletariats of Hungary and Bavaria the better for everybody concerned.

3. Theses of the West European Bureau of the Third International

The following sets of theses are all products of the Amsterdam conference of the West European Bureau of the Third International held in February 1920. They represent a much lesser known set of programmatic documents of the early Third International, which are in continuity with the positions adopted by its founding congress but draw primarily on the experience of the working class in the advanced capitalist countries of western Europe and America.

The work of the West European Bureau itself, which existed for less than six months, is still a neglected episode in the history of the Third International, and many of the texts it produced have never been published.[6] Its formation and activities, particularly its one and only conference, provided an important focus for the communist movement in the USA and western Europe, and for a brief period promised to be a decisive influence on the evolution of the International itself.

With Russia besieged by the armies of the 'democratic allies', in early 1919 the ECCI decided to establish bureaux outside Russia, which would undertake propaganda and promote the growth of communist parties to help spread the world revolution. Bureaux were subsequently created in Scandinavia, the Balkans and Central Europe, as well as the south of Russia and Latin America. In the strategically important region of western Europe the ECCI simultaneously put in place a provisional secretariat based in Germany, and a provisional bureau in the Netherlands. Membership of the secretariat, decided beforehand in Moscow, was exclusively from the right-wing leadership of the KPD, while that of the bureau was to comprise representatives of both the left and right wings of the Dutch Communist Party, including Pannekoek, Gorter and Roland-Holst for the left.

The ECCI's delegate, Rutgers, arrived in the Netherlands in November 1919 to establish the bureau and organise an International conference as soon as possible. A conference of the Western European Secretariat in January had already been announced, and the provisional bureau in Amsterdam sent texts to Berlin while also preparing its own conference, making visits to Britain, Switzerland, Belgium and France. Delegates from Britain and America began to arrive in the Netherlands during January, and when no word was received from Germany, the Dutch comrades decided to go ahead, producing a bulletin with a set of propositions and theses for the conference, which opened on 3 February 1920 and lasted for four days before being broken up by the Dutch police. A full report of the conference appeared in the Workers' Dreadnought, *which also published its theses and resolutions.[7]*

Statement on parliamentary action

(from *Workers' Dreadnought*, 28 February 1920)

The theses on parliamentarism drafted before the conference (probably by Rutgers) did not reject the use of parliamentary action in pre-revolutionary conditions, but commented that the ECCI's position on this question, as set out in its circular of September 1919, had since proved insufficient in all practical cases (this was a reference to the controversy in the KPD on participation in elections). The theses posed the need to abstain from parliamentary activity where the workers had created their own organs of power, and it was against this that Lenin polemicised in his pamphlet Left-Wing Communism, An Infantile Disorder. *The dangers of parliamentary action for the Third International, and the need for communists to adopt an abstentionist position, were made more explicit in the revised set of theses, probably drawn up by Pannekoek, and presented to the conference for future discussion.*

The question of participation in parliamentary action being merely one of tactics, it can only be decided according to local conditions. The various communist parties and groups adhering to the Third International must be left free to adopt parliamentary action or to reject it if they choose. It would be dangerous and cramping for the Third International to prescribe it as an essential tactic.

In some phases of the struggle between the ideology of bourgeois democracy and that of the soviets and the proletarian dictatorship abstention from parliamentary action is necessary.

Young communist parties, whose policy and discipline is not yet strong and coherent and whose theory is not yet firmly grounded, may easily be corrupted and revert to Second Internationalism by a plunge into the parliamentary contest.

It must be recognised that in the highly industrialised western countries, of which Britain is at once the extreme and typical example, the feeling of the revolutionary sections of the working class is turning ever more definitely from parliamentarism and from all parliamentary tactics.

It would be a fatal mistake for the Communist Parties to allow the question of parliamentary action to divide them from the revolutionary masses.

When the workers have passed through trade unionism and Labour parliamentarism, through industrial unionism, and developed a Marxian appreciation of the class war, and are striving to build up amongst the workers within their own industries the organisation and consciousness from which the soviets will spring, they are unlikely to turn their attention to parliamentarism in any form. Even those who have not yet arrived at a full appreciation of communism and the soviet structure may be assisted in their development to this point of consciousness, rather by teaching developed from the point at which they have arrived, than by an attempt to drag them back to parliamentarism.

It must be recognised that as the bourgeoisie discovers that parliament is being used as a platform for propaganda by those who do not intend to use parliament for legislative objects, but whose object is to destroy its influence parliaments will take steps to protect themselves from such a case by adapting their procedure to meet the case. The British parliament has already gone far in this direction. There is a stage in the revolutionary struggle when parliamentarism can no longer be used to advantage; only those who are engaged in the revolutionary struggle in each country can decide when that moment has arrived.

It is imperative that the Third International should guard itself against a drift towards the right, using this present period of comparative quiescence in the revolutionary struggle outside Russia. Such a drift towards the right might lead to a revival of reformist parliamentary action within the Third International itself. It must be guarded against with the utmost vigilance and repudiated with strong emphasis should it appear.

Communist unity and separation of communists from the social patriotic parties

(From Workers' Dreadnought, 20 March 1920)

The most important resolution passed by the conference was undoubtedly that concerning the basis for communist unity. The section explicitly calling for no compromise with parties belonging to the Second International was proposed by Pannekoek.

1. The social patriots and opportunists, particularly when catering to the 'left' tendency, constitute a most dangerous enemy of the proletarian revolution.

2. To associate or co-operate with these corrupt and counter-revolutionary elements means seriously hampering the development of the conscious communist movement. Rigorous separation of the communists from the social patriots is absolutely necessary.

3. The toleration of opportunist or social patriotic elements in a communist party on the plea of unity, means violation of the only unity promoting the revolution – unity, consisting, not merely in formal acceptance of general principles, but agreement on fundamental action.

4. It is necessary that communist groups still in the old reformist and opportunist parties (even if these repudiate the Second International) should sever their compromising relations and unite in the Communist Party (or form a Communist Party if necessary).

5. Unity depends upon local conditions; but must be animated not alone by formal acceptance of communist theory, but uncompromising emphasis on the revolutionary practice developing out of that theory. In general, the fundamental considerations in establishing unity are:

   (a) The uncompromising class struggle of the proletariat – no compromise with the bourgeois or social patriotic parties, with parties affiliated with the Second International, or with the agents of capitalism in the labour movement.

   (b) Mass action of the proletariat as the means for the conquest of power, the Communist Party as the conscious and directive force in the development of this mass action.

   (c) Dictatorship of the proletariat (and consequent repudiation of bourgeois democracy).

   (d) The soviet system as the necessary form of the proletarian democracy.

Theses on trades unionism

(From *Workers' Dreadnought*, 20 March 1920)

The theses on trade unionism which appeared in the Bureau's bulletin adopted a compromise position which saw the existing trade unions as necessary for both the workers and the bourgeoisie, while recognising the bureaucratisation of the old craft unions and their role for capitalism in strangling the development of wildcat strikes. The main tactic proposed was to organise a revolutionary opposition within the unions, while at the same time supporting the formation of new, industrial union-type organisations.

A different set of theses, written by the American communist Louis Fraina, were agreed unanimously by the conference and are presented here. These are still contradictory but go much further, calling for a struggle against the unions, which with the rise of imperialism have become integrated into the state, and advocating the use of a variety of tactics, including moves to strengthen rank and file control, and the formation of shop stewards' and workers' committees, and industrial unions; although they also include a critique of industrial unionist ideas, and end by affirming the need for mass action and the construction of soviets.

The debate in the conference focused solely on whether workshop bodies, like the shop stewards and workers committees in Britain, and the factory committees in Germany, should be admitted to the Bureau. The workers' committees were seen as embryo soviets, open to all workers, while the International was a communist political organisation. Fraina and Pankhurst argued strongly against admitting what were essentially non-communist bodies; there should be a separate industrial international body. The vote was for admittance, but as this was against a decision at the CI's founding congress it was deferred.

1. Unions are necessary organisations in the economic struggle of the workers against their employers, since, in spite of their limitations, the unions are meant for resisting, and often improving, the most inhuman conditions of labour. Nor are the unions transitory in character, since they can, particularly as industrial unions, become active means of revolutionary struggle, and a factor in the communist reconstruction of society.

2. The trade unions, persisting in the defensive struggle against capitalism, do not materially improve labour conditions; the rise of wages is, in general, exceeded by the rise of prices; while the policy of compromise, wage agreements and industrial peace weakens the fighting spirit of the workers.

3. The trade unions arose during the epoch of small industry, and with its consequent division of the workers into crafts and trades. The artisan conception prevailed that a worker's craft or skill was a form of property, developing a property and bourgeois ideology; and this, together with the circumstance that trade unionism acquired power during a period of intense national economic development (1870-1900), produced the concept of limiting the proletarian struggle within the limits of capitalism and the nation.

4. Trade unionism represented (and still largely represents) the upper layers of the working class, excluding the bulk of the unskilled workers; and where these workers are organised in trade unions, they are dominated by the concepts

and practice of the upper layers – the 'aristocracy of labour.'

5. The development of imperialism merges the trade unions definitely in capitalism, the upper layers of the working class being bribed with a 'share' in the profits of imperialism by means of slightly higher wages, steady employment and labour legislation.

The 'aristocracy of labour', dominant in trade unionism accepts imperialism, uses the unions to assist capitalism in 'stabilising' labour in industry, and becomes the source of the corrupt ideology of social imperialism. The decisive factor in the collapse of the old International was the immersion of socialism in trade unionism, with its practice of social imperialism, petty bourgeois democracy, and its fundamental counter-revolutionary tendency.

6. Trade unionism (as typically expressed in the American Federation of Labour) is impotent to improve materially conditions of labour, or to conquer power, since the division of the workers into craft or trade organisations splits them into innumerable unions, each antagonistic to each other, making hopeless the struggle against concentrated capitalism, which largely expropriates the worker of his skill, eliminates the craft divisions of small industry, and brings masses of the proletariat together regardless of particular occupational functions. The general mass strike alone is capable of decisive action against concentrated capitalism; but trade unionism, in form and spirit, is antagonistic to the mass strike.

7. Trade unionism comes to realise its economic impotence, and proceeds to parliamentary action, which, represented by Labourism (as typically expressed in the British Labour Party), is as impotent as trade unionism to accomplish fundamental conquests, since Labourism necessarily accepts the dominant union concepts and practice. Labourism unites with petty bourgeois democracy against the proletarian revolution – that petty bourgeois democracy which is seduced by imperialism.

8. The governmental form of expression of Labourism is state capitalism, the merger in the state of the capitalists, the small bourgeoisie, and the upper layers of the working class dominant in the trade unions; the state is used to regulate equally industry and labour, for purposes of imperialism, the proletarian masses being compelled to accept this arrangement by means of deception and force.

9. The tendency is for Labourism and Socialism to unite (either formally or by means of trade union domination of the Socialist Party) each necessarily accepting social imperialism, since their activity is limited within the limits of capitalism and the nation; and, under the ascendancy of monopoly and finance capital, the 'prosperity' of a nation depends on imperialism.

10. Labourism becomes the final bulwark of defence of capitalism against the oncoming proletarian revolution; accordingly, a merciless struggle against Labourism is imperative. But while, politically, Labourism expresses itself as state capitalism and petty bourgeois democracy, its animating impulse and force is in trade unionism. The struggle against this form of unionism, accordingly, is an inseparable phase of the struggle against Labourism, proceeding:

(a) In general by means of agitation by the Communist Party to drive the unions to more revolutionary action.

(b) By encouraging every movement in the unions that tends to break the permanency of the bureaucracy, and placing control in the masses by means of delegates being subject directly to instructions and recall.

(c) By the formation of organisations such as the shop stewards, workers' committees, economic workers' councils and direct branches of the Communist Party in the shops, mills and mines, which are not alone means for moving the masses and the unions to more revolutionary action, but which at the moment of crisis may develop the soviets.

(d) By endeavouring to transform the trade unions into industrial unions, that is, a unionism in *form* paralleling the economic integration of modern capitalism, and in *spirit*, animated by the struggle for political power and economic mastery.

11. The agitation for, and construction of, industrial unions provides, in an immediate and practical way, the opportunity to articulate and mobilise the militant spirit of discontent developing in the old unions, to carry on the struggle against the corrupt bureaucracy and the 'aristocracy of labour.' Industrial unionism, moreover, provides the opportunity of calling to action the unorganised unskilled workers, and to release the unskilled organised in the trade unions from their bondage to the reactionary upper layers of the working class.

The struggle for the revolutionary industrial unionism is a factor in the development of communist theory, and for the grasping of the power.

12. Unionism trades and industrial must not limit itself to economic strikes but must acquire the concept and practice of the general political strike – co-operate with the Communist Party to develop the general mass struggle of the proletariat against the bourgeois state. The concept that industrial unionism alone is necessary for the conquest of capitalism must be decisively rejected. It is sheer utopia to imagine that all the workers, or an overwhelming majority, can be organised in industrial unions under capitalism; economic conditions interfere; the upper layers of the working class, being the impulse of Labourism, will necessarily reject revolutionary industrial unionism; while the lower layers will not move very rapidly until thrown into action by the impact of revolution itself. Moreover, the concept that the workers under capitalism must in their industrial unions acquire the experience and technic [sic] of management of industry, 'growing into' the new society by the industrial unions' gradual acquisition of industrial control, identical (although inverted in form) with the proposals of parliamentary socialism – that the working class must gradually 'grow into' socialism by acquiring experience of state affairs and 'absorbing' control of the bourgeois state. Each concept, in its own way, rejects the fundamental problem of the revolutionary conquest of state power.

14. [sic] The conquest of the power of the state is the objective of the revolutionary proletariat. Neither the parliaments nor the industrial unions are the means for this conquest of power, but mass action and the soviets; mass action to rally the workers, organised and unorganised, in the open revolutionary struggle for power; the soviets to constitute the mechanism of the revolutionary proletarian state, the dictatorship of the proletariat.

At the moment of active revolution the struggle becomes, not a struggle for industrial unions, but for the construction of soviets.

15. After the conquest of political power and under the protection of the soviet dictatorship; industrial unionism comes actually to function in the economic reconstruction of society on a communist basis; and the stronger the industrial unions, the easier the process of reconstruction. The government of soviets, of proletarian dictatorship; is political and transitory in character, the necessary agent of repression to expropriate and crush capitalism. While industrial in its constituents and representation, the government of soviets functions

geographically and politically; but alongside of itself it constructs a central administration of industry – wholly economic in character, equally in representation and functions, perfecting the organism of proletarian control and management of industry on the basis of the industrially organised producers.

4. The SLP and unity – an open letter to the party
by J.T. Murphy

(From the *Socialist*, 6 May 1920)

J.T. 'Jack' Murphy is best known as the intellectual leader of the wartime shop stewards' movement and author of the influential pamphlet The Workers' Committee *(1917). Less well known is that, like Pankhurst, he made extensive contacts with the early Third International and, under the influence of these contacts and his direct experience of the German revolution, he developed a distinctive analysis of the danger of opportunism facing the International, which led him to very clearly warn against any compromise with centrism in the formation of a communist party in Britain.*

Murphy left Britain for Amsterdam in early 1920 to attend the conference of the West European Bureau as a delegate for the shop stewards' movement (and as observer for the SLP). After the conference's break-up he took part in discussions with the ECCI's representative, Borodin, and other delegates, before travelling clandestinely with Borodin to Germany, where he wrote a series of open letters for the Socialist. *In the most extensive of these letters, presented here, Murphy analyses the different revolutionary tendencies in Britain in the context of the main trends in the international communist movement, explicitly identifying the dangers of opportunism and centrism within the International. He then provides a comprehensive refutation of the BSP's arguments for communists affiliating to the Labour Party, and ends by defining the main points of a programme for communist unity in Britain based on the Amsterdam resolutions. Murphy's in-depth analysis is one of the most significant attempts by the left in Britain to identify the roots of the opportunist danger in the International. (He produced a more extensive version as a report to the CI in preparation for its second congress.)*

Alone of the former pro-unity SLP leaders, Murphy did not immediately endorse the formation of the Communist Unity Group, and warned against any compromise with opportunism in forming the Communist Party. Practically, however, he was in no position to argue for this line within the SLP, or to play an active role in the unity negotiations, and he simply drifted away from the party. From Germany he travelled to Petrograd for the CI's second congress, after which he became involved in the setting up of the Red International of Labour Unions (RILU), returning to Britain in December 1920.

During the past fifteen months the whole socialist movement in Britain has been agitated by appeals for unity from one source or another. Under the influence of the Russian revolution certain parties have moved towards the left, while the extreme left (SLP) has shown a strong element moving towards the right in the desire to help Russia. The conflict within the party and the negotiations with the other parties have thus produced a most critical situation, from which must proceed developments destined to have a tremendous effect upon the future of the revolutionary movement in Britain. The choice before our party is, in view of the BSP Easter Conference decisions in particular, one between a muddled large organisation and a smaller organisation strictly disciplined, with a clearly defined structure, communist platform, policy and practice.

The situation in the socialist movement of Britain is similar in kind to the international situation. And the choice before the SLP is also the choice before the much greater Communist International. The Second International has been shattered, and its remnants seek a new home. The old birds are sprouting new wings on the left side which hamper them considerably in their flight. Almost all and sundry are declaring their affiliation to the Third International. The Socialist Labour Party of Spain, without expelling the right and the centre, have declared for the Communist International. The left wing of the German Independents, the left wing of the French party, the BSP, which still clings to the Labour Party although the latter hangs onto the Second International; the American Socialist Party, which expelled 40,000 communists, and consists now wholly of the centre and the right, declare for the Third International. So also a section of the ILP.

The tremendous struggle of the Russian proletariat has generated a profound sympathy for the revolution, and this, coinciding with the disintegration of the Second International, is responsible for the leftward movement which has not yet clarified itself and become sufficiently daring to throw off its compromising policy. Therein lies the danger and the challenge to the communists; the danger of the International becoming a radical socialist body, and the challenge to fight these elements and retain the revolutionary integrity of the Communist International.

Even within the Communist International signs are not wanting that the spirit of compromise has already crept in. The Italian Socialist Party, affiliated to the Communist International more than a year ago, has not yet rid itself of the right and centre. The Communist Party of Germany (Spartacusbund) is compromising with the Independents, with what tragic consequences those who have witnessed the recent upheaval in Germany can bear witness.

The things essential in the International today are clearness of vision and uncompromising adherence to the fundamental communist principles and practice. The International is in its formative period, and any toleration of confused elements in it now will be paid for later in mistaken plain tactics and weakness in action. It is therefore imperative for every Communist Party to purge itself of compromise and refuse fusion with other parties until they have done likewise, for its own sake and for the sake of the International.

The four parties in Britain claiming adherence to the Communist International are the SLP, BSP, WSF and South Wales SS. There is a closer affinity between the two latter and the SLP than there is between the BSP and any of the parties. Each has a different historical background. The WSF and the SWSS are the youngest parties, and are practically agreed anti-parliamentarians, though neither party has developed a specific programme and policy. Indeed, none of the parties are fully developed in this respect. It should be observed that the Russian revolution has affected the SLP and BSP differently. The communist programme of the Third International partly accepts and partly supplements the principles and programme the SLP has fought for since its inception. Its uncompromising waging of the class war, its advocacy of industrial unionism and revolutionary parliamentarism, and its insistence on the impossibility of using the parliamentary state to accomplish the revolution and the necessity of extra-parliamentary action, have received a dynamic impulse from the revolution and the realisation of the need for the intermediate soviet state with the dictatorship of the proletariat. This is a development of its first principles. The BSP, on the other hand, in adhering formally to the Communist International, has had to reverse its previous policy. Trailing with it all the traditions of the SDP, its opposition to industrial unionism, its reformist parliamentarism, it has had to pass through a process, and it has still to pass through a further process of internal change. It rid itself of the National Socialists, Hyndman and company, and then later the reformists, Fairchild and Alexander. It accepted industrial unionism and revolutionary parliamentarism nominally and automatically. So also soviets and proletarian dictatorship, etc.; but its practice is still the same. The unity discussions produced an alignment on practically every occasion of the SLP, WSF and the SWSS against the BSP. Each party subscribed to the soviets and proletarian dictatorship. That was to be expected. But on the questions of revolutionary practice the differences were, and are, profound. Here let it be said that the manner in which a party applies the principles it professes provides the acid test of the value of the party, whether for revolution or anything else. All the four parties agreed on anti-parliamentarism as understood by the rejection of the parliamentary institutions as an organ of proletarian government. In practice, however, we find the BSP a part of the Parliamentary Labour Party which believes in parliamentary democracy. It has members on the local municipal councils accepting duties in administrative departments – thus doing exactly the same as the ILP.

Under the pressure from the International and the SLP, the BSP Executive decided to withdraw from the Labour Party under protest. That means it does not change its mind in the least, and this is clearly indicated in its later decisions to send a special plea to the Executive of the Communist International and its proposal for local autonomy in the Communist Party on the matter of Labour Party affiliation. The latter proposal had already been defeated in the unity conference. Local autonomy in any matter of policy must be absolutely rejected by any revolutionary party.

In every phase of policy the BSP revealed its reformist character; and how automatic is its acceptance of communist principles. In its plea for affiliation with the Labour Party, in its attitude towards the trades union bureaucracy and unionism in general, the same compromising characteristics are manifest.

The BSP's reasons for affiliation to the Labour Party and the answers we give are summarised as follows:

1. The Labour Party is the working class organised, and it is essential for the Communist Party to be within the Labour Party to maintain contact with the working class.

The Labour Party is not the working class organised politically as a class, but the political reflex of the trades union bureaucracy and the petty bourgeois. Contact with the working class is not, and never has been, dependent upon contact with the Labour Party.

2. The Labour Party is different to the Socialist parties of France and other countries, being a federation of trades unions, co-operative societies, and politi-

cal parties, and hence not a political party in the usual sense of the term.

The fact that the Labour Party is the political federation of the trades unions, co-operatives, etc., condemns it to parliamentary democracy, which is in fundamental contradiction to the principles of communist struggle.

3. Affiliation to the Labour Party by the Communist Party is similar to the Bolsheviks staying in the soviets when these were dominated by the Mensheviks.

In no sense is there a parallel in the two situations. The soviets are the instruments of revolution, the future governmental machinery of the proletariat.

The Labour Party is a parliamentary party, an instrument of reaction, a body to be destroyed. The soviets were created in the heat of revolutionary struggle. The Labour Party is a product of counter-revolutionary conciliation with capitalism.

4. Affiliation is necessary because in many places there exists no other organisation of labour, and the Communist Party must be within it to get a hearing by the use of its platform.

The workers are always accessible in the workshops, the streets, the unions; and the creation of an independent communist platform is better than going cap in hand to the Labour Party for a hearing.

5. Affiliation is necessary in order that the Communist Party may be represented at the Labour Party conferences, and influence its decisions by the Communist Party putting forward its own resolutions.

This implies that the Communist Party is either intent on capturing the Labour Party or passing revolutionary resolutions for reactionaries to carry out. If the first, the policy is fundamentally wrong, because the Labour Party, in composition and form, is not a revolutionary organisation; its members are neither communists nor revolutionists, and it is structurally incapable of mobilising the masses for revolutionary action. It is a product of capitalism, and fit only to be used for the maintenance of capitalism. If the second, then the masses are betrayed and their revolutionary fervour used to strengthen the forces of reaction. This proposition also indicates that the BSP does not clearly understand the functions of a Communist Party in its struggle for power. It is evidently content to be a spur to another party for whose actions it refuses responsibility, instead of a strong revolutionary party leading the masses to action.

6. The local Trades and Labour Councils are the nuclei of the soviets of the revolution. They would be augmented by the Workers' Committees, shop stewards, and the like.

The Trades Councils are not the nuclei of the soviets. Their ineptitude in all industrial disputes provides ample proof of this. They possess no executive power over the unions, and action comes either through delegates from the workshops, etc., or the local district committees of the unions, which bodies improvise strike committees composed of stewards and the district committees, etc., leaving the Trades Councils in the background or playing a reactionary part. It will be in such manner that the soviets will be formed, and not through the Trades Councils, as suggested.

7. Members may be elected to parliament on the Labour Party ticket.

This is sheer parliamentary vote-catching opportunism and a repudiation of independent political action. It is also confusing to the masses. The Communist Party must go into elections not on vote-catching excursions, but for revolutionary agitation, and to familiarise the masses with itself as the party of revolution.

8. As the workers become more revolutionary they will throw over the reactionary leaders such as Henderson and Macdonald, and turn to the Communist Party leaders.

This implies that a Communist Party will be out to capture the Labour Party – a proposal which must be rejected. The Communist Party must seek to destroy the Labour Party as an enemy to the proletarian revolution. This can be done by working in the unions for disaffiliation of the unions and building independently a strong Communist Party free from the entanglements of opportunism.

9. Affiliation, maintains the BSP, does not mean acceptance of the Labour Party programme.

This is an argument for political tricksters. The masses do not follow the winding paths of politicians, and are confused by such practices. The masses reason more simply, and think that those in the Labour Party are of the Labour Party and responsible for its deeds. The Communist Party can best make its antagonism to the policy of the Labour Party clear to the masses by being neither in it nor of it.

10. This affiliation is temporary, as when the Labour Party comes into power the Communist Party would have to separate.

This acknowledgement indicates that there is a fundamental antagonism between communism and the Labour Party policy and programme, otherwise there would be no reason to part company at such a moment. Such a policy is not only confusing, but it weakens the confidence of the masses by encouraging hopes that cannot be realised. It is far better to make clear the antagonisms now and build the Communist Party strong and independent, so that, instead of having to explain to the masses why the party retired at such a moment, it can proceed with revolutionary vigour and confidence to attack the capitalist-cum-Labour government as it attacked its predecessors.

On unionism and mass action the BSP is equally confused. It formally accepted industrial unionism at its conference, but has failed to apply the principles it formally accepted. As in politics it looks to the Labour Party, so in unionism it looks to the trades union bureaucracy for action. The resolution passed at the last BSP conference indicates not only this fact, but also that the BSP is confused as to an understanding of mass action and direct action. The resolution reads: "In the opinion of this conference, the present social condition of the world is such that if the trades unions were to unite in joining all striking forces at one time instead of striking individually there is every prospect of a successful overthrow of the wage system, with less suffering and expenditure". This resolution implies that we can get a general strike of the unions by our propaganda within them, a possibility an infant in trades union history would repudiate. It implies that the overthrow of capitalism can be attained by the general strike alone, a further proposition repudiated by history. No finer example of a general strike can be cited than the recent strike in Berlin. But it did not achieve the social revolution. More than the strike was required communist leadership, the seizure of arms, an open, united military struggle for power. The repeated limitation of mass action to direct action (a syndicalist limitation) by the BSP is either an indication of lack of foresight into the needs of revolution or moral cowardice expressing itself in a fear of an open declaration that revolution cannot be carried through without resort to arms.

But there exist not only these differences on policy in relation to things external to the party, but also differences on internal organisation and discipline. The resolution on Labour Party affiliation stressing local autonomy indicates ideas on party organisation and discipline of a very loose character. A revolutionary party needs strong leadership, strong centralisation, and rigid discipline; local autonomy cannot give any of these essentials.

In view of these vital differences the BSP must purge itself of its reformist notions and dare to swing into real revolutionary practice before there can be any real unity between itself and the other three parties.

The situation in Britain demands that whatever forces can unite truly and fundamentally should do so. In order, therefore, that the efforts already made in this direction shall come to fruition or the impossibility of any unity between any of the parties be clearly demonstrated, I would urge that the three bodies, the SLP, WSF, and the SWSS, which have been in general agreement throughout the negotiations, draw up a joint programme and thesis, presenting not only basic principles, but also their specific application to the proletarian struggle, and should include:

1. No compromise with the Labour Party.

2. No compromise with the trades union bureaucracy, but an intensification of the propaganda for revolutionary industrial unionism.

3. No compromise with the centre parties, such as the ILP.

4. Strong centralisation of the party and rigorous party discipline.

5. An intense struggle by the Communist Party to attain the leadership and the domination of the party in all aspects of the proletarian struggle.

The international communist movement, by its present conditions, demands the utmost vigilance on the part of those who desire to maintain its revolutionary integrity. I therefore call upon the revolutionary communists in the parties enumerated not to follow either parochialism or the desire for a large party or immediate circumstances to limit their visions or dull their revolutionary character by compromise. There must be no compromise with the BSP. Better a Communist Party without the BSP than a party including the BSP, trailing with it the spirit of compromise to hamper the party in its revolutionary practice.

We must move firmly and earnestly towards a real Communist International composed of revolutionary communist parties daring to apply the principles they have proclaimed.

20 April 1920

5. A world movement. The Third International and international communism
by Sylvia Pankhurst

(From *The Workers' Dreadnought*, 16 October 1920)

This article, dating from the period following Pankhurst's return from Moscow as a committed supporter of unity, sets out her reasons why the left should work within the Third International for a change of line. It serves to refute the notion that the British communist left simply capitulated in the face of Lenin's arguments at the Congress, and shows that the decision of its main representatives to accept the discipline of the International was based on thought-out perspectives which took as their starting point the interests not of the British but of the international communist movement.

The article itself was written as a response to Edgar Whitehead, national secretary of the CP(BSTI). While Whitehead's arguments are omitted here, their flavour can be judged by the following example: "Those of us who have spent some years on the continent were well aware how absolutely different the Britisher was from all other continentals..." Pankhurst clearly rejects the 'little England' mentality of those who objected to 'interference from Moscow' because 'British communists knew best', and offers a clear, practical explanation of why the working class must unite its struggles on an international level. Her extensive quotes from the CI's 'Theses on Parliamentarism' have been retained in full here; not only because they help to show how closely the British left followed the general orientation of the second congress, despite disagreements on parliamentary activity, but also because they help to underline the Theses' own original revolutionary intentions, after many years of falsification and distortion in support of the grossest parliamentary and electoral activities.

With the further downturn in the revolutionary wave in 1921, Pankhurst's optimism that the International would swiftly abandon its unworkable position on parliamentary action was of course to prove tragically misplaced, but this does not negate the importance of the main political arguments presented here.

The class war is international

Comrade Whitehead writes of '*Our* communist problem' and 'the class war for Britain'. He fails to realise that capitalism is international, that the class war is international, that communism must either be international, or it cannot succeed.

Soviet Russia is not yet communist, because Soviet Russia exists in the midst of a capitalist world. Soviet Russia is, therefore, part socialist, part capitalist still.

Moreover, Soviet Russia could not be even so much socialist as it is were Russia not enormously vast in extent and rich in the products alike of arctic and tropical climates. Soviet Russia contains within her own borders at least a minimum supply of all those things which are absolutely essential to the maintenance of civilised life. Were Russia entirely lacking in anything without which the Russian people could not exist, Russia could not stand alone. We in the British Isles are less able to stand alone than are the Russians.

Capitalism is international

If the population of Soviet Russia were not enormous, the capitalist governments of the rest of the world would easily have vanquished the military resistance of Soviet Russia; but, even as it is, international capitalism has forced Soviet Russia to remain always at war, constantly sending the most devoted, the ablest, and strongest of her sons to fight in the trenches, instead of attending to the productive and administrative work of communism. The class war is international; the capitalists are banded together internationally; they act internationally, and devise their tactics and strategy internationally.

The capitalists, of course, desire that the workers shall not band themselves together to fight internationally. Capitalism would, of course, prefer that the workers should not band themselves together at all; it would, of course, prefer to fight them as weak and isolated units. The workers are terribly slow to realise this, and to understand that they cannot defeat capitalism unless they act together. Hence we find them clinging to the old craft unions for minor personal reasons, instead of banding themselves together industrially. Thus we find that when the railwaymen were on strike, the workers in other industries took no sympathetic action, and during the present crisis, whilst the miners have been on the verge of striking, even those unions which are in the Triple Alliance with them have announced their refusal to give them active support. This, too, in Germany, when the workers of Berlin were fighting capitalism in the guise of a bourgeois republican government, the workers in other parts of Germany were unready to act, and the workers of Berlin were vanquished. The same thing happened when the workers of Munich set up a soviet and when the workers in the Ruhr and other parts of Germany rose to attack the capitalist system. In the international field also, Russia, Hungary, and Finland have fought the life-and-death struggle with capitalism, whilst in the countries adjoining them the workers made no move to assist the workers' revolution, and even allowed themselves to be used by the capitalists against it.

Narrow sectionalism of the nationalist

We need not be surprised that those who have not enlisted in the class war should fail to realise that this, the class war, is international, but every communist in anything more than name, must clearly realise that fact, and must act always in conformity with that realisation. No far sighted communist revolutionary can possibly adopt the attitude that the communist movement in each country is sufficient unto itself, and that the rest of the world is unimportant.

Comrade Whitehead asks: 'Can British communism be directed from Moscow?' The question is misleading. It ought to be: 'Can British communism be directed by the Third International?' That question necessarily involves another: it is: 'Can the Third International direct the international revolution; can it influence the national movements in the various countries so that they may act together with international effect?'

I think that the answer is: 'Yes. The Third International can and must combine all the various national movements into an international force against capitalism'. Our party was emphatically of this opinion at the time of its formation, for it not only made adhesion to the Third International one of its principles, but even attached the words 'British Section of the Third International' to its name as a sub-title.

The principle of 'give and take'

International action, like national action, entails a certain amount of give and take. Extremists who believe their extreme stand to be justified may sometimes have to wait and be content to find themselves in a minority for a time. More moderate elements may have to swallow policies that are a little alarming to them. If this sort of compromise is carried far, the party, whether it be national or international, will lose coherence and definiteness and become deprived of driving force. On the other hand, unless without some reasonable give and take we should each of us find ourselves in a party consisting of one member.

We of the Communist Party do not find ourselves in agreement with the Third international on every point. Therefore we must ask ourselves:

(1) Whether the points on which we disagree are fundamental.

(2) Whether these points are minor questions of tactics, or major questions of principle.

(3) Whether these points of disagreement will be so rigidly enforced as to hinder us in revolutionary action.

(4) Whether these points are likely to remain a permanent part of the policy of the Third International, or whether, owing to the fact that there is a growing tendency in the Third International to reverse the policy with which we disagree these points of difference may shortly disappear.

I will answer the last question first. The most definite point of difference between ourselves and the Third International (and remember it is with the International, and not with 'Moscow' as comrade Whitehead puts it, that we are dealing), is in regard to parliamentary action. The Third International, at its Second Congress, was [sic] approved parliamentary action.

Will the Third International adhere to parliamentary action?

I think it unlikely that the Third International will continue to approve of parliamentary action. I believe that the next conference of the International will either reverse the decision, or so modify it that parliamentary action will only be tolerated in a few countries and under certain special conditions. In Italy, the communist abstentionists, though still a minority, are a growing power, their policy is the most communist of the communist fractions of Italy in other questions as well as on this. In Germany the strong anti-parliamentarian elements are those which fought in the Ruhr, those which are readiest for revolution. These are outstanding examples; but the communist abstentionists are to be found in every country, and their number grows. I believe they will presently win the day in the Third International.

Does the approval of parliamentary action by the Third International constitute a fundamental difference between us and the Third International?

I do not think so, because I believe that the Third International will abandon the use of parliamentary action, and because the International has already declared itself for the destruction of parliament, and so whittled down its approval of parliamentary action, and so hedged it round with conditions that it seems like a poor shrivelled chrysalis from which the butterfly has flown away, a chrysalis that is just left as a memorial to a past epoch, in order not to seem disrespectful to the honoured socialist dead who believed in it in the days that are gone.

To prove that the Third International has itself lost faith in the parliamentary weapon, I quote the following passages from the thesis on parliamentarism adopted by the recent Second Congress in Moscow.[8]

At the moment when the class struggle turns into civil war, the proletariat must inevitably form its organisation as a fighting organisation, which cannot contain any of the representatives of the former ruling classes; all fictions of a 'national will' are harmful to the proletariat at the time, and a parliamentary division of authority is needless and injurious to it; the only hope of proletarian dictatorship is a republic of soviets.

The bourgeois parliaments, which constitute one of the most important apparatus [sic] of the state machinery of the bourgeoisie, cannot be won over by the proletariat any more than can the bourgeois order in general. The task of the proletariat consists in blowing up the whole machinery of the bourgeoisie, in destroying it, and all the parliamentary institutions with it, whether they be republican or constitutional-monarchical.

Consequently, communism repudiates parliamentarism as the form of the future; it renounces the same as a form of the class dictatorship of the proletariat; it repudiates the possibility of winning over the parliaments; its aim is to destroy parliamentarism. Therefore it is only possible to speak of utilising the bourgeois state organisations with the object of destroying them. The question can only and exclusively be discussed on such a plane.

Every class struggle is a political struggle, because it is finally a struggle for power. Any strike, when it spreads through the whole country, is a threat to the bourgeois state, and thus acquires a political character. To strive to overthrow the bourgeoisie and to destroy its state by any means whatever, means to carry on political warfare. To create one's own class apparatus – for the management and suppression of the resisting bourgeoisie – whatever such an apparatus may be means to gain political power.

This work within the parliaments, which consists chiefly in making revolutionary propaganda from the parliamentary tribune, the denunciation of enemies, the ideological uniting of the masses, etc., must be fully subordinated to the objects and tasks of the mass struggle outside the parliaments.

The following conditions are indispensable: (1) The absence of all autonomy for the parliamentary communist groups, and their unconditional subordination to the Central Committee of the Party; (2) constant control and direction by the Party Executive Committee; (3) the adaptation of parliamentary demonstrations to those going on outside the parliament; (4) revolutionary attitude in the parliament, i.e. the absence of all 'principled' fear of overstepping the limits of parliamentary regulations; (5) the execution of part of the work outside the parliament, especially in connection with the mass demonstrations, by the communist members of parliament; (6) to be in touch with the illegal work and to profit by parliamentary immunity, as far as it exists, for those purposes; (7) an immediate remand or exclusion from the party of any member of the parliamentary group who violates in his parliamentary work any orders of the Party.

In complying with all these conditions, the parliamentary work must present a contrast to the dirty 'politics' which is practised by the social democratic parties of all countries, who enter parliament with the object of supporting that 'democratic' institution or, at best, to win it over.

At the same time we must constantly bear in mind the relative unimportance of this question. If the centre of gravity lies in a struggle for the power outside of parliament, then naturally the question of a proletarian dictatorship and a fight in masses for it is immeasurably greater than the secondary one of using the parliament.

Will the approval of parliamentary action by the Third International interfere with revolutionary action in this country?

I do not think so. In the first place there will probably not be a parliamentary election in this country until after the next congress of the Third International, when this year's decision may probably be reversed.

In the second place, the thesis on parliamentarism itself provides many reasons for abstaining from the elections:

On the other hand, an acknowledgement of the value of parliamentary work does in no wise lead to an absolute, in-all-and-every-case acknowledgement of the necessity of concrete elections and a concrete participation in parliamentary work. The matter depends upon a series of specific conditions. In certain combinations it may become necessary to leave the parliament. In other circumstances a boycotting of the elections may be necessary, and a direct violent storming of the parliamentary bourgeois clique, or a participation in the elections with a boycott of the parliament itself, etc.

In this way, while recognising as a general rule the necessity of participating in the elections to the central parliament, and to the institutions of local self-government, as well as in the work in such institutions, the Communist Party must decide the question concretely, according to the specific conditions of the moment. Boycotting the elections of the parliament, or leaving the parliament, is allowable, chiefly when there is a chance of an immediate transformation into an armed fight for the power.

It is important that the British communists should remember that the founders of the Third International were those who had made the Russian revolution and are eagerly looking to the world revolution to relieve them from the task of fighting the entire world of capitalism.

The object of the Third International is to accelerate the international communist revolution. In pursuing that object, the Third International is far more likely to prove harassing to the right-wing communists than to the left. Thus the Third International has refused to admit the affiliation of the great Italian Socialist Party unless it changes its name to Communist Party and unless the reformist leaders, Turati, Treves, and Modigliani be expelled from the Party. The orders of the Third International are now about to be obeyed by the majority of the Italian party. Stringent conditions have been sent to the French and German parties, as well as the British ILP. The Italian Socialist Party has, moreover, been rapped over the knuckles by the Third International for its failure to throw itself into the struggle for the factories carried on by the Italian metalworkers. The Third International has congratulated the Italian metalworkers on their fight, but has pointed out that in order to achieve success they must not merely seize the factories, but also the banks and the centres and forces of government, in order that the capitalists may not be able to use money and militarism to put down the workers' revolt.

6. The united front. With labour or with capital?

(from the *Workers' Dreadnought*, 11 February 1922)

This is the first part of an unsigned editorial probably written by Pankhurst in response to the news of preparations for the conference at Genoa in April 1922. This conference saw the culmination of the Russian state's attempts to make an accommodation with the major imperialist powers by accepting their right to exploit Russia's natural resources.

The article is a clear example of the Dreadnought *group's attitude at this time towards the degeneration of the Russian revolution; while clearly warning the working class against the disastrous consequences of the CI's united front policy, and denouncing the soviet government's concessions to European capitalism, the group was very circumspect in drawing definitive conclusions from this 'ignominious surrender' of the CI's original revolutionary principles, still seeing the main enemy as the capitalist governments themselves, who, with the active support of social democracy and the trade unions, were attempting to draw Russia back into the orbit of world capitalism and destroy the last proletarian vestiges of the revolution.*

The second part of the article, which deals briefly with the conference in Paris between the Second and 'Two and a Half' Internationals, has been omitted here.

Chicherin praises Lloyd George

The delegates of Soviet Russia to the conference of capitalist governments at Genoa are appointed: the conditions of capitalism are accepted. Comrade Chicherin, whom we thought would have known better, having lived here, has praised Lloyd George for his policy of peace and trade. It is strange that our Russian comrades have not learnt the little value of the gilded talk of Lloyd George and his ministers. All the world of capitalism speaks of 'perfidious Albion' today: yet Soviet Russia has been more treacherously dealt with than any other country by this government of tricksters: Soviet Russia, would-be communist Russia, has surely more reason than any other country to distrust Lloyd George and his capitalist masters.

Lloyd George is for peace and trade, says Chicherin, adding that Soviet Russia's object is the same. Soviet Russia's object was not that when it hoisted the red flag: Soviet Russia was for communism and not for trade.

We do not like at all the statements emanating from the Soviet Foreign Office: there is much talk now of united fronts: we hope that what we are about to see is not a united front between Soviet Russia and British or Allied capitalism.

It is obvious however, that what the capitalist governments are demanding as a condition of coming to any commercial agreements with Soviet Russia, is the security of tenure for capitalism in Russia, and the co-operation of Russia in establishing European capitalism.

Comrades should brush away the cobwebs of sentiment and look that fact squarely in the face.

The united front with Labourism

The soviet government and the Third International, which it controls, has blundered disastrously in its international policy. So lately as the Third Congress of the Third International last summer, it boasted of having split the workers' parties of Italy and France, and driven out the reformists – that was its policy in all countries originally. Even whilst the Third Congress was sitting, whilst it was loudly boasting of driving out the reformists, it was working to secure a united front with those same reformists it had driven out.

At the Second Congress, in 1920, the Third International was already yearning towards unity with the British reformists, and it had leanings in that direction, even for Germany, though it was vigorously working to secure the split in Italy and France.

During the last few months we have already shown, week by week, how the Third International Executive was abandoning the revolutionary policy, and endeavouring to establish unity between itself and the Second and 'Second and a Half' Internationals; as well as between its own creation, the Red International of Labour Unions and the Yellow Amsterdam International.

The *Communist*, organ of the Third International right-wing parliamentary communists in this country, suppressed all information as to the doings of the Third International Executive in this direction. Reluctantly it at last withdrew the veil and, on January 28th, published the following statement:

The Communist International approves the demand for a united working class front. The Communist Party in every country will enter into negotiations with every other working class organisation (right, centre or left) to establish a common fighting programme. The Communist International is prepared to enter into negotiations with the Second International, the 'Second and a Half' International and the Amsterdam International, to establish a programme of common action.

This is, indeed, an ignominious surrender; the more so as it has been preceded by the expulsion from the Third International of the Communist Left, the real revolutionaries.

In Germany, not only were the anti-parliamentary, industrial revolutionary communists, who have formed the KAPD and the Fourth International, cold-shouldered out of the Third, but all who took part in the splendid revolutionary fight in the Ruhr in 1920 are expelled from the German Communist Party on Moscow's order.

The ignominious surrender of Moscow's International to Geneva and Amsterdam, which they arose to destroy, is, moreover, fruitless. The old guard refuses to negotiate with Moscow's faithful servants: it may come to terms with Moscow presently, because Moscow has governmental power and money; but only on condition that the Muscovite Communist Parties are sacrificed.

In Germany the Communist Party proposed a united front with those whom it had flouted, the Social Democrats and the Independents, on the basis of a programme of capitalist reconstruction, some bourgeois-pacifist phrases, and the eight-hour day. The Social Democrats refused the communist overtures, preferring to support the capitalist centre block, including the Stinnes Party. The Wirth government, which the Social Democrats welcomed, now makes ruthless war on German trade unionism, even going so far as to seize the funds of the

German railwaymen and imprison their officials, because they are on strike.

When the wave of working class fervour, floating on war-wage prosperity and the mobilisation-born scarcity of labour swept through the world, Moscow formed the Third International. Now that the trade slump has brought depression and a sense of weakness to the workers, Moscow would find strength by uniting with the reactionary Labour officials, who have betrayed the workers, according to Moscow's own dictum, and will endeavour to do so again should desperation cause the workers to rebel.

The old guard of Trade Union-Social Democrats, however, wants none of Moscow on Third International lines; it wants none of *Communist* Moscow. The old guard is nestling under the wing of capitalism and means to stay there. That has been shown in Germany: it is plainly to be seen here.

Notes

1 Texts of the anti-parliamentary and council communists have not been included here; not for political reasons but because a substantial collection of articles has already been reprinted by Wildcat in *Class War on the Home Front* (1986). Although this is now out of print it is available at a number of locations on the internet (e.g. http://www.geocities.com/knightrose.geo/contents.html, 28 March 2005).

2 Sir Frederick , 'F.E.', Smith was a Conservative Unionist MP and fervent supporter of the Protestant Ulster Unionist bourgeoisie. He held a seat in the cabinet throughout the first world war.

3 The full text of the Zimmerwald Manifesto (in a different translation) is available in J. Riddell (Ed.), *Lenin's Struggle for a Revolutionary International, vol. 1, Documents: 1907-1916 The preparatory years,* Monad, 1984, pp.318-321.

4 Guesde, Vandervelde, Hyndman, Henderson and Südekum were all right-wing social democrats who supported the war. The Union of Democratic Control was a grouping around E.D. Morel comprising political figures and liberal academics from the left wing of the British bourgeoisie, including Ramsay MacDonald and other Labour Party leaders. It saw the main cause of the imperialist war as 'secret diplomacy' and called for 'parliamentary control' over the war effort. Needless to say it was not anti-war but provided a 'pacifist' left cover for British imperialism.

5 *Vorwärts* was the paper of the German Social Democratic Party (SPD).

6 A collection of unpublished papers and handwritten translations of reports is in the Pankhurst Papers. Details of the Amsterdam conference can be found in the *Workers' Dreadnought,* 20 March 1920.

7 For a fuller study of the Amsterdam Bureau's activities in the context of the history of the Dutch and German lefts, see *The Dutch and German Communist Left,* ICC, 2001, pp.140-143.

8 The full text of the 'Theses on Parliamentarism' (in a different translation) is available in *Second Congress of the Communist International, Minutes of the Proceedings, vol. 2,* New Park, 1977, pp.49-59.

List of abbreviations

AAUD	Allgemeine Arbeiter-Union Deutschlands (General Workers' Union of Germany)
AAUD-E	Allgemeine Arbeiter-Union Deutschlands – Einheitsorganisation (General Workers' Union of Germany – Unitary Organisation)
APCF	Anti-Parliamentary Communist Federation
AWRU	All Workers' Revolutionary Union
BSISLP	British Section of the International Socialist Labour Party
BSP	British Socialist Party
CI	Communist International
CNT	Confederacion Nacional del Trabajo (National Confederation of Labour)
CP(BSTI)	Communist Party (British Section of the Third International)
CPGB	Communist Party of Great Britain
CUG	Communist Unity Group
CWP	Communist Workers' Party (later Movement)
ECCI	Executive Committee of the Communist International
FAI	Federacion Anarquista Iberica (Iberian Anarchist Federation)
GIC	Groep(en) van Internationale Communisten (Group(s) of International Communists)
ILP	Independent Labour Party
IWW	Industrial Workers of the World
KAI	Kommunistische Arbeiter-Internationale (Communist Workers' International)
KAPD	Kommunistische Arbeiter Partei Deutschlands (Communist Workers' Party of Germany)
KPD	Kommunistische Partei Deutschlands (Communist Party of Germany)
NEP	New Economic Policy
NUWM	National Unemployed Workers' Movement
PCI	Partito Comunista d'Italia (Communist Party of Italy)
PSI	Partito Socialista Italiano (Italian Socialist Party)
RCP	Revolutionary Communist Party
RILU	Red International of Labour Unions
RSL	Revolutionary Socialist League
SDF	Social Democratic Federation
SDP	Social Democratic Party
SLP	Socialist Labour Party
SPD	Sozialdemokratische Partei Deutschlands (Social Democratic Party of Germany)

SPGB	Socialist Party of Great Britain
SWSS	South Wales Socialist Society
USM	United Socialist Movement
UWO	Unemployed Workers' Organisation
USPD	Unabhanginge Sozialistische Partei Deutschlands (Independent Socialist Party of Germany)
VKPD	Vereinigte Kommunistische Partei Deutschlands (United Communist Party of Germany
WES	Western European Secretariat (of the Third International)
WIL	Workers' International League
WSF	Workers' Socialist Federation (before May 1918 Workers' Suffrage Federation)

Sources of original material used in this study

Baillie's Library, Glasgow

British Library, London

British Library of Political and Economic Science, London

British Newspaper Library, Colindale

Comintern Archive (microfilmed copy in British Library of Political and Economic Science, London)

Communist Party of Great Britain Archives, National Museum of Labour History, Manchester

Gallacher Memorial Library, Glasgow Caledonian University

Marx Memorial Library, London

Modern Records Centre, University of Warwick

National Library of Scotland

Pankhurst Papers, International Institute of Social History, Amsterdam (microfilmed copy in British Library of Political and Economic Science, London)

Tait and Watson Collections, Stirling University Library

William Morris Papers (microfilmed copy in British Library of Political and Economic Science, London)

ICC Publications in English

International Review
The quarterly theoretical journal of the ICC.

World Revolution
The paper of the ICC in Britain. Ten issues per year.

Internationalism
The paper of the ICC in the USA. Six issues per year

Visit the ICC website
http://www.internationalism.org

Subscriptions
(At the time of publication)

	POSTAL ZONES			
	A	**B**	**C**	**D**
World Revolution	£10.00	£13.00/$18.00	£13.00/$18.00	
International Review	£12.00	£12.00/$17.50	£15.00/$22.00	
Internationalism	£5.50	£5.50/$9.25	£5.50/$9.25	$6.50
Airmail postage supplement (WR)			£6.00/$8.00	$8.00

COMBINED SUBSCRIPTIONS

WR/International Review	£22.00	£21.00/$33.50	£28.00/$40.50	$40.50
Internationalism/Int Review		£15.00/$24.00	£16.00/$25.00	$31.50
Inter/Int Rev/WR	£27.50	£26.00/$41.00	£33.50/$49.00	$47.00
Airmail postage supplement			£6.00/$8.00	$8.00

SUBSCRIBER/DISTRIBUTORS		**Postal Zones**
World Revolution	£32.50 (6 months)	**A) United Kingdom**
International Review	£20.00 (6 months)	**B) Europe (Air Mail)**
		C) Outside Europe
		D) USA/Canada

Subscriber/distributors receive 5 copies of each publication per month, by airmail outside UK.

Payment and Postage
1) Payment may be made either to our London or New York addresses. Payment to London may be made by cheques, drawn on a UK bank, or by international money order (Giro) in **sterling** made out to INTERNATIONAL REVIEW and sent to our London address. 2) Payments to New York should be made by cheques or money orders in **dollars** made payable to INTERNATIONALISM and sent to our New York address. 3) Postage in the UK is second class letter. Postage to Europe is by letter rate. Postage outside Europe is by surface mail for WR and pamphlets. An air mail postage supplement is available for subscriptions to WR. Air mail rates for pamphlets supplied on request.

ICC Pamphlets

ICC Pamphlets

	Prices		Postage		
	£	$	A/B	C	D
Unions aginst the working class	1.25	2.00	£0.30	£0.75	$0.75
Nation or Class	1.25	2.00	£0.30	£0.75	$0.75
Platform of the ICC	0.50	1.00	£0.30	£0.60	$0.75
The Decadence of Capitalism	3.00	4.50	£0.30	£1.20	$1.25
Russia 1917: Start of the World Revolution	1.00	1.50	£0.30	£1.00	$1.00
Communist Organisations and Class Consciousness	1.75	2.50	£0.50	£1.40	$1.00
The Period of Transition from Capitalism to Socialism	2.00	3.00	£0.50	£1.80	$1.00
2nd Conference of Groups of the Communist Left vol 1	1.50	2.25	£0.50	£2.10	$2.00
2nd Conference of Groups of the Communist Left vol 2	1.50	2.25	£0.50	£2.30	$2.00

Prices in dollars applicable only to orders from the USA/Canada placed with INTERNA-TIONALISM, in New York. POSTAL ZONES: A=U.K., B=Europe, C=Outside Europe, D=USA & Canada for orders placed in the US.

ICC Books

	Prices		Postage		
	£	$	A/B	C	D
The Italian Communist Left	10	9	£2.00	£8.00	$3.00
The Dutch and German Communist Left	14.95	21			

Political Positions of the International Communist Current

* Since the first world war, capitalism has been a decadent social system. It has twice plunged humanity into a barbaric cycle of crisis, world war, reconstruction and new crisis. In the 1980s, it entered into the final phase of this decadence, the phase of decomposition. There is only one alternative offered by this irreversible historical decline: socialism or barbarism, world communist revolution or the destruction of humanity.

* The Paris Commune of 1871 was the first attempt by the proletariat to carry out this revolution, in a period when the conditions for it were not yet ripe. Once these conditions had been provided by the onset of capitalist decadence, the October revolution of 1917 in Russia was the first step towards an authentic world communist revolution in an international revolutionary wave which put an end to the imperialist war and went on for several years after that. The failure of this revolutionary wave, particularly in Germany in 1919-23, condemned the revolution in Russia to isolation and to a rapid degeneration. Stalinism was not the product of the Russian revolution, but its gravedigger.

* The statified regimes which arose in the USSR, eastern Europe, China, Cuba etc and were called 'socialist' or 'communist' were just a particularly brutal form of the universal tendency towards state capitalism, itself a major characteristic of the period of decadence.

* Since the beginning of the 20th century, all wars are imperialist wars, part of the deadly struggle between states large and small to conquer or retain a place in the international arena. These wars bring nothing to humanity but death and destruction on an ever-increasing scale. The working class can only respond to them through its international solidarity and by struggling against the bourgeoisie in all countries.

* All the nationalist ideologies - 'national independence', 'the right of nations to self-determination' etc - whatever their pretext, ethnic, historical or religious, are a real poison for the workers. By calling on them to take the side of one or another faction of the bourgeoisie, they divide workers and lead them to massacre each other in the interests and wars of their exploiters.

* In decadent capitalism, parliament and elections are nothing but a mascarade. Any call to participate in the parliamentary circus can only reinforce the lie that presents these elections as a real choice for the exploited. 'Democracy', a particularly hypocritical form of the domination of the bourgeoisie, does not differ at root from other forms of capitalist dictatorship, such as Stalinism and fascism.

* All factions of the bourgeoisie are equally reactionary. All the so-called 'workers', 'Socialist' and 'Communist' parties (now ex-'Communists'), the leftist organisations (Trotskyists, Maoists and ex-Maoists, official anarchists) constitute the left of capitalism's political apparatus. All the tactics of 'popular fronts', 'anti-fascist fronts' and 'united fronts', which mix up the interests of the proletariat with those of a faction of the bourgeoisie, serve only to smother and derail the struggle of the proletariat.

* With the decadence of capitalism, the unions everywhere have been transformed into organs of capitalist order within the proletariat. The various forms of union organisation, whether 'official' or 'rank and file', serve only to discipline the working class and sabotage its struggles.

* In order to advance its combat, the working class has to unify its struggles, taking charge of their extension and organisation through sovereign general assemblies and committees of delegates elected and revocable at any time by

these assemblies.
* Terrorism is in no way a method of struggle for the working class. The expression of social strata with no historic future and of the decomposition of the petty bourgeoisie, when it's not the direct expression of the permanent war between capitalist states, terrorism has always been a fertile soil for manipulation by the bourgeoisie. Advocating secret action by small minorities, it is in complete opposition to class violence, which derives from conscious and organised mass action by the proletariat.
* The working class is the only class which can carry out the communist revolution. Its revolutionary struggle will inevitably lead the working class towards a confrontation with the capitalist state. In order to destroy capitalism, the working class will have to overthrow all existing states and establish the dictatorship of the proletariat on a world scale: the international power of the workers' councils, regrouping the entire proletariat.
* The communist transformation of society by the workers' councils does not mean 'self-management' or the nationalisation of the economy. Communism requires the conscious abolition by the working class of capitalist social relations: wage labour, commodity production, national frontiers. It means the creation of a world community in which all activity is oriented towards the full satisfaction of human needs.
* The revolutionary political organisation constitutes the vanguard of the working class and is an active factor in the generalisation of class consciousness within the proletariat. Its role is neither to 'organise the working class' nor to 'take power' in its name, but to participate actively in the movement towards the unification of struggles, towards workers taking control of them for themselves, and at the same time to draw out the revolutionary political goals of the proletariat's combat.

OUR ACTIVITY

Political and theoretical clarification of the goals and methods of the proletarian struggle, of its historic and its immediate conditions.
Organised intervention, united and centralised on an international scale, in order to contribute to the process which leads to the revolutionary action of the proletariat.
The regroupment of revolutionaries with the aim of constituting a real world communist party, which is indispensable to the working class for the overthrow of capitalism and the creation of a communist society.

OUR ORIGINS

The positions and activity of revolutionary organisations are the product of the past experiences of the working class and of the lessons that its political organisations have drawn throughout its history. The ICC thus traces its origins to the successive contributions of the *Communist League* of Marx and Engels (1847-52), the three Internationals (the *International Workingmen's Association*, 1864-72, the *Socialist International*, 1889-1914, the *Communist International*, 1919-28), the left fractions which detached themselves from the degenerating Third International in the years 1920-30, in particular the *German, Dutch and Italian Lefts*.